THE CAMBRIDGE MISCELLANY

X

SOMETHING BEYOND

SOMETHING BEYOND

BY

A. F. WEBLING

CAMBRIDGE
AT THE UNIVERSITY PRESS
1933

CAMBRIDGE UNIVERSITY PRESS
Cambridge, New York, Melbourne, Madrid, Cape Town,
Singapore, São Paulo, Delhi, Tokyo, Mexico City

Cambridge University Press
The Edinburgh Building, Cambridge CB2 8RU, UK

Published in the United States of America by Cambridge University Press, New York

www.cambridge.org
Information on this title: www.cambridge.org/9781107632240

First published 1933
First paperback edition 2011

A catalogue record for this publication is available from the British Library

ISBN 978-1-107-63224-0 Paperback

To

EDMUND BLUNDEN

with affection and gratitude

CONTENTS

PREFACE

I HAVE no great love for prefaces, holding that, as a general rule, a book should give a sufficient account of itself. Yet the reader may care to know that what is here set down is essentially a transcript from life. Since, however, the book is a picture rather than a photograph, the judicious will expect certain disguises and reticences, and will understand that the author has here and there exercised some freedom in the use of his material.

A. F. W.

December 1930

SOMETHING BEYOND

"AN UNSUBSTANTIAL FAERY PLACE"

My father was a horse-dealer. An industrious person, he
was at the age of eighty still peering into horses' mouths,
and he once told me that he started to earn his living when
but twelve years old.

He was a man of some force of character and had risen
from poverty to a considerable degree of affluence. But he
was no miser. In middle age he freely scattered what he had
so painfully gathered.

He had a turn for games of "let's pretend", and had persuaded himself that on three days in the week, while summer
reigned, he must run a stage coach between a West London
hotel and what was then a sequestered village in Kent.

Behold him, then, in a fawn-coloured livery adorned with
an unnecessary number of buttons (his tilted chin defying
criticism), driving his team of chestnuts through the Kentish
lanes, and rousing each little village that dozed in the sunshine with the notes of the post-horn which he had learned
to blow—in all the glory of "let's pretend".

Sometimes I accompanied him, sitting by his side, my
small legs dangling from the high box seat, when, as often
happened, there were no other passengers. I think that a
love of country sights and sounds (a love that has grown with
the lapse of years) was first awakened in me by my visits to

the noble park, deep set in the heart of Kent, in which, on these occasions, I used to wander.

In the haze of June lay those smooth lawns, those glades where the deer moved silently, those dim avenues beechen-shaded, the vistas that opened into fairyland.

I once saw a magnificent stag, erect and motionless, near the southern entrance of the mansion. I conceived that the owner had caused to be commemorated in stone some patriarch of the neighbouring herd. I drew nigh to see, whereupon the statue came to life, and, with a toss of the head, glided away and merged into the shadows.

Through a chance-open wicket I looked into the walled garden and held my breath at sight of the massed glories of colour. Here, beside the grass walks you had the Euphuist's jillyflowers, carnations, sops-in-wine, sweet Johns. Towering above was the Tudor mansion, dreaming in the sunshine, a haunt of immemorial peace.

The pleasance was undisturbed by clap of shears or plunge of spade, for even the gardeners appeared to have succumbed to the genius of the place. Bees' murmur and doves' low croon were almost a part of the hush that had fallen on that happy plot. It was not of the world I knew; an enchantment lay upon it. It seemed sun-kissed into silence, awaiting the touch of some magic wand which would bring upon the scene those who had planned it all and looked upon it lovingly three hundred years ago.

I never saw this place except in the tranced stillness of summer afternoons and vaguely I imagined it ever thus, preserving a serene content within its nest of sheltering trees. . . .

2

Then the return journey, the beat of hoofs deadened by the powdered dust of mid-June; the rattle of harness suggesting odd rhymes to the sleepy little boy.

The twilight lanes gradually gave way to miles of streets, the glare, and the harsh confused noises of the swarming city.

I had been ill for some time with a childish complaint. The turning-point came when I awoke to consciousness one sunny morning after a long refreshing slumber. The sound of soft music broke very pleasantly on my drowsy senses. My brother, in a distant room, was playing an old Welsh air, with a merry lilting iteration resolving into chords which touched some spring of emotion within me, and I repeated over and over to myself lovingly, like a refrain, the name of the little melody, "The Bells of Aberdovey". And at the repetition of these sounds there broke upon my mind's eye the vision of a dewy landscape, fresh as Eden and tremulous with awed anticipation at the opening of a cloudless summer day.... One flash of glory and it was gone....

The period of my convalescence was granted magic privilege by the gift of a book of Breton fairy legends, illustrated with engravings after the style of Gustave Doré. I would close my eyes, bedazzled by these wondrous pages, and see with the inward eye enchanted castles clinging to the summits of precipitous rocks, their turrets catching the rays of the setting sun, whilst far beneath, forests clothed the lower hills. Beyond, into infinite distance stretched a wide champaign, half the Breton land of legend and story and half the realm that existed within my own mind.

3

These glimpses of mysteries hinted in flashes so transient and beyond all power to convey their splendours are so closely interwoven with what I suppose were the purely objective experiences of my younger days, that, looked back upon across the silence of forty years, I seem indeed to have lived in two worlds.

My father's turn of mind was romantic, and this fact coloured what theological ideas he possessed. He once remarked that he derived greater benefit from listening to an opera than from hearing a sermon. I gather that his hazy theology was of a liberal order. Full of an argument in which he had been engaged, he once called me to his bedside, and, indicating a position on the counterpane, he explained that that was Heaven. Then, with eager forefinger he drew a number of lines all converging upon the point previously marked and bade me observe by how many different roads one could journey to Paradise. I might justly have enquired by which road he considered himself to be travelling, for at that time he was carrying on an intrigue with a woman for whom he afterwards deserted my mother.

His was an incurable romanticism. He had brought up a family with unceasing toil. Affluence came to him in middle life and a new world opened to him. Had my mother shared his buoyant spirits, his pleasure-loving disposition, and his zest for fresh ventures in the art of enjoyment, all might have been different. But she, dear soul, next to her God, loved her children and the quiet duties of home. My father looked for companionship elsewhere, ignorant of the fact that youth's raptures cannot be revived in after years. They had

4

once been spontaneous and came by the way; they could not be bought with money and arranged at will.

The moth fluttered for a time before the final and inevitable leap. At length flight was agreed upon. But my father, whether depressed by the gloom of a sombre midwinter day, or moved by some feeling of compunction, almost at the last hour despatched from the hotel at which he was waiting a letter which cancelled the arrangement made. This done, he sat gazing for some time at the dying embers of the neglected fire.

Presently he heard the sound of an approaching cab, scarcely audible though it was, for snow had been falling heavily. He hastened to the window. A gas jet flared from the hotel doorway, and through the flurry of snowflakes he discerned that the appointment was to be kept after all. The deep snowfall had delayed his messenger; the letter had not been received.

His chivalry prevented my father from speaking of the message he had sent. She had taken the risk; he would do the same, but roses and rapture must have been far to seek as darkness shrouded the close of that winter day.

What might be anticipated duly followed; business was neglected, and consequent upon the poverty that resulted for him and his, I did not become the prosperous tradesman, but was forced by hard necessity to strike out into other paths leading to undreamed-of opportunities.

A grandmother lives in my memory; a bright-eyed little woman, upright and alert, her cap-strings a-quiver at any imagined inattention; shrewd, worldly, and almost untouched by religion. My father was kind to her, especially during her last illness. Once he sent her a barrel of oysters. "They may say what they like of your father", she remarked to me, "but I am sure his principles are good, or would he have done so much for his mother? Above all, would he have sent me oysters?"

A question worthy to be discussed together with that subtle point which Charles Lamb tells us used to be so pleasantly debated at Saint Omer....

A kindly professor was presenting a book to each of the men who had attended his lectures. When he was told my name for the purpose of inscribing it on the flyleaf, he said, "Wolfe? A great name that! Wolfe—Guelph. You may read of the origin of the feud between your family and the Ghibellines (a quarrel which rent Europe) in the Novelle of Ser Giovanni Fiorentino". It is possible that my ancestors ruffled it with the best, in mediæval Germany, and pitted Pope against Emperor, but, if so, the family glory has departed. My paternal grandfather, a shrivelled, weather-worn personage with face and head encircled by a fringe of white hair, and crowned with a black velvet smoking cap gaudily embroidered and tasselled, drove, in his younger days, a cab or an omnibus. That, at least, is the idea that lingers in my mind. I have never taken the trouble to verify it.

I was born in a noisy thoroughfare in Camberwell—one of the many place-names of London which preserve so pathetically the memory of bygone rusticity. When William Blake knew it Camberwell was "a large and pleasant

6

village". I passed the first twenty-six years of my life mainly in London, the City and its suburbs. I am imbued, therefore (being what I am), with a loathing of town life.

Late-Victorian happenings are bound up with the memories of my young days, and from the conversation of my elders I knew something of mid- and early-Victorian times, which probably accounts for the fact that, mixed in my mind with the dreams and fancies of childhood, this period possesses for me something of that strange charm which invests antiquity.

When my father's coach journeyed to that village (not in Kent, but in fairyland) on those bygone summer days it did not take so long to pass the farthest tentacle of the monster city as it took me lately when I travelled over the same ground, although I moved more rapidly. Gone is the country inn I looked for, the ostler who always carried a flower in his mouth, the neat, pretty barmaid with clustered ringlets (my early love), who mixed for me one chilly evening my first and only glass of hot shrub. Was there ever such a room as the bar-parlour of the "Beehive" on a cool, dark evening! The ruby and amber of sunsets in those lands from which they came hovered yet (a Shechinah glory) about decanted port and sherry; the fire crackled and spluttered; the little boy warmed his hands around the tumbler in which steamed the generous (though prudently diluted) cordial.

Instead of these delights I found a vast red-brick structure bearing still (in mockery) the old name, but not the old sign, and not the charm of other days.

7

Could I be transported, by some spell, back into the surroundings of my childhood, would they produce upon me
anything of the feeling of mystery and wonder which they
then inspired? That scrap of back garden in the suburban
street to which I returned one autumn, after three months'
absence, and found a forest of sunflowers, their broad discs
yellow-rayed towering above the jungle of stalks and leaves
—which I ranged incredulous—would it now hint things
unutterable?

A passing scent has power to cross the gulf of almost half
a century. The odour of a certain sort of paint recalls a
scrapbook, the pictures in which, gaudily coloured by some
oily pigment, opened magic casements.

The fragrance of violets re-creates a wood in springtime
where, one evening, holding my mother's hand, I first
heard in my heart the birds sing. From a childhood's experience I assumed that the sickly, undertakerish odour of
polished wood was natural to churches, and when I come
across it now I am again in the ugly mid-Victorian, suburban building. A smell of hot painted tin—and I am back
forty years, trimming the wicks of the footlights of a cardboard Theatre Royal. In front of the stage is an alert but
silent orchestra, the leader conducting with graceful gesture
an endless overture. On either side of the stage rise tiers of
boxes containing whiskered gentlemen and rose-wreathed
ladies whose dress begins beneath their shoulders.

The stage itself, viewed with half-closed eyes, and head
held level with it, presented scenes of wonder (cut out, and
painted with no sparing brush by myself):

"Scene: The Pirates' Lair" (the entrance of a cavern

8

screened by palms; the black ship at anchor in a sea of ultramarine). "Scene: Sherwood Forest. Enter Robin Hood", which he did, attached to a flat piece of tin propelled by a wire, and invariably falling over in the process.

Another scene, where two cloaked bravoes stood communing in a patch of sunlight deep in an avenue of giant oaks, gave my imagination wings. I feel the spell as I recall it now. Again, I press on in thought far down that mysterious pathway out towards a land beyond.

My mother's maiden name was Berkeley. The labours of a painstaking genealogist might, therefore, provide me with a noble ancestry on her side as well as a royal one on that of my father. My immediate forbears, however, claimed no ancestral dignities. I recollect hearing some relation reverently spoken of as "a gentleman who had never soiled his hands with work". The relatives whom I knew were tradesfolk.

One day in early summer (being then about nine years old), I left London for a three months' visit to my maternal relatives who lived in a town in Gloucestershire. I have never seen the place since, and although I have an urgent longing to re-visit it, I am afraid of destroying a little country of the mind in which I have enjoyed pleasures now for over forty years.

So frequently are dreams compacted of the things that chiefly interest us in waking life that I am not surprised that in sleep I often re-visit the Gloucestershire town. Alas! I cannot present to the student of psychic phenomena a case of travelling clairvoyance, for the scenes I pass through in

9

my dreams have little resemblance to those I treasure in my memory.

Although this visit gave me for the first time several weeks of rural life, my relatives did not live in the country, but in a wide, paved street on the outskirts of the town.

I was introduced to my maternal grandmother, who sat in state on a high-backed armchair in a room which I now know to have been filled with a curious and valuable assortment of furniture, prints, miniatures, and ornaments—the still unravished brides of quietness, uncontaminated by the dealer's calculating gaze, and not yet dissipated by an owner unconscious of their worth.

Two only, out of all those treasures, are mine. One is a sampler upon which a verse of a hymn is displayed amid the appropriate surroundings of six strictly symmetrical trees, certain crimson animals supposed by imaginative persons to represent dogs, and a cottage, from the two chimneys of which plumes of smoke float in opposite directions. To establish the whole as the authentic work of my grandmother there appears along the lower border a legend in green silk lettering: "Anne Roberts, aged 11 yeares, her work. Staverton House Academy. 1823".

The other treasure is a spoon which, since it was used only to stir the pigs' pot, was black with the accumulated slime of many decades. I cleaned it, and discovered a silver spoon of Charles the Second's reign. *Ex pede Herculem!*

My grandmother, when first I saw her, fitted her surroundings as hand to glove. She was dressed in black with a white lace collar and cap; the latter, tied with lilac ribbon and adorned with a row of little lilac silken balls, framed a fine, dignified face, with a complexion which had borrowed some of the ruddy glow of the sunshine of seventy-five summers, although life's wintry days had ploughed deep furrows too.

"This, Mother, is Priscilla's boy, Arthur." I recall the introduction but nothing else. I expect I was anxious to be set free to explore my new and wonderful surroundings.

I must have seen my grandmother again, but I have no recollection of it, and what little I know of her is derived from trifling matters related by my mother. "I never asked the Lord for anything but my prayer has been granted", was one of her sayings. "But", she would add, with a shy sidelong glance towards you, "of course I never asked for a carriage-and-pair and that sort of thing." Her constant words in trouble (with which she was well acquainted) were, "The Lord will sustain". A simple, sweet, evangelical piety was hers, untouched by speculation, yet with no harsh, dogmatic outlines. My mother inherited it. "It is enough", she once told me, in her later years, "to believe in a Heavenly Father who loves you, in a Saviour who died for you, and in a Holy Spirit who puts good thoughts in your heart."

My grandmother's house was small, but for me it contained infinite riches in a little room. Although the house stood on the very outskirts of the town, and one would suppose ground space to have been of no great value, yet it had seemed good to the builder to place the kitchen underground. Of all the rooms this was the most fascinating. One reached it by a steep flight of stone steps, and it received light through a fair-sized grating let into the pavement of the street above. Through the window which opened to the grating, bars of sunshine streamed in, on bright days, and dappled the opposite wall, but the greater part of the place was wrapped in a perpetual twilight. The kitchen had its characteristic odour, compounded principally of the perfume exhaled from the black pot in which simmered unendingly the swill destined for the stay and comfort of the pigs. With this mingled the fragrance of successive meals—the roasting joint that twirled on the jack, or the grateful aroma of spluttering bacon and foaming coffee in the early morning hours.

The pigs' pot provided the witches' cauldron; there was the appropriate gloom. What wonder, then, that here I should make my first acquaintance with the idea of the occult. In a corner of the kitchen was a large cupboard wherein reposed an assortment of brass ware of the kind which one seldom sees now except in the shops of antique dealers: warming-pans, copper saucepans, inverted cones of metal used for heating beer, candlesticks of strange shapes, discarded roasting-jacks, and the rest, the accumulation of two centuries. This cupboard and its contents became associated in my mind (by what process of childish reasoning I know not) with a gruesome narrative related to me by one of my uncle's men, the climax of which was that, long after darkness, and exactly at the stroke of nine, there appeared a spectral female figure clad in black, accompanied by an even more awful personage in white. I, therefore, preferred the kitchen by daylight when it was only delightfully mysterious. At night time it was eerie.

12

Having made my first inspection of the house, I wandered out into the narrow strip of garden, and there encountered a stout and jovial looking personage clad in a white smock curiously pleated about the neck, who bore upon his shoulders a wooden yoke from either end of which depended a burnished milk can.

Easing himself of his burden, he wiped the back of his hand across his forehead, enquired after my health, and said, "Hot, bean't it?"

With loftier ideas of the extent of my grandmother's establishment than the circumstances warranted, I remarked to my mother afterwards, "I have just been talking to one of the milkmen". "That", she replied, "is your Uncle Tom."

All honour to his memory! He loaded me with benefits which I, child-like, received without reflection and as my right. Not least of his gifts to me was this, that through him I first became acquainted with Shakespeare.

I recall him as he used to sit of an evening, in his ladder-back armchair. By his side was the tankard of beer which stimulated eloquence and refreshed the mind wrestling with high themes. Then would he tell me of Lear, his eyes moist at the old man's unmerited griefs; of the treachery of the Highland chief; of Iago's knavery. I see him scanning my face with wistful gaze, eager to mark if I appreciated duly the sorrows of which he told.

Usually my uncle's talk was of bullocks. He had had little education, but he was a shrewd and capable man of business. He made money, and he invested it with an in-

stinct which hardly ever led him astray. He became a fairly
wealthy man, although he continued to live with the utmost
simplicity.

One of the few enjoyments involving expense which he
allowed himself was an excursion by train. Attracted by a
reduction of the fare, he would travel great distances in extreme discomfort in order to spend a few hours wandering
forlorn through strange cities. He once got so far as Paris,
and the impressions left on the mind of the simple Gloucestershire countryman by three days' acquaintance with
that centre of pleasure would, if recorded, I think, present
Paris in a new light.

On one of his wanderings through far-off cities his rustic
appearance gained him the attentions of some mendicant
who expected an easy prey. The harpy finished his harangue
with a manly confession of poverty, trusting to the other's
good sense to draw the necessary inference. "Hard up, are
you?" said my uncle. "I can sympathise with you. I am
hard up myself. I thought, when you stopped, you were
going to help me."

This man, shrewd in all that appertained to his craft,
wandered with the delight of a wondering child through
the pastures of our native literature. He knew his Shakespeare well, with the intuitive apprehension of the heart,
owing nothing to the commentators.

Desiring to enlarge his acquaintance with the poets he
approached the attendant at the Public Library.

"I want", said he, "to read some poetry."

"What poems do you require?"

"I have not the slightest idea."

14

"Well, sir, I have here a set of the English Poets. There is a whole shelf of them."

"I will take the first volume now", said my uncle, "and the rest in order."

Thus, as I firmly believe, he read steadily from Beowulf to Browning.

A big-bodied and big-hearted man, my uncle loved a broad jest. A favourite book of his was the *Contes Drolatiques* which he possessed in the translation published by John Camden Hotten in 1874, with innumerable woodcuts in Doré's characteristic style. Supposing that Balzac always wrote in this strain, he purchased a complete set of that author's works in an English translation, and, hoping against hope, read them through. He once sent me two sovereigns, one for myself, "for my trouble", and one with which to purchase for him the *Decameron*. "I find", he explained, "that to read a chapter or two of a book of that sort sends me to bed in a good humour, and I sleep soundly."

He was well acquainted with the great English novelists of the eighteenth century, and I have realized since that there must have been somewhat of a Shandean flavour about his relations with my aunt.

My Uncle Tom was shrewd and whimsical. My Aunt Vashti, a small, thin, brown, toothless woman, was simple and austere.

At one end of the thoroughfare in which they lived was a solid Georgian church. The bell tower which topped its pillared portico commanded a view of the whole length of the street, and appeared to mount guard over it. It might be supposed difficult not to fall under the influence of this perpetual silent watch, but my uncle was unmoved, and parried with gentle raillery all his sister's attempts to persuade him to acquaint himself with the inside of the building, with the exterior of which he was so familiar.

The usual arrangement was that my uncle should cook the Sunday dinner while my aunt went to church. All that I recall of the service is the pleasure I experienced at the re-appearance of the clergyman, just before the sermon, garbed in a preaching-gown of black silk with snowy bands, he having but a few moments before disappeared into the vestry clad in voluminous white. This divine, who wore horn-rimmed spectacles and whose grey hair was brushed upright on either side of his forehead, presented, to my childish delight, when in the pulpit, the appearance of an owl. Of his godly admonitions I remember nothing. I recollect only a text from which he once preached, and which recurred throughout the sermon as a kind of refrain: "And God remembered Abraham". The solemn and repeated enunciation of these words exercised upon my aunt something of the influence of a mantra. She crooned them to herself on the way home. "Ah, Tom," she said to my uncle, in a fluster of pious exaltation, "you ought to have been at church this morning. We had such a beautiful sermon."

"So you have come home full of good things?" my uncle replied.

"Indeed I have."

"In that case you won't want any dinner?"

My aunt could make nothing of this.

The claims of orthodoxy having been reasonably met by an attendance at church on Sunday mornings, my aunt felt herself at liberty to nibble in other pastures at the evening service. For some weeks she and I fed at the hands of a dark, tall, earnest young shepherd, who had abandoned the ministry of the Church of England for one he deemed more in harmony with the Gospel pattern, to wit, the Presbyterian. Of all the spiritual provender dispensed by him I retain but a morsel. I was deeply affected when he closed a sermon (denouncing God's vengeance on sinners and indicating the only way of escape) by expressing the desire that upon his tombstone should be inscribed the words of his text: "A broken and a contrite heart, O God, shalt Thou not despise". I pictured his early and untimely decease. I have since learned that there is a type of mind which, unable to body forth imaginatively the implications of its belief, grows fat and is nourished to old age on thoughts of Death and Hell.

I attended a meeting of the Salvation Army, then in its buffeted but undaunted youth. My aunt did not accompany me herself; she deemed it scarcely proper, but she was unwilling to debar me from any possible spiritual profit. This militant organization being a new thing in those days, its meetings provided an outlet for the ebullience of bucolic wit. Accompanied by a farmhand eager for fun, I entered the hot, gas-lighted hall, fetid with the odour of unclean humanity. Amid many interruptions, most patiently borne, a converted prizefighter witnessed for God. Of what he said I have kept only the memory of the deep compunction with which he spoke of the mauling of an adversary in some combat (meriting its Homer) of his unregenerate days.

We sat, too, my aunt and I, at the feet of an itinerant Baptist preacher who announced the true way of salvation to a handful of (mostly incredulous) people in a public hall which he hired for the purpose. Once I witnessed the baptism of a half-dozen female converts who, clad, apparently, in some waterproof material, walked down to a large tank let into the platform where, with ecstatic fervour, they were immersed by the minister amid the tittering of young men who had come to scoff, and adhered to their original intention.

The minister once appealed for gifts of flowers for the sick. My aunt obtained from the florist a bouquet encircled by a cardboard holder with filigree edges, as the custom then was. In order not to offend the susceptibilities of my uncle, or point the shafts of his raillery, I was instructed to convey the offering out through the back entrance of the house surreptitiously, while my aunt emerged with due dignity from the front door, appointing a trysting place at the end of the street. Alas, for these benevolent intentions!

"What are you doing with those flowers?" said my uncle.

I forget what lie sprang readily to utterance. I rejoined my aunt and recounted archly the story of my address.

"God does not like little boys to tell lies", was her comment, and I conceived, I think for the first time, the idea of a silent, invisible, and most accurate observer, to whom I was responsible for what I did.

I scan these memories, probing them for knowledge of

anything that might show me what manner of religious belief I held in the days of my childhood. The picture suggests
that I entertained a legalistic conception of God. An elderly
person, of somewhat irascible temperament, prone to take
an arbitrary and magisterial view of things. Thus, when my
uncle read me Dickens's pamphlet *Sunday under Three
Heads*, I felt a thrill of horror, as I perceived that the writer
advocated "Sabbath breaking", an offence which I supposed to be of the most heinous description. How I reconciled my conception of God as an omniscient policeman
with my lying and petty pilfering I am unable to explain.
Childhood's beliefs are not more logical in their effects than
those of adult years.

I sat one evening in June in a summer-house at the end of
my uncle's garden. The westering sun shone on a multitude
of pictures cut from the illustrated papers of the period and
pasted upon the wall. Queen Victoria opened the Great
Exhibition side by side with an Australian aboriginal standing on a headland overlooking the Pacific. A Mandarin
jostled a gauze-draped ballet girl.

My companion was a lad a good deal older than myself.
"Do you know how babies come?" he asked. Upon my
quite genuine profession of ignorance, he volunteered an
astonishing perversion of physiological fact.

Silence fell, and I looked again at the pictures on the wall,
now a rabble-rout dancing a maze in the waning light of the
setting sun. Thus the Serpent entered my Eden, but no Voice
of the Lord sounded, minatory, in the cool of the evening.

The consequences of this initiation into the mystery of

sex (hitherto a sealed book to me) I do not reckon as
necessarily a sign of moral declension. I stumbled, lacking
guidance. Yet, so strangely manipulated, as by an unseen
designer, are even the seeming misfortunes of my life, that
this early vitiated knowledge, and my fancied misde-
meanours consequent thereon, made realities to me what
might otherwise have been merely theological terms. I owed
to them soul-rending experiences of remorse and contrition,
and the calm of sin forgiven.

My nature was timidly sensitive. The occasional slaughter
of animals on my uncle's farm, valued by the neighbouring
youth as a pleasing and gratuitous entertainment, made me
sick. I fear it was a physical repulsion rather than a feeling
of sympathy with the poor frightened things. Indeed, I was
thoroughly self-centred.

My elder brother's birthday was at hand. His kind heart
pictured me anxious to present him with the appropriate
gift, but hindered by impecuniosity. He sent me two shillings, refraining, delicately, from explanation. I wrote,
thanking him warmly for his kindness, and spent the money
on myself.

At length, my long stay in the country drew to an end, and
I returned to London, my home for the next seventeen
years. One day, perhaps, I may re-visit that town amid the
Cotswold Hills, and recall at each well-remembered spot the
memories associated with it. I shall go in the midsummer
and walk slowly down the quiet street, and crave admittance
to the house which once sheltered the two people for whom
my love has grown with the passing years.

If those who live there now show themselves to be courteous and understanding folk, I will ask leave to wander
about the house for a few minutes, alone. Then, first, I shall
descend the flight of stairs that leads to the gloomy subter-
ranean apartment, and imagine my aunt still busy about her
household tasks, while simmering yet upon the hob will be
that cavernous pot exhaling strange odours. Or I shall
fancy it the close of day (no difficult feat in that dim light)
and then I shall feel once more the alarms of the dark cupboard in the corner with its spectral associations.

Coming upstairs, in the room behind the shop I shall see
again my uncle, ruddy-jowled, with close-cropped hair and
twinkling grey eyes. Again he will discourse, and the little
boy all agog will drink in the wondrous tale.

Upstairs I shall go, slowly, thoughtfully, for down those
stairs once were carried the bodies of my friends. I shall
visit the bedrooms in turn.... My own little room; the
chamber above the street where my aunt slept; my uncle's
room looking out on the green countryside, and to the hills
beyond. Then, last of all, I shall enter that chamber where
first I saw my grandmother. Once again the old pictures
will adorn the walls, silhouettes, samplers, miniatures, the
copy of da Vinci's Last Supper, inscribed by the engraver
Alla Santita di Pio VII, Pontifice Massimo, Felicamente
Regnante, and set in a rosewood frame. I shall peer once
more into desks and workboxes of cedarn fragrance, awe-
struck at their varied contents. Again will come back to me
a certain Sunday morning in summer when as a child I sat
in that room. There was a Sabbath calm, a deep brooding
peace. Not a sound. The sunshine poured in at the open

window, a myriad motes were quivering in the gold, and for one flashing moment I had that strange experience of awareness of something just beyond sense-perception. I was on the point of discovery, but, before I could behold it, the vision had been poised for flight. I do not expect to recapture that feeling, but it will be good to recall it.

Then I shall remember with deep and true love the kindness I once received in that humble home. I shall think those gentle spirits still linger there, and I shall thank them, and kneel for pardon as I remember all their un-requited, unrealized goodness.

Then out into the sunlight, and I shall take the path I have trodden in thought a thousand times; through the garden gate; down the lane; a turn to the left, past the end of the two or three streets dated by their old-world names which linger still in my memory. A turn to the right by a farm-house, and so along the winding lane where I used to hide half-pence in the hedges to enjoy next day the thrill of dis-covery. At last I shall walk once more in the meadows of my uncle's farm, and shelter from the blaze of noon be-neath the shade of the elms which border the pastures where the quaker-grass grows, and breathe deep, deep the fra-grance of new-mown hay. Again I shall taste the lump of bread and the morsel of bacon which the haymakers so generously gave me from their little store. Then I shall lie back and gaze at the blue sky and the masses of white cloud floating silently above me, and float with them silently into that other Country, which all my life long, as it seems to me now, has lain close about me, though often undiscerned.

II

THE SNAIL'S PROGRESS

THERE rises to memory the picture of a thin, pale little boy, with satchel on back, scurrying to school, and in a panic lest he should be late. His hands are clasped together and his eyes are closed as he prays feverishly that he may escape punishment by being in time. When he opens his eyes he sees a companion, grinning cheerfully, and mimicking his action.

The incident suggests that the school discipline was keen. The schoolmaster was a red-haired Irishman named Bourke, a born bully. He seemed to derive satisfaction from the flagellation of the flock committed to his charge. When caning a boy, he punctuated each stroke with such ejaculations as: "What a lark!", "That was a good one!", "O what fun we're having!" Only once did I hear addressed to me the dread words, "Hold out your hand". I had failed in answering questions on the fourteen-times table. The master left the room to fetch his cane. "Blub", advised a friendly soul. "Blub away like anything and he won't lick you so hard." I needed little encouragement, and the result was fairly satisfactory.

I wonder now how any sane creature could suppose it necessary for a small boy to know the fourteen-times table. I have not been handicapped in life by failing to memorize

23

its details. If, at any time, I should require to know how much fourteen-times anything amounts to, I should perform a simple sum in multiplication, and all would be well. But the same characteristics marked the methods followed in all the four schools I attended: instruction was given rather than education. The duty of the schoolmaster was to furnish the mind with an assortment of facts. But my mind was so constituted that it seldom retained a fact unless it was linked on to some feeling or emotion. Once, when the class was asked to name the Twelve Apostles, and Peter, James and John had been duly recorded, my piping voice contributed Bartholomew. The meed of praise accorded to so small a boy for remembering so difficult a name was undeserved. Peter and James and John had no association with anything in my mind, and so passed by me like the idle wind. Bartholomew remained as a pleasant and enduring possession, for the word's last syllable linked it to the voice of a favourite cat.

The prevailing odour in the stuffy schoolroom was that of ink, with which it was lavishly bestrewn. Lapse of time effected nothing against this, for fresh mishaps ensured a continuity of the characteristic fragrance. As the report of the gun follows the pressure of the trigger so followed hard upon the sound of the overturned inkpot the invariable sentence: "Six strokes now and a pennyworth of oxalic-acid to-morrow morning". I liked the sound of the name of the master's chosen ink eraser. "You don't know what they call the stuff you get blots out with", I said to my brother. He meekly confessed his ignorance. "Well, it's ox-ally-gaskell", I said, unwilling to hoard knowledge. He

24

received the tidings with the deference that human nature pays to the voice of authority.

The schoolhouse was ugly and dingy. In winter my frozen fingers could scarcely hold a pen. In summer, when a shaft of sunlight stole through the dirty window and came within my reach I would quietly draw from my pocket a glass "drop" from a broken "lustre". It acted as a prism and spread bands of colour over the page of my soulless book. A glance up at the drooping leaves of an attenuated tree which overhung one of the schoolroom windows: then my head sank, the drone of voices faded, and I was far away in the hayfields in Gloucestershire, resting beneath those shadowing elms.

A change in the place of the family abode necessitated a change in schools. I was placed in the charge of an impecunious Irish clergyman who had a large family to support, and who tried (I fear with little success) to add to the income he received as curate in a neighbouring church by undertaking the instruction of youth.

He was a learned person, with the refined face of the scholar, florid, and with white, closely cropped side-whiskers. I admired his appearance in cap and gown as he entered the schoolroom on my first morning there. I thought that he only needed to carry a cane to be the perfect school-master. Next day he bore the rod of office and I felt that the picture was complete. He was a kindly man and the cane was laid upon the table merely as a symbol of authority; he would as soon have thought of using it to belabour the shoulders of his charges as would the Speaker design so to profane the majesty of the Mace.

25

A priest-schoolmaster, he must have given much instruction on the Bible, yet I can recall nothing connected with it except his enunciation of the words, "Until Shiloh come; and unto Him shall the gathering of the people be". The sentence impressed me with the thought of silent throngs journeying beneath the Eastern stars, attracted towards some compelling Personality.

Once when I made a low stool more convenient for use by putting a Bible on it, he said, "I don't think I should use a Bible to sit on. It is hardly reverent to the word of God". Did that courteous hint first awake in me a befitting respect even for inanimate things? I am uneasy still if I pass a wild flower tossed by careless hands on to the road, unless I place it where its frail loveliness will at any rate be safe from the crush of oncoming wheels.

Of this kindly, pious, simple soul, harassed perpetually by the *res angusta domi*, I shall always think with respect and affection. Any definite dogmatic teaching he ever gave me I fear I neither grasped nor remember; but I am sure I must have been influenced, all unknowingly, by contact with a good man. His acceptance of tardily bestowed preferment in Ireland brought to a close what was for me a period of not unhappy days.

"Fairchild House Preparatory School for Young Gentlemen" opened next its friendly doors to me, as to one born out of due time. Over this modest establishment presided two elderly maiden ladies, adherents of the Baptist sect. The senior of the two was a frail little woman with thin, veined hands, who always appeared in a white shawl fastened by a

gold brooch, and a muslin cap from beneath which peeped
a couple of tiny grey curls. By reason of advancing years,
she occupied somewhat the position of a professor-emeritus.
She hovered in the background, the court of appeal before
which recalcitrant youth was haled. Yet that was no very
awful experience. I had once been ejected from the classroom for my misdeeds, and was discovered by the old Head.
She led me into her drawing-room, and questioned me about
my crime. My confession received, she took my hand,
stroking it gently as she talked. In a few minutes I was
shedding tears of contrition.

"Ask the Lord to help you to be good," she said, "and
when He shows you what to do, obey. I was very wayward
myself in my earlier years." She proceeded to relate an instance of this youthful turbulence. "I am afraid I was rather
a rowdy girl", she said. "I remember riding once, all by
myself, on top of an omnibus. But, wilful though I was,
God always seemed to lead me by the hand and say, 'Not
that way, but this, my child'." The old lady dismissed me
with her blessing and an apple.

Each morning, standing in two rows, we spent a quarter
of an hour, not unpleasantly, in religious exercises. We committed to memory certain notable passages of Scripture,
learning to recite them together in solemn monotone. I see
an affinity between the unsophisticated child mind and the
really great in literature in the fact that to this day I can
repeat with ease whole passages of the Bible committed to
memory at that time, whilst much acquired, painfully
enough, from other books has vanished.

The more to interest us in those inspired utterances, it

27

was the custom, on birthdays, to invite suggestions for a "motto text", to be suitably transcribed (up-strokes thin, down-strokes gradually thickened to a meridian corpulence) and presented publicly to the fortunate recipient.

The words, "Well done, good and faithful servant. Enter thou into the joy of thy Lord", once suggested for a grubby, tiresome child, one supposes to have been a hopeful anticipation of better things to come.

For the natal festivities of our venerable preceptress was offered Joshua's counsel to the backsliding Israelites: "Choose you this day whom ye will serve".

Into the dovecote of Fairchild House there swooped one day an eagle in the shape of Miss Grimwood. A volcanic soul, housed in a frail tenement, dark-eyed, swarthy-skinned, with black hair in coils, Medusa-like. She took fierce views of things, and worshipped the super-man. Napoleon had previously been represented to us as just sufficiently great to make Waterloo worth our winning. He was the god of her idolatry.

Uninterested in much that she had to teach, she often grew listless. Our attention flagged: we indulged in whispered conversation. It was patiently disregarded. We grew more ostentatiously offensive. Outstepping the bounds of her forbearance, a biggish boy was ordered to leave the classroom. He refused to go voluntarily. She put him out by force. I recollect the flushed face, the tumbled hair, the heaving of the gallant little bosom.

When she was indifferent to the information that necessity compelled her to impart, her manner was lifeless. She

28

was roused to torrential eloquence when her heart was touched.

She was with us for but one term. Vague whispers circulated that she had been discovered to be an Atheist, and had been solemnly cast forth with the appropriate maledictions. The gentle old ladies of Fairchild House could not have been harsh to the most abandoned. One of them remarked, "Dear Clara had, unfortunately, some strange ideas, and we thought she would be happier in other surroundings". That was all.

I am truly thankful that, visited by genuine compunction for my share in the annoyance she had suffered at our hands, I wrote to her after she had gone away, expressing my shame and regret. She replied that she recollected of me nothing but what was good. Dear, brave little Atheist (if so you were), I pay you this tribute now. I own myself debtor to the Greek as well as to the Jew.

The only other gust of the odium theologicum which I remember ever to have ruffled the prevailing charity of Fairchild House was a lecture delivered with the object of putting our tender minds in a state of timely watchfulness against the errors of the Roman Church. A violent harangue was made by a friend of one of the mistresses. He stirred us with fierce denunciations of idolatry, both the genuine Roman article and the hybrid variation of the Puseyites. I subsequently discovered that the lecturer was a disciple of the school which keeps sentiment strictly separate from business, for he was head of a firm which existed to supply altars, crosses and candlesticks, and the rest of the paraphernalia of idolatry.

29

But Fairchild House was not narrow. The old Head must have retained something of the daring of her youth, for, despite her theological affinities, she caused to be held each week in winter a dancing class at which the sexes were mingled in the mazy whirl, or (more accurately to describe it), the mistresses piloted round awkward little boys in tight shoes who beat the earth with lumbering tread.

There were annual festivities, too, at the end of the winter term, when "old boys" performed little plays in appropriate costume, and, at intervals, certain small youths of our company especially selected for their gifts in improving and delighting an audience by their elocutionary accomplishments, were set up upon a chair to recite; starting off with the simper of gratified vanity, and not seldom ending in tears and a hasty escape when memory proved treacherous.

The slight sketches enacted on these exhilarating occasions were not my first introduction to the drama, for my elder brother had already taken me to the theatre.

The memory of one play that I witnessed is still clear in my mind. It was a musical drama of the simple, hearty, old-fashioned sort, the once popular *My Sweetheart*.

The performance I attended was given in a public hall. One reached the building at the end of a long passage. Half-way down this passage was the entrance to a smaller hall, in which a religious service of some sort was proceeding, as one could perceive through the open door, outside which two earnest young men stood inviting all who passed to stay their heedless steps, and marking with sad eyes our guiltily averted looks. This was my first visit to the play and there flashed through my mind certain cryptic words which had once been read out to us during a dictation lesson at Fairchild House: "With [a thrill of horror the youth recrossed the threshold of the theatre".

Despite the warning thus providentially conveyed, with beating heart I pressed on.

My nature has always had two distinct strains in it, as I realize after much pondering upon the past. From my father I get the adventurous, romantic, sceptical and decidedly worldly side of my character. From my mother the streak of orthodox, timid, Puritan leanings. As often as the spirit of adventure and speculation urges me forward, so often does a cautious conservatism startle me with misgivings. But the last word in the argument is almost always "Onward!"

So was it now, and I found myself in the cheapest seats at the back of the hall, looking eagerly for those delights which as yet were screened behind the curtain.

A sorry affair it all was, no doubt, the whole having been got up by, and produced principally for the satisfaction of, the leading lady, a "talented amateur" whose stage-name was Miss Pauline Siddons. In private life she owned a scared-looking little husband and eight children. The latter provided her with no small portion of the juvenile part of the caste. An extremely youthful member of the family had been given the part of the child who is nursed with great effect by Tony during the song, "Go to sleep, my baby". But the moving impression sought for was somewhat marred by the fact that, as the child was dandled to and fro in Tony's arms, the romantic-looking overall he wore rode up and revealed, in the glare of the footlights, two circular portions of his hinder-parts of considerable extent visible through long-neglected rents in his apparel. Cheerful, honest little melodrama! Virtue (long defamed and oppressed) at length proved victorious; the curtain shut out the moving scene (sober reality and deadly earnest to my unsophisticated soul) and my brother and I passed out into the night, hugging to our hearts a visionary loveliness.

Fairchild House, as has been narrated, did not altogether ban the drama. Nor did it look unkindly on English literature, but its tastes were not recklessly catholic. Once discovered reading *The Arabian Nights* I was informed that there were limits to the wide freedom allowed, and that I had overstepped them. "That kind of book is not permitted in Fairchild House", I was told to my utter surprise.

I wonder what my fair monitress would have said about a certain bundle of paper-covered novels which my brother purchased cheaply and brought home about that time, and amongst which I was permitted rights of free pasturage? I see them now, each with an enchanting coloured picture on the front cover. There were Fielding and Smollett, Lytton, Scott, Dickens, Harrison Ainsworth, and Marryat. I recollect taking a copy of the last-named author's *Phantom Ship* to bed with me one night. I began to read at daydawn the next morning, and nearly finished it—terror-struck but fascinated—before I got up to breakfast.

"O fortunatos nimium sua si bona norint" might truthfully be said of all small boys who were as happy as we were at Fairchild House, but alas! as we grew older we waxed wanton and sighed for other worlds to conquer.

32

I fell a victim to this spirit of unrest, goaded thereto principally by a companion who attended a secondary school belonging to one of the great City Companies. He wore a cap adorned with a crest, and spoke of adventure and perilous doings, commiserating with me on my unhappy state of pupilage in feminine leading-strings.

I clamoured to be allowed to enter the great world, and, being now nearly twelve years of age, my mother decided that the change should be made.

Alas! the meed of vaulting ambition was mine. My schooldays henceforth were a repetition of my first experiences. The headmaster, a somewhat vulgar-looking personage with untrimmed beard and bulbous fiery nose, struck terror to my soul on such occasions as I came into contact with him.

The daily religious exercises of the school consisted of a short lesson from Scripture followed by the recital of the Lord's Prayer. In his reading of the former the headmaster frequently indulged in buffoonery, caricaturing the subject-matter by intentionally exaggerated intonations; and in our repetition of the prayer we were not seldom pulled up for being too fast or too slow, and ordered to commence the mechanical and meaningless performance over again.

I was exceedingly afraid of many of my schoolfellows, and would seek a sequestered part of the playground in order to avoid their rough horseplay.

My father had chosen to set up his new household in the very next road to that in which the school was situated. The facts became known, and I remember the agony of shame with which I heard, amid the babel of voices in the play-ground, "His father has got two wives". A mirth-provoking topic it proved, capable of ingenious handling.

Schoolboy cruelty is to be expected, but that older folk should join the hue and cry is surprising. I often exchanged visits with my companion who had lured me from the temperate joys of Fairchild House. One day he said to me, "Mother doesn't want you to come to our house again. It's because of the way your father is carrying on". I submitted, of course, to this particular application of the vengeance denounced on the offspring of the ungodly. My friend's mother was an earnest churchwoman and doubtless felt gratified at the opportunity of identifying herself with the Divine Will.

I suppose I added somewhat to my small stock of knowledge while at this school, but I had no zest for my work, and performed it as a task.

A brighter side to my memories of the place is supplied by my recollection of three of the under-masters with whom I had to do.

The first was a kindly young North-countryman who taught chemistry to the school in addition to conducting the form in which I was placed on my admission.

He loved his chemistry demonstrations. It did him good to see our admiring gaze at the successful outcome of some experiment. "Ah, we chemists can do rather wonderful things", he would say with modest pride. Occasionally the experiment did not eventuate as predicted. "With these materials, treated as you will see me use them, I shall shortly present you with a cake of soap." But the soap refused to materialize. "Ah, we chemists can do some rather wonderful things!" murmured the inevitable wag.

He was a man of many interests and with a kindly heart. "You boys put your books down," he would sometimes say when we drowsed on a hot summer's day, "and if you will keep quiet I will read you a story."

Once he was entrancing us with some legend of northern climes, a tale of gnomes and trolls. The door opened and the Head appeared on one of his surprise visits, looking suspiciously as the master paused in the full flood of oratory. But our man was a North-countryman and not easily disconcerted. "Tomkins, let me hear you spell gnome." "Ah, a spelling lesson in progress!" The situation was saved.

About this time the romance and adventure part of my mental make-up, which I suppose myself to have inherited from my father, first found a harmless outlet in literary composition. Later on I turned novelist and produced works of a vigorous and truculent sort, a medley, of course, of ideas I had gleaned in the course of my multifarious reading. I have the manuscripts still, although they were offered to various publishers of books for boys. They had the instinct of the migratory bird and never failed to return to the point of departure bearing the printed message which plunges in gloom the aspiring soul.

But it was not altogether wasted effort. I might have been less innocently employed, and the practice served to keep up my right to wander at will in the land of dreams. I recall one golden Sunday evening in summer when my mother chid me mildly for not laying aside on the Sabbath so worldly an occupation as story-writing. I was only seeking a way of escape from the ugly suburban street; in fact, at that moment I was conducting a perilous adventure on a green island shimmering beneath the liquid blue of southern skies.

And yet the practical, commonsense side of my nature (my mother's gift) had an important part in the plans I now began to entertain for my future career. Our straitened means and entire lack of influence limited my choice, and, after much thought, I concluded that there was no opening for me in anything but the commercial world.

This decided, I set to work after an entirely practical fashion to bring about the ultimate accomplishment of my purpose. I was due to be moved into a higher form at school at the opening of a fresh term. This was a parting of the ways, for the choice lay between a form in which we commenced to learn Latin, and another which professed to specialize on subjects useful in a commercial career.

I chose the latter blithely and confidently, and have never ceased to regret it.

By some mistake, however, I was sent for one day, at the commencement of the new term, into the classroom that sheltered those who essayed to adventure the lower reaches of the steep Parnassian ascent. Their straggling steps were directed to the beaten track by an Irish clergyman. I have wondered since if Irish influence in English education is so considerable as my experience might lead one to suppose.

The priest, seated on the throne of office, was presiding over the mysteries. With infinite gusto he repeated, "Amo,

Amas, Amat", beating time with the ruler held in his right hand, while in his left he grasped a thick slice of bread-and-dripping with which at intervals he refreshed nature weakened by the mental strain. The attendant neophytes, with reverent upturned gaze, squeaked in chorus, "Amo, Amas, Amat".

The mistake in reference to myself was at length put right. A message was delivered to the servant of the Muses that I had chosen the commercial side.

"Is this so?" he asked, with pain.

I agreed.

"Go then, counter-jumper", he said scornfully.

I found myself next morning amongst the commercial magnates of a future day. I cannot, however, remember having been very much the more fitted for a business life by what I learned in their company. I studied the art of making out invoices and bills of lading. I mastered some of that jargon in which otherwise intelligent persons feel it necessary, apparently, to express themselves in commercial correspondence. But little else.

Perhaps this was partly the fault of our instructor, a mild man, lost for the most part in a dreamy abstraction, and blinking through his spectacles in a bewildered way at his unruly flock. He was a Doctor of Philosophy of Jena. What did he in that uncongenial galley? God had created him to expound Teutonic transcendentalism to earnest young metaphysicians, instead of which he was compelled by a hard fate to hammer figures into unintelligent skulls.

His forbearance, or rather, his utter obliviousness to much of the vexation offered him was a thing to marvel at.

37

"You are nearer the stove than I, Dr Tanner", said one impertinent youth, thrusting some waste paper into his hand. "Would you have the goodness to consign this to a fiery grave." A gesture of mild impatience. But he complied with the request.

A common custom was to cut squares of cloth out of the skirts of his gown even as it hung on his back, for use as penwipers. He never observed the indignity, and by the end of the term the bottom of his diminished robe hung in tatters. Before the next term gentle fingers had made an effort to repair the mischief (I wonder, with what tears?), and the dingy garment, grey-green with use, was botched with black patches.

Peace be with him! He must be dead now many years. May his simple, kindly soul, lapped in Elysian calm, devour, in undisturbed leisure, the ghostly counterparts of the ponderous tomes he loved during the time he suffered the indignities which befall wayfarers such as he in the wilderness of this world.

These were the masters who strove to guide my youthful steps along the path of learning, I fear with scant success, for it was not until some time after I had left school that I became conscious of an enthusiasm for the acquisition of knowledge. Hitherto I had regarded learning as a task. One had to memorize a certain number of facts or one was punished. As soon as the occasion for reproducing the facts passed, they were allowed to fade from the mind. Unless a fact set up a responsive vibration in my imagination, or touched my emotions, it meant nothing to me. Most of the information offered me at school did not succeed in doing either. The better part of such education as I received in my earlier days was acquired, therefore, out of school. It came to me principally through reading the books I enjoyed, imaginative books, mostly of an adventurous type. I attained knowledge, too, by contact with persons. I was affected by their point of view. Things that happened set me thinking; and so, from very different sources, I gathered material which, all unconsciously, was woven into the stuff of my mind. It was only the information which was offered me of set purpose which, speaking generally, failed to effect a lodgment.

The labours of my spiritual pastors were scarcely more fruitful than those of my masters.

When my mother first left her childhood's home in the Gloucestershire town, and came to London, she travelled each Sunday from church to church in quest of a sanctuary where, amid all else that was strange, she might find something of the glow of a spiritual home.

Her search was in vain. Formal services, stilted and unhelpful preaching, and a cold aloofness on the part of her fellow-worshippers, produced in her earnest and affectionate nature a feeling of spiritual starvation.

Someone chanced to speak warmly of the ministrations of a certain Dissenting divine, and urged her to test their efficacy.

She did so. Upon entering the chapel her right hand was grasped by an effusive deacon, while into her left was thrust a hymn-book. She was conducted to a front seat, in a flutter of pleasure at such unwonted marks of interest and kindli-

39

ness. Moreover, the discourse of the pastor afforded the spiritual nutriment she craved. At the conclusion of the service she was accompanied to the door by attentions similar to those which greeted her arrival. She was invited to come again, and she did. Thus the Church of England lost an adherent, and her children naturally went with her. There are, of course, those to whom Dissenting effusiveness is simply offensive. Yet, in a world in which one's experience consists so largely of the indifference of one's fellow-men, one should scarcely feel affronted by the appearance of kindness in however ungainly a form it may chance to present itself.

The mingling of the adventurous and boldly speculative with the cautious and timid, which make up my mental outfit, revealed itself early. As a very young child I recollect surprising myself by whistling a comic song one Sunday. This was Sabbath-breaking, of course, and would bring down upon me divine retribution. I was going for a holiday next week. That would afford Providence its opportunity. I should somehow be prevented from going. Then the thought came, "I don't believe it will make the least difference". I resumed my interrupted melody. For all that, there was still the element of fear. I was taken to hear a famous Presbyterian preacher. He had once been a railway porter, and he had developed a truly terrific voice. From time to time, in the course of his harangue, he raised his voice to full strength. He thundered denunciations. The congregation coughed, and shuffled uneasily. I sat paralysed with terror. The Pit opened her mouth at my feet.

40

Of equal skill in touching the chords of fear in simple souls was the celebrated Baptist preacher, Spurgeon, whom also I was once taken to hear. He had no pulpit, but roamed about a platform, provided with table, lamp, chair and a sofa. I recall the great building in which he ministered, with its semicircular galleries fringed on the lower side with a row of gas jets. After my recent experience of famous preachers I dreaded what lay before me. But the old lion was not roused, and it may be taken by whom it pleases as a proof of the value of hell-fire preaching that, when on this occasion he was all mildness, his words roused no responsive echo in me, and I have no recollection of them whatever. I do, however, remember seeing the great man drive off after the service in a carriage-and-pair.

About this time my elder brother had come under the influence of the later developments of the Tractarian Movement. That tempest which swept over the placid waters of the Establishment was now well on into its second stage. It had ceased to be a powerful force in the University, but was making itself felt in the world outside.

Earnest and devoted, if not particularly intellectual men, red-hot with conviction, were carrying the fiery cross throughout the country. Those were the days when religious conviction was a real thing, and, argument failing to demonstrate the truths they held, men fell to blows.

My youthful mind, upon which pastors of such varying sorts had striven to produce an impression, was now subject to the efforts of the sect everywhere spoken against.

My brother took me to a mission church over which presided a tall, thin young man who used to hasten to the

41

west end and shake hands with the people as they left the building after the service. A significant innovation.

The ceremonial here was considered advanced in those simple days. The altar hangings changed with the seasons. I recollect the thrill of æsthetic satisfaction I experienced in the change from sombre violet to dazzling white or glowing red. We had processions on festivals, and high days were further marked by the use of two harmoniums instead of one, and the presence of a cornet player.

For a short time I was a choirboy here. I felt awed when, for the first time, I vested in cassock and surplice, nor was the impression weakened by the fact that I wore my surplice inside-out in accordance with the instructions of a young wag who prevailed upon my innocence to believe that that was the correct way of wearing it.

My brother was deeply, though but temporarily, impressed by his new teachers. He crossed himself before meals, to the alarm of my mother. One Good Friday evening he revealed to me with gloomy satisfaction that he had subsisted throughout the day on half of a hot cross bun.

As time went on he became less satisfied with the moderation exercised in the ceremonial of the church he attended. He went further afield in search of a more heady wine. He found it in an East London church to which he journeyed every Sunday by the Underground Railway. I was sometimes taken too. We reached the gloomy gas-lighted station, its walls exuding slimy moisture, the tunnel-opening vomiting clouds of sulphureous vapour, and hurried through the surrounding slums to the great church.

I recall the red sanctuary lamps, the clustering tapers, the rich banners carried in procession, the contrast between the solemn dignity within and the herded misery outside the building. I inhaled with pleasure the fragrance of incense. I was mildly interested, but, strange as it seems to me now when I think of what these things meant to me later, I was not deeply moved or impressed. Possibly I was prejudiced by the talk I had heard at home and elsewhere. Certainly I was too young and too ignorant to feel the forcible appeal to the imagination of that for which these externals stood. I remember with shame that I was futile enough to mimic, for the benefit of a young companion, the ringing of the sanctus bell and the accompanying genuflections.

My brother's departure from home brought to an end my earliest acquaintance with Anglo-Catholicism. I had been very little affected by it, and returned with indifference to the services of the Dissenting Chapel to which my mother had continued faithful, and it was here that for the remainder of my schooldays, and for some time after, I regularly attended.

Of those whose devotion to the common weal deserves a recognition which it does not always receive are the admirable lovers of mankind who, in most cases, after six days of toil, voluntarily surrender a moiety of the seventh in the effort to train that errant twig, the Sunday School scholar.

I well remember one of this praiseworthy company, a nervous, irritable, warm-hearted little man whose instructions I received for two or three years. We gathered first for the common devotions of the whole school. Teachers "led in prayer" each Sunday in turn. Self-confident teachers

43

addressed the Creator with genial loquacity; the less experienced, with a tendency to take refuge in certain set forms of Nonconformist speech—an indication of the probable origin of a fixed liturgy in Christian worship.

We sang hymns too. Poor doggerel, much of it, I doubt not. It is significant of the bent of my mind that the only memories I retain of what we sang are of lines which touched my imagination:

> There are sandy wastes that lie
> Cold and sunless, vast and drear,
> Where the feeble faint and die—
> Grant us grace to persevere....

> There are soft and flowery glades
> Decked with golden-fruited trees,
> Sunny slopes and scented shades—
> Keep us, Lord, from slothful ease.

On summer afternoons we sang words which had a certain pathos when uttered in a stuffy hall by the lips of pale little children penned within square miles of bricks and mortar:

> Summer suns are glowing
> Over land and sea,
> Happy light is flowing
> Beautiful and free.
> Everything rejoices
> In the mellow rays,
> All earth's thousand voices
> Swell the hymn of praise.

These devotions concluded, the senior classes departed to various small rooms for the lesson. My memories of the

44

room I knew are associated in my mind principally with
dark winter afternoons, when, for light and warmth, two
gas jets flared. The atmosphere of the place grew almost
unbearable; moisture poured down the walls.

The patience of our good preceptor was sorely tried by
his ungrateful flock. The ringleader in what we regarded as
our legitimate diversion was a youth who had a genius for
asking inconvenient questions. A lesson on the Jewish rite of
initiation was in progress. The teacher went all round the
subject. He discussed Faith and Works, the Old Covenant
and the New. Presently the dreaded question came: "What
exactly, sir, took place when the rite was performed?" The
unhappy man wilted. He plunged again into analogies and
types and symbols. At length, to his deep joy, the bell rang
which warned us that we must now reassemble for the close
of school. He gathered up his notes and fled from the classroom. "But, sir," the plaintive tones of the aggrieved seeker
after knowledge followed him, "what did they really do?"
Nonconformity, at any rate in those days, accurately reflected the nervous prudery of the respectable middle-classes.
In the Church of England, its people being fortified by
familiarity with Tudor outspokenness, a spade is called a
spade.

The shepherd who tended the flock of which this Sunday
School formed a part was, in outward appearance, the
typical Dissenting divine of the days when it was easier than
now to distinguish him from his Anglican brother. He had
a straggling beard; his upper lip only was shaven; his long
damp hair lay about his collar. His smile was described as
oily by those who disliked him. He wore a black frock-coat,

45

light tweed trousers, and a straw hat. He would also have worn tan-coloured boots had they then been invented.

Beneath this unpromising exterior was the soul of a saint and a lover of all things beautiful and good. Flowers, in those days, were slightly suspect by the ever-sensitive Nonconformist conscience. Their presence in a chapel was held to savour of Rome. Yet did this temerarious divine take his courage in both hands and place each Sunday on the table before the pulpit two vases of flowers. The strange ceremony was seriously debated, but the action was not challenged. A point in its favour was that the flowers were provided at the minister's own charges.

Waxing bold at this immunity, he proceeded, further, to inaugurate a May Day Service to which all who attended were exhorted to bring spring flowers, either in bunches or in their native pots. These gifts were afterwards carried to the local hospital. At seven in the morning we gathered on these occasions. The good man, with beaming face, and always with a sprig of lily-of-the-valley pinned to his black gown, conducted devotions which celebrated the return of spring. Two or three times during the service he bade us hold high up our offerings. Then, for a few moments, was the dingy chapel a gay parterre bedecked with gleaming blossoms and the faces of children with round eyes and parted lips.

I had now reached the age at which it was considered desirable that I should "join the Church". This admission to adult privileges is, of course, the Nonconformist equivalent to Confirmation. It shares with Confirmation, also, the fate of being regarded by many young people as a formality to be complied with in response to the solicitations of their elders.

So was it, I fear, with me. Our good pastor, wistfully probing me for signs of a saving faith, asked, "And why do you desire to join the Church, Arthur?"

"Because, sir," I replied, truthfully enough, "my Sunday School teacher asked me to."

My answer was an obvious disappointment, but he was not one to quench the smoking flax, and in due course I received "the right hand of fellowship".

This admitted me to the Lord's Table, and my mother used always, before the monthly Communion, to offer prayers with me in her bedroom, employing for the purpose (with sublime indifference to theological propriety) a communicant's manual compiled by an Anglo-Catholic.

I was somewhat impressed by the service, conducted, as it was, in the solemn calm which succeeded the noisy withdrawal of the greater part of the congregation. But it had no effective point of contact with anything in my then very imperfect mental and spiritual endowment, with the consequence that I accepted Nonconformity—its teaching and practice—as passively and ineffectually as I had submitted to the instruction of the Anglican teachers who had sought to enlighten me.

47

III

SHADES OF THE PRISON HOUSE

By this time I had attained to a knowledge of the commercial subjects dealt with in my class at school such as I then deemed sufficient to enable me to enter upon a mercantile career with every prospect of becoming, in due course, some great one in industrial affairs.

Not that I had any passion for a commercial calling; that was to be merely a path which would lead ultimately to prosperity and ease, and, above all, an affluent, leisured life in the country. My imagination wrought upon the topic until I had the edifice complete from foundation to turret. These detailed plans for the arrangement of my cloud-castle country-home bewildered my mother's matter-of-fact apprehension of the state of the case.

"What nonsense you talk, dear," she said, "you haven't even obtained a situation yet."

"But that", said I, "is easily remedied. I am now about to seek one."

Enquiry led me to suppose that a certain firm of "Colonial Produce Merchants" (as they styled themselves; they were wholesale grocers) needed the services of just such an aspiring youth as I.

My mother and I, furnished with an introduction, attended for an interview with the great man who was to preside over my entrance into the world of commerce.

Facing the door, as one entered the sale room, was a kind of pulpit in which sat, intent upon his books, a clerk. I think of him now as a type of that conscientious toiler in commercial affairs which I was not destined to become. He was method itself. He had done the same thing each day, for six days in every week and for fifty weeks in every year, through well nigh half-a-century—whilst the honeysuckle had glistened in the showers of May; the snipe had drummed in the twilight; the shadows lengthened from where the sheaves drooped in the glow of the autumn sunset; whilst the first snow fell silently at nightfall, and morning had revealed the countryside vested in unearthly purity.

For him all this was not. His task was to be first to arrive in the morning, and open the doors; to be last away at night after bolting and barring securely.

Legend had it that his nourishment was regulated by unchanging law. Each day (as careful observers affirmed) he brought with him a cold pork chop, a two-penny loaf, an ounce of butter, and a pennyworth of milk. These he placed in his desk. At certain fixed hours his head was hidden inside the desk. When it emerged his cheek was seen to be distended. He ruminated its contents after a bovine fashion.

Yet some feeling for the yon-side of existence manifested itself even in this poor drudge. He was married, but childless. It was rumoured that he adored his wife, and that his fairly substantial salary was for the most part devoted to enabling her to enjoy the amenities of life. Music, literature, art, he thus savoured by proxy, content with such scraps from the feast as she chose to interpret to his bedazzled soul.

My mother and I were conducted, by this pattern of what Commerce loves to see in her lesser satellites, into the august presence of a greater planet of that firmament. The interview was brief, but satisfactory. I was to enter upon my duties on the following Monday morning at a commencing salary of ten pounds per annum.

So it fell out, and for twelve years (no less) I made entries in books; added up figures; wrote letters and posted them; wrote more letters which also were duly forwarded. Thus the tale. Monotony, extending over twelve long years—those precious years, moreover, during which the youth becomes the man.

Had that period of slavery something for me of a salutary discipline? At least it showed me that I possessed endurance; that I was capable of a heart-seared tenacity of purpose. Though summer succeeded summer and I passed them amid surroundings which I soon began to hate with a fierce silent rage, realizing that year after year of my life was being filched from me; still I went on. I changed, indeed, my plans as to how release should be achieved, but never faltered in the resolution to escape, at long length, from this soul-destroying drudgery into a way of life in which I could move for the few years granted to me in this earthly paradise with leisure to make its enchantment a part of myself.

In the mid-season of this prison existence, a window was opened for me looking towards Jerusalem. I became acquainted with the poetry of Shelley and Keats.

The ignorance of uncultured youth hid a great part of Shelley from me. But at least I had sufficient wit to enable him to lead me out of London into another country, of which some features were those of Italy and Greece, but the main part whereof was a land I had known long since but was likely to have lost.

I was intoxicated by the loveliness of Keats. As with Shelley so with him, my ignorance hid from me much of his greatness, yet even I could be one with him as he sat, on that still autumn day, when for him the busy world was hushed, and life's fever almost over. I felt his trembling fingers set down the deathless lines, and heard with him the passionate song that lured my soul, too, into the dim forest glades, and onward toward a land of far distances.

What, now, but that I also (poor fool) should attempt to describe the indescribable? It was nothing that what can be set down in words has already been uttered by those ethereal spirits who have pushed the bounds of speech so far as to make the sign almost one with the thing signified. The creative faculty cannot but seek expression; or, at least, the imprisoned spirit must find an outlet. However ludicrous the failure in utterance, out of the abundance of the heart the lips must speak. I turned poet.

In after years I submitted to one, himself of the authentic band, what in those days I wrote with conviction so real, with passion so intense. He is one who loves all and speaks kindly of the least. "Your poems gave me pleasure", he said. "They are an echo of the great Romantics, are they not? They pleased me with a certain gentle, pensive beauty."

Be that their epitaph. A charitable account of what is dead. But I feel that there was something not altogether incongruous with the dignity of man's immortal soul in that other self of mine. Outwardly, a thing that journeyed by train each day; that calculated the sum-total of figures; that ate frugal meals at cheap eating-houses. Inwardly, a dream-struck thing passing from eternity to eternity, sustained by faint glimpses of the glories which seemed to lie beyond.

And so, on the top of omnibus or tramcar; while waiting for the train at the noisy City terminus; and also (alas! with true contrition I must write it) when I ought to have been hard at work helping to fill the brass-edged tomes that now keep an incommunicable sleep in the strong room of a certain firm of London merchants, I committed to paper those stanzas after the (outward) manner of Spenser in which I sought to relieve my pent-up emotions. A blessed escape from actuality without which I truly think that some of those twelve slow-moving years would have been unendurable.

Yet there were days when the charm was broken, when fancy could not hold out against the grim reality. One such time impressed itself indelibly on my memory. It was a most splendid day of early summer. The streets of the vast crowded city sweltered in a blaze of sunshine. Blinds were drawn; we sat at our desks and toiled on. I was summoned to take a message to a house of business a mile away. I emerged into the sunlight and, passing through a quiet by-way, in the unwonted hush I heard an itinerant musician playing on the harp. He played an air I had never heard before, nor have I heard it since, but I recollect it, note for note, now after more than thirty years. As I stood with the little knot of people who gathered round the harper, listless on that

52

June day, his music touched some spring of feeling which, blending with my constant thoughts, gave me a most poignant sense of homesickness for the glory of the divine country. I knew that at that moment the cattle were sheltering under the elms, knee-deep in streams which threaded the living green...that in the southern counties there must now be the scent of new-mown hay...that along the coast of Devon the tide was running over crescents of snowy pebbles, lapping around the rocks, swaying the filmy red seaweed. I looked out of a cavern in the cliff side and saw, framed in ebony, a fragment of the sea; white sails filled to the breeze that blew in to me sunny and brine-laden.... The cuckoo's note was changing as it reverberated among the lonely hills....I walked beneath a canopy of branches down a lane deep set in the heart of Gloucestershire. It opened upon the silver and gold of uncut meadows....

Thus, in a flash, as it were, I saw England as God made it, and as God means it to be on one of those days when earth takes on the semblance of heaven.

And then the music ceased; the pageant faded. The harper removed his hat and laid it, inverted, upon the ground before him, in mute appeal. The minstrel was gratefully rewarded, albeit not as my desire, nor his, may have conceived as his due. I passed on with a tension at the heart that was almost physical suffering.

The harping of that harper (to me an incarnated wanderer from the celestial company whose music fell upon the ear of the writer of the Apocalypse) and the response which he awoke in me mark, in my memory, the high tide of this kind of emotion, as I experienced it at that time.

Human nature, fortunately, cannot sustain continuously over long periods any profound emotion. I sank into apathy. At times I was, in a manner, contented. My situation corresponded to the almost invariable rule—it did not lack alleviations.

The office in which more than a decade of my life was spent sheltered a curiously diversified company of persons, brought promiscuously together and united by one sole tie —the necessity of earning a living.

I was too reserved to make friends, and too simple (oddly enough) to be harmed by the greater part of the indecent talk which I might chance to overhear. One man I recollect as the ringleader in this. A person of unhealthy complexion, of clammy and trembling hand, who offered you furtive glimpses of continental photographs. He appeared from time to time with unsightly skin eruptions and was redolent of disinfectant.

A contrast to him was a tiny man with a disproportionately large moustache; an earnest soul who heard Mass at a High Anglican church every Sunday morning and, in the afternoon, raised by a soap box to the level of his contemporaries, strove to incite the stolid throng to bloody revolution.

The nearest approach to friendship which I reached was with the occupant of the next desk to mine. His passion was the drama and his custom was to read during his lunch hour a tattered copy of Shakespeare printed in the smallest type by someone interested, plainly, in the trade in optical instruments. Into my attentive ear would he whisper immortal verse while our pens lay idle between our fingers.

"Ah, Mr Wolfe," he would say, "could you but have heard Ellen Terry utter those words as I heard her speak them when she was young. It was the first night of the production. I had waited hours for a seat. I sat down at length, exhausted. But the moment the curtain rose upon the enchanted scene I was transformed. I entered another world. I sat in an ecstasy of unspeakable delight as beauty succeeded beauty, and the deathless lines lived upon golden tongues.

"At last the curtain fell, and I started up as from a dream. I came out into the London streets echoing with raucous noise.

"But I could not tear myself away. I must hang about at the stage door until the lady I worshipped appeared. I raised my hat as she passed me, and her smiling bow lifted me, sir, into the Heaven of Heavens.

"Then, with my hat dashed down over my eyes, home to my miserable lodging; but no sleep for your humble servant that night. Backward and forward, up and down the floor of the garret, ranting and raving, mouthing the speeches, picturing myself the Romeo to that incomparable Juliet, acknowledging the frenzied applause of the audience.

"The next day, sir, the gentleman who occupied the apartment below me sent up his compliments, and would take it as a favour if I went through my training exercises at any hour outside one to five in the morning.

"In me, Mr Wolfe, an abject and broken slave ignominiously toiling for a pittance, you behold one who (had the gods been kind) might possibly have left behind him a name. As it is, he will go down to the grave (very shortly,

I believe) unwept, unhonoured and unsung. And now, for a complete change, suppose we both get on with our work."

Gentle soul! Your life of drudgery accomplished, the last entry (in your wonderful Italian penmanship) completed, may you be admitted to a symposium of the immortals of the dramatic art and duly honoured for what you might have been.

The only occasion when the entire staff of the office met for any other purpose than work was at an annual dinner which was held at an hotel near by. The first of these functions which I attended impressed me greatly, because I had had no previous acquaintance with a meal of six courses. I feasted with Lucullus. Also it revealed to me in an entirely undreamed-of light the men I thought I knew.

It amazed me to perceive the senior partner acknowledging another god than Mammon in the grace with which he solemnly opened the banquet. I was overcome at hearing the principal cashier racily reminiscent, and a junior clerk, with genial badinage, bidding him stop talking and pass the cruet. It was as strange to listen to the weighty affairs of the office being discussed in humorous vein as it would be to overhear a monarch's connubial confidences after a State function. A veil was withdrawn and a little company of human beings was revealed.

The cloak-room waiter courteously assisted me to put on my overcoat. Deferentially I enquired if there was any charge. "I leave that to you, sir", he replied. I gave him sixpence. It was the sum-total of the wealth I carried with me.

56

Next morning the imperturbable countenances of our great ones betrayed no recollection of the ungirded ease of the night before. We were caught up again into the machine.

An apparently trivial circumstance, which occurred when I had followed this course of life for about three years, was destined to carry me ultimately into a new world.

I had wandered during my lunch hour into one of the City churches. I found the incumbent conducting a few visitors over the building. I joined them, and was struck by the facility with which the clergyman translated the Latin inscriptions on certain ancient monuments.

It occurred to me that it was a highly desirable thing to be master of this great language. What stores of interest were unlocked to such an one. He could reel off the meaning of crabbed inscriptions to awe-struck listeners. And more. Was there not great Latin poetry the beauty of which was lost in translation, the delicate charm inherent in the language in which it was written?

I must know Latin! I purchased a grammar and plunged with ardour into deep waters. I declined and conjugated as I journeyed daily in the train to and from the City.

Books on Occultism insist that the written word is insufficient; there must be the guru, the master, to interpret orally to the disciple. Alas, I had no master, and the mysteries of quantity and accent were hidden from me. I pronounced Latin as fancy dictated, and to this day I fear to venture upon an oral quotation, in terror of a false quantity.

Yet, it was thus that I entered into possession of one of humanity's choicest treasures—the pure delight of acquiring

57

knowledge. For this I had never had the least desire during my schooldays. I must have been seventeen years old before I experienced a deep joy in the exercise of the capacity to know. I became ashamed of my ignorance. I grew conscious of the romance of pushing out on the great ocean of human learning. I think I did not then love knowledge simply as knowledge with the scientist's impassioned quest of the fact. I coveted knowledge for the fresh fields it provided in which the imagination could find pasture. It promised me a world of wonder and delight. I dwelt upon the thought with a kind of poetic ardour.

I have never had the vivid consciousness, enjoyed by some, that the unseen powers have been sufficiently interested in my welfare to intervene directly in my small affairs. And yet, as I look back upon the strange variety of causes which acted together to determine the nature of my life's work, it is hard to resist the feeling that, without any kind of coercion, I was yet being led along a path which I knew not. Circumstances having, apparently, no kind of relation with each other, combined to produce a definite result upon the whole of my future life.

Amongst these oddly miscellaneous occurrences was one which gave pain to the excellent Nonconformist divine, whose ministrations I was at that time attending. He suffered the lot, not uncommon to his kind, of being driven to abandon his charge owing to the vexatious conduct of his flock. Had he been an obscure person, or an elderly man realizing that his market value was decreasing year by year, he would have been compelled to pray for a double portion of the spirit of Job, and go on. But he was in the prime of life, and a man of some note. Consequently he resigned, and responded hopefully to a call elsewhere.

His departure brought to an end my mother's connection with Nonconformity. This second change in her allegiance betokened no sort of inconsistency on her part, nor on that of her children, who followed her lead. She had attached herself to Nonconformity because she thought that there existed, in the particular Dissenting community with which she had come into contact, a devotion, a warmth of feeling, a sense of Christian unity which was lacking in certain Church of England congregations with which she had associated on first coming to London. She abandoned Nonconformity upon discovering infallible proofs that envy, hatred, malice and all uncharitableness existed side by side with an extreme religiosity in the only Nonconformist assembly she knew well.

But between her early acquaintance with Anglicanism and her final experience of Nonconformity great changes had taken place in the Church of England. Despite the many and glaring faults which still exist within its borders, few would deny to the Established Church the credit of a change for the better since the days when Dickens and Thackeray voiced the popular contempt into which it had deservedly fallen.

My mother was as indifferent to theological niceties as are the majority of the inhabitants of the southern portion of this island. She shared their view of religion as being something which stimulates the good in us; which gives some kind of expression to our unformed longings after

59

better things; which offers us a working explanation of life and its problems; and which affords, in some one of the many forms of ecclesiastical organization, the help and encouragement of fellowship with other wayfarers bent upon the same quest.

Of the points of doctrine and church order which distinguish the Church of England from other religious bodies she had but the vaguest ideas. Amid a life of many sorrows and great trials, she sought help wherever she might find it, and was indifferent to the theological affinities of the source from which succour came.

A kindly Evangelical clergyman relieved the transition of the least sense of embarrassment, and henceforth my mother and her children were to be reckoned amongst those who extend to the Church of England that somewhat vague but quite real allegiance which is the despair of our dogmatic purists.

For my own part, I accepted the change with the same passivity with which I had passed into Nonconformity from the Tractarian influences of my childhood. I certainly preferred the ordered worship of the Church of England to the changes and chances which wait upon those who hazard their devotions to the vagaries of extemporaneous utterance. Our good pastor being absent through illness, I once heard his substitute desire Omnipotence to teach that gentle, suffering soul to "realize that there is a Divinity which shapes his ends, rough-hew them as he may".

The church we now attended being of the kind known as Evangelical, the services were simple, but we chanted the Psalms and Canticles and Responses, and I discovered a real pleasure in that "Anglican" Church music which is so grievous an infliction to lovers of Plainsong.

I was confirmed with more or less the same feelings with which I had "joined the Church" in my Nonconformist days. The course of preparation conducted by an Evangelical clergyman did not lead me to attach any profound sacramental significance to the rite. I regarded the ceremony as one of initiation into adult membership in the Church of England, of which body I was willing to become an adult member, and with that the matter, for me, ended.

The most vivid recollection of the Confirmation service which I retain is of the organ playing an opening voluntary while the church bells were still pealing. The two sets of sounds combined harmoniously, and deeply affected me.

I had been a communicant Nonconformist, and my first experience as a communicant in the Church of England did not provide me with any fresh spiritual experience. I felt something of an unusual solemnity in the early morning hour at which the service was held. The gleam of the celebrant's surplice against the red velvet of the altar far away at the east end of the church touched me with some kind of awe. The act of kneeling to receive the hallowed symbols was something new and strange. My communion was attended, too, by the feeling that such an act was incompatible with a life lived on a level of indifference to the claims of religion and morality.

Next in order of the events which combined to fix my vocation was a visit, paid to the office in which I worked, by a former clerk who had abandoned commerce to become a clergyman. The great man was received with due deference by his late colleagues, although a wag recalled to the memory of the embarrassed divine some escapade of his less-ordered days.

I watched the young man in his black garb, the neat gold watch chain with the tiny dependent cross (odd collocation!), the narrow white collar. I speculated on his present manner of life; I envied his freedom from the drudgery of the office stool. I pictured him with time for study and thought, moving through a round of useful but not irksome duties, enjoying the society of cultured people; able, in a word, to live as I desired to live.

The thought struck me (and I flushed hot as I realized what I was thinking): "Why not take up the same career?"

There were mountains of difficulty in the way, I knew. I was a plebeian and but little educated, without money, without influence, and I supposed that these deficiencies would be almost insuperable barriers for one who aspired to Holy Orders in the Church of England. But this man before me had achieved the impossible!

And what an object for which to work and struggle! Should I not be able to satisfy my newly born desire for learning? And the life of a country clergyman presented itself to me as the one vocation in which I could both gratify my thirst for study and at the same time move amongst those scenes of Nature to enjoy which I was consumed with so passionate a desire.

I realized, in a vague way, that the objects which led me to seek the priesthood were not of the highest kind. An utter devotion to God, a burning love of the souls of men, a gospel which I was compelled to proclaim—these, I knew, were possessions which many would hold as indispensable in one seeking so exalted an office.

I had to admit to myself that none of these compelling motives was mine. Yet I argued that many men were useful ministers who did not strive to wind themselves too high. I would be one of these. I should take a genuine delight in conducting worship in the stately liturgy of the English Church. I could preach, I thought, not unhelpfully, with the whole wealth of the literature of the Bible as subject-matter. I would visit my people conscientiously. I would live an upright, honourable, useful life. Was not that enough?

And so, for good or ill, whether with worthy motives or unworthy (with mixed motives, in reality) my resolution was taken. It was a resolution to which I held with un-deviating purpose, and with a perseverance which over-came the most formidable obstacles, over a period of eight long years, until my object was achieved.

Thus it fell out that the casual translation of a Latin in-scription, the vexatious behaviour of a certain Dissenting congregation, and a chance visitor to a London office brought it about that the life of one whom none of these things had concerned personally was completely changed.

The resolution being taken, the next step was to deter-mine how best to bring about the accomplishment of my desires. I had no definite information as to what is required of candidates for Holy Orders in the Church of England,

and, in my existing circumstances, I was too shy to make enquiries. I knew, however, that the possession of a degree must be a considerable step on the way. Good! I would take a degree.

Obviously, a university which required residence was out of the question, but I knew that the University of London granted its privileges to those who attained to the necessary standard of knowledge without any stipulations as to how that knowledge should be acquired.

I obtained the syllabus of subjects for matriculation and at once saw that before I was competent to undertake work on the prescribed matter it would be necessary for me to acquaint myself with the rudiments of each subject set, of most of which I was ignorant.

For a year, therefore, I worked by myself at elementary books and, towards the end of that period, chancing to see a notice that a class for preparation for this examination was about to commence at a college on the outskirts of the City, I joined it.

The two years which followed were devoted, therefore, to office work by day, and to the classes and home preparation in the evening. Our instructor was a mild, amiable man who, having obtained first-class honours at matriculation, had belied the fair promise of his first essay by subsiding into a pass degree. But he was a capable and painstaking teacher, and I found myself in an atmosphere congenial to keen and enthusiastic work. We were not schoolboys being driven reluctantly along the paths of knowledge. We were young men and women all anxious to know things; eager enquirers; assiduous toilers.

And so, at the end of two years, I found myself one June day in the hall of some institution on the Thames Embankment, lent for the purpose, about to undergo my first serious examination.

O, the terrors and the joys of those five summer days! The grave person in charge of the proceedings hands round the slip of paper bearing the dozen or so of questions. With beating heart I scan its contents. Yes! I can deal with this—and that. Ah! And that was the very matter we discussed at length in class last term! I recollect exactly how our instructor summed it up. I can recall his terse accurate dicta, and the examiner shall have an answer in abler words than mine.

Wisely cautioned, I attempt first those questions of the correct replies to which I am most sure. These despatched, I enter debatable ground, and trust to luck. There are still, perhaps, two or three questions to which no conceivably possible answer presents itself in response to the anxious conning of probabilities. But it is no matter, I feel sure I have done enough to secure a pass, and with a sigh I lay down my pen.

I look around me and perceive on all sides persons in various stages of emotion, ranging from him whose face expresses placid content as his pen travels without haste and without rest over the paper, to him whose eyes seek inspiration from the ceiling, and the end of whose pen remains between his teeth.

At last the five days are over. A rush from the examination room to the station, and the blissful prospect of nine days in a quiet village near the coast of Kent. Nine days only, for the examination has taken from me five of those precious periods of my brief annual holiday.

And now, to possess my soul in such patience as is possible until the result of the examination is made known. Days of alternate hope and deep gloom. How often do I weigh the chances, and cling with desperation to someone's cheering prophecy: "O, you won't be ploughed unless you were very bad".

At length, a great printed sheet reaches me. It contains first the names of those illustrious persons who have achieved "Honours". But I do not exercise myself in great matters. My eyes scan the "Pass" list and there (my name for the first time in print) I read, set out at full length, "Arthur Berkeley Wolfe". I repeat it to myself and rehearse my honours—"Matriculated Student of the University of London".

My feet are on the ladder. Excelsior!

Greatly encouraged, I turned my thoughts now to the next step—the Intermediate Examination in Arts. A class in preparation for that, too, was announced at the institution which had helped me previously.

On the day and at the hour specified, I was ready at the notified place and eager as a war-horse for the battle. I waited for a long time, and, no one else arriving, I enquired at the office, afraid that I had mistaken the appointed time.

I received my first setback. A class for this examination was in the nature of a pious aspiration of the authorities. If a sufficient number of entrants did not appear it was not held. Such was the case now.

Very sorrowfully I returned home, and for a few days was greatly perplexed. Fortunately, I came across a notice from which I learned that tuition for my next examination could be obtained by correspondence. In using this method one would miss two very valuable helps—the living voice of an instructor and the stimulus and assistance of fellow-students. But it was the only way, so far as I could see.

My means were so limited, that, to save expense, I resolved to get up two of the set subjects (those with which I thought myself best acquainted) without help.

In a few lines I can describe the two years' work which followed. But, as I recall it, I think it was a valiant effort. Let him who, after a thorough grounding at a Public School, proceeds in due course to one of the two greatest of our Universities, ponder these things and give thanks for his happy lot.

Would he, I wonder, have laboured all day, year after year, in a stuffy office, and then have shut himself up, during almost the whole of his leisure time, alone with his books?

Would he have toiled like that when springtime summoned him out into a world of sudden greens, and the song of birds? Would he have closed his eyes to the lure of summer days? Known that autumn was calling to him to bathe his soul in glory, and yet have turned away?

Would he have sat on many an evening of biting wintry cold, clad in an overcoat, and with a rug wrapped round him (for the little room I used as a study had no fireplace), yet at his books while all the house was still and he alone working far into the night?

I toiled terribly, held up, sometimes, for an hour, puzzling over some difficulty which a friendly tutor would solve for him in two minutes.

O, happy, happy youth, for whom the rugged path of learning is smoothed into verdurous slopes opening ever upon fresh delights!

In after years a warm-hearted old General of my acquaintance, who knew something of my early struggles, was wont to add "M.A." to my name in addressing letters to me. "I am not entitled to this distinction", I remonstrated. "But, begad, sir, you deserved it", was his argument.

Achievement, however, does not always follow desert. At any rate, I was to learn that in my case desire outran performance.

A further two years' work accomplished, again I took my place in the examination room.

In due course I scanned the list of successful entrants. My name was not among them.

Upon enquiry I found that I had passed in the three subjects in which I had been coached, and failed in those two in studying which I had relied on my unaided efforts.

For a few days I was mentally stunned. Two years of unremitting toil had gone for nothing, I told myself. It is true that I had learned a good deal, and, on the whole, I had thoroughly enjoyed the process. But for my immediate purpose those years were wasted, since fresh subject-matter was set for examination annually, and one must take over again all five of the divisions of the syllabus.

Well! there was no help for it. I must begin again. And

now, not with the inspiring sense of going forward, but with the feeling of attempting to recover lost ground and with the haunting remembrance of past failure.

Thus I struggled on for about two months, and then there happened that which any observant and experienced person could easily have foretold.

It was one evening in autumn. In all the orchards of England, doubtless, the trees bowed beneath their rich fruitage. Homing rooks would now be seeking their native haunts after a noble foraging in the stubble. The sun was going down in a blaze of splendour. I knew it, for ruddy gold dappled the wall of my little room. Rustic lovers, bronzed with wind and rain and sunshine, clear-eyed and in all the vigour of radiant health, would be whispering along quiet lanes. . . .

I turned again to my books. I became conscious that I read but did not comprehend. I read again. I could not grasp it. Once more I made the attempt, but a heavy, dull pain at the back of my head, and an alarming feeling of acute tension warned me to stop.

I took up a book of illustrations and glanced over a few pages to rest my mind, and then tried to read again. In vain. Something, I knew, had gone wrong with me. That faithful, willing servant, my brain, had toiled too hard. It had responded over and over again to the demands I made upon it. But now it was like a worn-out steed put to an impossible task, which, conscious of whip and spur no longer, staggers a few steps and collapses.

I did not realize all this at the moment. Gradually, however, it dawned upon me that for a time, at any rate, I must lay my books aside. I dared not contemplate what this might mean to all my hopeful plans.

So now, instead of spending my evenings within doors, I went into the open air. But I was like a prisoner released from a darkened cell. I was unused to the light. I did not know how to employ my unaccustomed liberty. I walked aimlessly to and fro, and sought by violent exercise to relieve the tension of my mind. Change of work (for such was my unintelligent rushing from a sedentary indoor life to the opposite extreme) proved no recreation to me. I endured bodily fatigue in addition to mental; that was all.

My acutely sensitive, over-taxed mind now became a prey to a variety of alarming ideas. I imagined myself in the earlier stages of mental alienation. I know perfectly well, now, the nature of my malady, and I realize that it followed an entirely normal course. I shared the lot of such as have overstrained the mental faculties. George Borrow and Leigh Hunt, to name but two out of many, have given accounts of their experience of it. Both sufferers outlived the agonizing trial, and, given a certain amount of resolution, the phantoms of acute depression and paralyzing fear can be outfaced, as I was myself to prove. But how much easier would the effort have been had I realized the intimate connection between bodily and mental health. At length, in my agitation and alarm, I summoned up sufficient courage to consult a doctor.

Had he been a fairy physician, carrying on a highly successful practice in Utopia, he would, after having listened to the catalogue of my woes, have addressed me after this sort:

70

"All the symptoms of which you speak have their origin in a single cause. You have overworked one part of your organization, and have neglected the rest. You can win back perfect health by recovering the balance. For this purpose you will walk out of my surgery to the Land's End, and return hither to report yourself cured, because, as has been truly observed: 'An excitement which vents itself in moderate bodily exercise carries its own sedative with it'. You will take a month to accomplish the journey each way, for you will proceed at the average rate of ten miles a day, strolling along at the speed of two miles an hour. The gentle exercise will soothe your mind and promote the metabolism which will result in gradually returning bodily and mental poise. Upon reaching your destination (the Land's End, you remember), you will, if the weather be fine, seek out a safe and sequestered cave facing south, and there, divested of your clothing, you will lie all day with your head in the shade and your body exposed to the warm sunlight, of which it has been starved. With every muscle relaxed, your mind will relax also, and you will yield your whole being, in a delicious sense of absolute repose, to Nature's healing powers. Also, since all this cannot be done without money, oblige me by accepting my cheque for one hundred pounds, the greater part of which you will spend on nourishing food (bread, cheese, ale and an onion for your midday meal; with a pint of good red wine at supper). Carry out these instructions and I promise you that all your symptoms will vanish like ghosts at cock-crow."

But alas! the doctor I consulted lived in our workaday world. He was a very busy man and had had a strenuous

71

day. His waiting-room was filled with other patients need-
ing help, and I was a case of "nerves", an ill from the
treatment of which the average doctor derives much trouble
but little glory. The consultant yawned frequently during
my recital, and at its end apologized. "I beg your pardon",
he said, "I am afraid I was not attending. What was it you
said? Ah, yes, yes! If you can't sleep take a tumbler of hot
milk before you go to bed, and I'll send you a tonic. Will
you ask the next patient to come in?"

The medical science at my disposal having failed to
minister to a mind diseased, I was led, I know not how, to
turn for help to the physician of the soul.

I chanced to take up a volume of sermons by a preacher
of whom I have already spoken, the once celebrated
Spurgeon. The force and earnestness, the strength of conviction of the man moved me deeply. I concluded that my
malady was a spiritual one. My trouble was that I had not
found salvation. My heart was not right with God. I had
not attained peace and joy in believing.

What must I do to be saved? To experience the radiant
joy, the sense of absolute safety, the deep tranquillity at the
heart, of which I felt myself in such dire need? The
preacher answered the question in unmistakable terms. I
must close with the offer. I must fall in with God's plan of
salvation. Believe in the finished work of Christ, simply.
Do nothing whatever save rest in full confidence on what
Christ has done for me. Such was the course I must pursue.
The joys of the believer were set forth in the sensuous
imagery (drawn from parts of the Old Testament) which
once exercised so powerful an influence over middle-class

72

minds of pietistic cast existing in drab surroundings, and possessing man's incurable longing for some outlet into the land of heart's desire.

I could picture the pale, eager faces of the throng assembled "in the Metropolitan Tabernacle, Newington, on Sunday morning, August 2nd, 1863", and how, on that bygone summer day, they were for a while translated from "these long corridors of dreary cells, which we call streets and houses", into another country, as they listened to the sermon entitled "Mealtime in the Cornfields". It opened thus:

"This morning we are going to the cornfields, not, however, so much to glean, as to rest with the reapers and the gleaners, when under some wide spreading oak they sit down to take refreshment. We hope there will be some timid gleaner here, who will accept our invitation to come and eat with us"

I yielded myself to the writer's limited but affecting eloquence. I cried mightily unto the Lord, as he bade me, and at times I really felt myself to be indeed one of those happy souls he described. I passed days in a sort of religious ecstasy. I pictured myself walking in green pastures, lying down by the still, deep pools of living water, sustained and guided ever by the rod and staff of the Lord my Shepherd.

I even extracted a curious comfort from the preacher's description of the fate of those who did not close with the offer, who rejected the plan of salvation:

"As the huntsman, when he goes forth to the battue, encompasses the beasts of the forest with an ever-narrowing

73

ring of hunters, that he may exterminate them all in one great slaughter, so the God of justice has made a ring in His providence about the sinful souls of men. No impenitent sinner can break through the lines; as well might a worm escape from within a circle of flame. I hear the baying of the dogs of death to-day, hounding the unbelieving to their doom...".

"My sufferings have been great", I thought, "but they are nothing to the tortures endured by the lost, where their worm dieth not and the fire is not quenched; where God Himself laughs at their calamity and mocks at their fear."

Thus, in my distress, I yielded myself to a theological scheme which in calmer moments I had regarded vaguely as being, no doubt, a true account of the facts, but which had no vital influence upon my mind and heart. In circumstances such as mine then were, one clutches at any and every means by which help may come. I cared not what was the source from whence succour reached me, providing that it kept me from being overwhelmed by the dark tides of despair that rolled over my soul.

I committed to memory some of the great Latin hymns, and at night time would endeavour to tranquillize my mind for sleep by repeating silently those immortal verses. I pictured the divine vitality flooding the empty soul as I chanted:

> Veni, creator Spiritus,
> Mentes tuorum visita,
> Imple superna gratia
> Quae tu creasti pectora....

74

How fervently did I utter Adam of Saint Victor's prayer:

> Donet nobis rectam mentem,
> In adversis patientem,
> In secundis humilem;
> Fidem puram, spem securam,
> Caritatem permansuram,
> Qua nihil est melius....

I tasted the rapture of Bernard's *Hymn of the Love of Jesus*:

> Jesu, dulcis memoria,
> Dans vera cordis gaudia;
> Sed super mel et omnia
> Dulcis ejus praesentia....

Thus, the eloquence of the unlettered Baptist peasant and the august music of the Catholic hymns would combine to give me that sense of a Power beyond myself, able and willing to help me in response to my acknowledged need. From time to time the peace of God slid into my soul and I experienced my first conscious impression of something vital and personal to myself in the strange conflicting phenomena of religion.

Especially do I recall a period, lasting for several weeks, in which I was possessed by an almost ecstatic perception of the truth of the Christian religion (as I understood it) and of its overwhelming importance to myself. I felt a passionate interest in sacred things; I read nothing but religious books and particularly the New Testament, every word of which seemed to me unspeakably precious. I longed for someone similarly affected with whom to take sweet counsel, and found him in a fellow-clerk to whom the Salvation

75

Army had imparted red-hot salvation. His boisterous greetings fell delightfully on my ear as he overtook me, trudging manfully through the slush of a dark wintry morning: "How are you, brother? A lovely, rainy, foggy day! Bless the dear Lord for all His goodness!" Strangely unembarrassed, I would reply, "Amen, praise His name!" And together we trod the Land of Beulah, and looked down from delectable hills. Again and again I told myself that this living from moment to moment in the realized Presence of God, with all its deep and hallowed joys, its absolute conviction of an interest in a Saviour's merits, and its consequent sense of power and peace, was life's most precious gift. I had a haunting dread that a time might come when the light would die away and I should drift back into dark uncertainty. Then the world would become an ordinary and dreary place instead of this adventurous battlefield through which I was passing with dreadful enemies on every hand but with Heaven's sunshine in my soul.

Alas, it fell out as I had feared. Slowly, imperceptibly, the ardour relaxed, the visionary splendour faded, and I returned to earth; yet enriched by an experience because of which the twice-born's stories of traffic with things eternal stir memories in me. I too have felt.

Although this period of divine intoxication passed, there remained alleviations. In the wide wilderness of London City there were certain oases which afforded me at this time some of the mental and spiritual rest and refreshment of which I stood in so sore need. I believe that the incumbents of the City churches now take a more generous view of their responsibilities, but when I knew them the buildings for the most part were kept locked, and their guardians appeared unconscious of the amazing privilege of being practically the only official representatives of religion in the heart of the metropolis of the world.

There were a few exceptions. From time to time a church was opened for an organ recital, and, although my knowledge of music was rudimentary, I sometimes found my way into fairyland borne upon the rippling melody of a barcarolle, or tossed by the tempestuous surges of a fugue as it thundered through its mighty course from the opening theme to those majestic chords that brought it to a triumphant and heart-satisfying close.

Even more potent was music when its appeal was enhanced by beauty presented to the eye. There was a fine church of Wren's building. It was for a time his own parish church, and contained the canopied pew, adorned with his initials, in which the master was wont to sit, placidly contemplating the fruit of his genius. The dim light that penetrated its painted windows fell in rainbow patches upon a wealth of carving in rich, dark oak, the authentic work of Grinling Gibbons, as the adornment of clustered peascods testifies. This church was in Anglo-Catholic hands, and upon festivals Mass was sung to the settings of some of the masters of ecclesiastical music.

I realize that my musical taste was uncultivated when I recollect that Gounod's *Messe Solennelle* impressed me most. But I still experience the wonted thrill whenever I hear what are to me the magic chords of the main theme of the Kyrie. It is associated in my mind, also, with the odd feeling

77

of being a French priest, and of walking through the rain-washed streets of an old Breton town early on a Sunday morning, a hundred years ago, on my way to say Mass in its cathedral-like church.

Although I was not unfamiliar with the kind of service held in this City church, since I had attended those of a similar sort in my boyhood, yet it was in this place that I first felt the attraction of Catholic worship. It was, I realize, almost entirely an æsthetic attraction. I did not understand the august and venerable conceptions of God and man for which it stood; indeed, as far as I did grasp its meaning, I was, for a time, repelled by it. I retained the conception, with which I had been subconsciously indoctrinated during my Nonconformist days, that the Mass was idolatry. "Nevertheless", I said to myself, "it is a very attractive and beautiful kind of idolatry."

I did not, however, trouble myself with the intellectual aspect of the matter; I only knew that I felt helped and uplifted by the service. The colour, the ordered movements, the perfume of incense (that unique and unearthly fragrance wedded to worship of kinds so various, from remote antiquity), the deep-toned organ, the beautiful singing of exquisite music—all combined to flood my soul with a sense of the wonder of holiness and beauty, and, thus far, to draw me nearer to God.

On one occasion, when listening to a certain passage of music which seemed to me of more than earthly beauty, I chanced to look up at a picture of the Transfiguration. I saw it with half-closed eyes. The scene around me faded. The music seemed to die away, and for a moment my spirit

78

was caught up into a place of eternal calm. This state of perfect tranquillity, combined with full consciousness, passed in a flash, and the silver chiming of the sanctus bell brought me back to earth. But I learned at that moment just enough to feel that while man remains man, retaining his mysterious intuitions of things that lie beyond, so long will the Mass afford to hearts attuned to its significance the most precious link between earth and heaven.

This church of which I speak was a home of ancient loyalties. On the thirtieth of January each year it commemorated the death of Charles the First with a solemn Mass at which an account of the martyrdom was read with faltering voice by the aged incumbent, and a tall, white-bearded personage, splendid in Highland costume, who attended as the representative of some Jacobite society, would call out the name of the *de jure* King of England at the two places in the service in which the Sovereign is prayed for.

Leaving the dimly lighted church, with the sound of the organ, as it thundered a closing voluntary, ringing in my ears, I passed into the noisy streets and was swallowed up once more in a world of external activities.

There was another City church, the incumbent of which did not share the view of most of his brethren that they had fulfilled all righteousness by preaching on Sundays to a congregation of six caretakers. It is true that in those easy-going days he was suffered to reside on the south coast, being incapacitated for work by extreme old age. But he had the grace to provide the ministrations of an earnest and indefatigable curate.

79

This church was one of the few that escaped the Great Fire, and to enter it was to go back through the centuries to mediæval London. The illusion was helped by the presence of all the customary adjuncts of "advanced" Anglo-Catholic ceremonial. Our Lady, beneath a canopy of blue silk, and embowered in flowers and a forest of tapers, smiled benignantly upon her clients from a niche in the wall. A film of incense floated perpetually about the ancient rafters. Plainsong was the only music used, and here I first heard, and learned to love, the *Missa de Angelis*. It was on Michaelmas Day (appropriately enough) that those divinely childlike melodies first fell upon my ear, and I was back in the days when radiant spirit-forms flashed visibly about the homes of men.

I record with hearty gratitude the debt I owe for many hours spent in these two churches, times of welcome refreshment and of pure and happy thoughts. If I try to analyse the impressions made upon me by what I saw and heard, I find that it did not produce in my mind any sort of clear-cut theological conceptions. Although I contemplated being ordained to the priesthood of the English Church I never for one moment imagined myself conducting services after the use established in those two churches. The doctrine and discipline of the Church of England as I understood it was of the kind described as moderate. I regarded Anglo-Catholic worship as a bold and interesting innovation, and its doctrine, as enunciated in many sermons which I heard, produced no lasting impression upon my habits of thought.

About this time, however, I made the acquaintance of a teacher who did exercise a formative influence upon my chaotic ideas. I was standing at a bookstall in a great London railway terminus. Around me surged the tide of humanity. I was, as almost always at that time, in a state of fret and fever, for I was still suffering from the mental over-strain of the past years. I was uncertain as to my future, the success of which seemed to depend so largely on mental efforts which I felt myself totally unable to make. Those acquainted with this phase of human misery know too well its distressing concomitants—the multitude of vague and formless fears; the definite nervous terrors of being in a crowd, of finding one's self shut in; the consciousness of hardly controllable impulses; the hideous fascination exercised by repulsive thoughts; the involved torture of dreading to be in dread; the horror of a great darkness....

> ...a brain confounded, and a sense,
> Deathlike, of treacherous desertion, felt
> In the last place of refuge—my own soul.

Listlessly I scanned the rows of books which the stall displayed. My eyes fell upon a small green volume inscribed with the title *Wordsworth's Poems*. I took it up, and chanced to open it at a certain page of the Introduction in which I read these words: "In this weary, work-a-day world, Wordsworth's poetry exerts a healthy, restful, calming, healing power, on thoughtful, downcast, and desponding hearts, brightening joy, and in times of grief, slowly but surely transmuting sorrow into strength and solemn joy".

I read no more until the little book was mine, and as my own possession it accompanied me everywhere for the next few months. I distracted my mind from gloomy thoughts by committing to memory some of the shorter poems, and would repeat them as I lay awake on many a sleepless night.

I did not at this time grasp in any adequate way the Wordsworthian philosophy of life. What I did get from him was a sense of calm and mental restoration in contemplating the idea of Nature as he portrayed it.

It is impossible to express the value to myself of this message of hope in those days of darkness. Such was the state of nervous distress in which I then lived that I was unable to read the two poets who in the past had been my chief delight. The frustrated longings of Shelley, the feverish despair of Keats, reflected in their poems, were feelings too closely allied to my own to be viewed with philosophic detachment. I could not but suck a poison with the dew.

Nature, as they conceived it (so I felt), was a beautiful, cruel, capricious mistress, a *Belle Dame Sans Merci* wooing to love only to cheat and destroy. The pageantry of Creation serves but to provoke reflections fraught with melancholy and despondency.

If I read Shelley's ethereal song, I was first caught up into the spheres with:

> Hail to thee, blithe spirit!
>   Bird thou never wert—
> That from heaven or near it
>   Pourest thy full heart
> In profuse strains of unpremeditated art.

And then cast to the depths by:

> We look before and after,
>   And pine for what is not;
> Our sincerest laughter
>   With some pain is fraught;
> Our sweetest songs are those that tell of saddest thought.

I believed that to be true. It was the summing-up of all life, and would be of mine. But I could not endure to have the thought so poignantly forced upon me. I put the volume back on the shelf. It no longer opened upon the frontiers of the morning.

Wordsworth also had sung of the skylark. But the wild joy of the little songster was no prelude to a threnody of despair.

He was acquainted with sorrow, truly:

> Alas! my journey, rugged and uneven,
> Through prickly moors or dusty ways must wind.

Yet, mark the characteristic sequence of his thought:

> But hearing thee, or others of thy kind,
> As full of gladness, and as free of heaven,
> I, with my fate contented, will plod on,
> And hope for higher raptures, when life's day is done.

The nightingale's song lured the dying Keats away into fairyland. But it was inevitably for him "a fairyland forlorn". And the mere utterance of the word brought him with the swiftness of a blow back to the wan reality of existence.

Wordsworth, too, sang of the nightingale, though incommensurably with the magic splendour of Keats's Ode. Characteristically he turns from that wild, untimely music breaking the silence of the sleeping earth, to the stockdove's homely tale:

> He sang of love, with quiet blending,
> Slow to begin, and never ending;
> Of serious faith, and inward glee;
> That was the song—the song for me!

I knew it for hempen homespun beside that starry texture, but to me it brought the dawn of a new day. The contemplation of Nature, I saw, need not heap fuel upon the fire of a fevered imagination. On the contrary, Nature was the divinely appointed ministrant of tranquil hope, and deep and quiet joy.

I obtained leave to take a sorely needed holiday. It was but for a week, yet, a memorable seven days, for then I saw the country for the first time after I had read something of Wordsworth. The true Wordsworthian will realize that that must be an outstanding event in one's life. He will understand. To others the recorded memories of such an experience will seem but an idle tale.

My destination was the Isle of Wight. I embarked at Portsmouth Harbour on one of the steamers which cross the Solent. It was a sunny day with a stiff breeze blowing. I stood as closely as I could get to the bows of the ship in order to watch it shoulder the rush of sparkling water, and thrust on either side a seething cream of foam. I delighted

84

to balance myself to the pitch and heave of the little vessel, and it was ecstasy to breathe deeply the cold sweet air and taste the sting of brine on my lips.

An ancient pony-carriage conveyed me from the pier gates and right through the town for the sum of sixpence. The driver received it with an expression of gratitude, for the primitive virtues still lingered in those days.

I was to stay at an institution provided by certain bene-volent persons for the entertainment of young men engaged in town occupations who needed rest and change. I shared a bedroom with a youth whose exuberant spirits I found somewhat overwhelming. Defying the rules of the house he smoked cigarettes, out of the window. He informed me that they were an Egyptian brand and contained a small quantity of opium.

The sedative effect of his tobacco, or more probably his abounding health, caused my companion to sleep soundly the moment after he had, for my entertainment, eased his mind of a mass of disconnected information. He then pro-ceeded to emit throughout the night an unbroken succession of raucous snores, whilst I, tossing and turning, and wide awake with the excitement of my unusual surroundings, listened, as far as was possible, to three nightingales who sang unceasingly in the moonlit garden below.

At breakfast next morning I observed a noteworthy phenomenon. The moment grace was said, every youth whose face was tanned thrust out an arm and seized an egg. Those whose countenances were pale fell with equal vigour upon ham and tongue. All scientific discovery is the result of painstaking observation and rational deduction, and by

85

these means I plucked the heart out of this mystery. The supply of eggs was limited, but there was an abundance of ham and tongue. Having secured the former one was sure of both, a fact which was duly appreciated by those whose brown skins proclaimed that they had been in residence long enough to acquire wisdom.

The aim of the generous folk who enabled us town-dwellers to live for a while in such healthy and beautiful surroundings was twofold—to refresh and restore our bodies and to nourish our souls. Consequently, when we had been soothed with ham and comforted with tongue, chairs were pushed back, Bibles and hymn-books were handed round and we fell to devotion.

The superintendent read and expounded a passage of Scripture and prayed. Then we sang a hymn. One verse of the hymn sung on this occasion lingers (I know not why) in my memory:

> The bride eyes not her garment,
>   But her dear bridegroom's face;
> I will not gaze on glory,
>   But on my King of Grace.
> Not on the crown He giveth
>   But on His piercèd hand,
> Where glory, glory dwelleth
>   In Immanuel's Land.

Lustily enough did fifty voices troll these words, and none with a more unctuous drawl than my young friend the cigarette-smoker.

I wonder greatly what impression of the Christian religion was produced on the minds of that mixed assembly of

English youth by the strange, sensuous oriental imagery of that hymn.

Me it moved chiefly because of the plaintive tune to which it was set, and because of the words "In Immanuel's Land". They gave me the same curious haunting sense of a country of unimagined glory as that which affects me as often as I repeat the first line of Goethe's poem: "Kennst du das Land? wo die Citronen blühn...".

Later on in the morning, it being Sunday, such of the assembled youth as professed religion went their various ways to the places of worship which provided services most in accordance with their several tastes.

The serious matter of the right choice was earnestly debated beforehand. One church was avoided by all. "It is half way to Hell", someone said.

Questioned as to his meaning, he replied: "Well, it is half way to Rome, and that is the same thing". This dictum was approved by all, apparently. I decided I would attend that church. And so I set forth.

It was at the beginning of June, and a day of summer weather. I walked through a sheltered lane, and then out into the dazzling splendour of the open countryside. Larks were pouring out a tumult of song, lost in the shimmering haze above, and presently, with a catch in my breath, I heard afar off the cuckoo. During my visit to Gloucestershire, as a child, I must have heard those two notes often enough with my outward ears, but to-day I listened to their echo in my heart enriched by a new world of association.

And so I wandered on in an ecstasy of wonder and delight. Not yet, however, had I attained to the true wisdom,

87

which, for me, consists in the attempt to subdue all violent emotion; for this, even if it be the emotion of joy, ultimately exhausts the capacity for delight. I know now that a serene and effortless contemplation is the right attitude of the mind in the presence of natural beauty.

> Until, the breath of this corporeal frame
> And even the motion of our human blood
> Almost suspended, we are laid asleep
> In body, and become a living soul;
> While with an eye made quiet by the power
> Of harmony, and the deep power of joy,
> We see into the life of things.

But at that time, as I have explained, I was ignorant of the profounder depths of the Wordsworthian gospel. I must "still be seeking", and become exhausted by the very rapture of delight.

I entered the church. I had almost to feel my way about it, so dim was its interior after the overpowering brightness of the world without.

Seven points of ruby light denoted the presence of the sanctuary lamps so dear to High Anglicans before learned ritualists commenced to fulminate against fancy ceremonial. Many tapers gleamed on and around the altar. Mass of the Holy Spirit was sung, for it was Whitsunday, and, as refreshingly as summer showers, there fell upon my ears the words of the hymn:

> And His that gentle voice we hear,
>   Soft as the breath of even,
> That checks each fault, that calms each fear,
>   And speaks of Heaven.

88

The God being worshipped within the church with that tender music, those stately movements, those gracious words, was one with Him whose splendours were pulsing and glowing in the perfection of all created things. "Heaven and earth are full of Thy glory: Glory be to Thee, O Lord most high."

All too rapidly passed those golden days. Every morning, with my little book in my pocket, would I set forth, in terror, until I was well clear of the house, lest one of its boisterous inmates should favour me with his company, for then the spell would have been broken and my dream-world dissolved.

I trod the short springy turf of the Downs, up and up, until, at the summit, I looked across the wooded plain, through which in the far distance a little toy train was hastening on its devious way. Then, beyond that, gleaming in the sunlight, the sea.

At the week's end I was homeward bound. The garish lights of the great city appeared as the train moved towards its journey's end. Two men, who had slept most of the way, roused themselves. "Well," said one, "I'm bloody glad to be back in little old London. But, Gawd! I'm hungry. I could do with a plate of good stew."

"I reckon", replied his friend, "I could manage a lobster."

IV

ALMA MATER

As I had now spent several months in comparative idleness (that is to say, I worked only eight hours a day in the office, and not during my leisure time as well), my health had improved sufficiently to make it possible to think of resuming my evening studies. But, persevering as I think I was, I could not bring myself to go on where I had left off. The thought of another year or two's incessant toil, with nothing at the end of it but the possibility that I might find myself exactly in the position in which I had confidently expected to be many months ago, was unendurable. I abated not a jot of my main purpose, but I felt I must take other means to accomplish it.

Very fortunately (as it fell out), I happened at the time to see an advertisement in one of the Church newspapers by which I learned that a degree was not indispensable to candidates for Holy Orders in the Church of England. I found that in one of the many institutions comprised within that extensive corporation, the University of London, there was a Faculty of Theology which granted a diploma accepted by most of the bishops in place of a degree. The diploma could be obtained ordinarily after a period of two years, but the kindly and thoughtful person who had drafted the rules (God rest his soul!) had arranged that the course could be extended over three years, during the first two of which students might attend lectures given in the evening, thus being enabled to earn their living during the day.

To this admirable provision the English Church owes some of her best priests, men who do not come raw and inexperienced to the work of the ministry, but such as have known something of the realities of life as lived by those who have had to earn the bread they eat.

I found that the fees demanded were not beyond my modest means, and I hoped to save during the next two years all I should require during the year in which I should be earning nothing.

I was duly entered, and on the first day of term, invested to my no small delight in scholar's cap and gown, I made my way to the lecture room. With some awe I entered the place which my due feet failed not to tread for the next three years.

There were about twenty young men present awaiting the arrival of the lecturer. This was a very elderly clergyman who was wont to be piloted to the college each week by a servant-maid who added to her domestic duties that of delivering her master safely, and waiting for him in the hall to conduct him home again.

The lecturer entered. We rose, bows were exchanged and the lecture (on Ecclesiastical History) was announced: "Our subject to-night, gentlemen, is the Period of the Benedictine Fervour"; and straightway it was begun.

Our tutor, bending closely to his notes, pursued the even tenor of his way for a few moments, when the young gentleman sitting next to me threw down his pen, and, with a sigh, exclaimed: "Whatever is he talking about?" Then, addressing the lecturer, he said solemnly, "You silly old boy. You've left your teeth at home again".

I was horrified at this totally unexpected levity breaking in so harshly upon the stately proceedings, and trembled to think of the punishment to which so audacious a delinquent must be doomed.

But the lecture continued, no notice being taken of the interruption. I realized at length that the lecturer was very deaf.

He was a truly lovable person, and on his birthday we presented him with a bunch of flowers. It was some time before he could be made to realize that they were intended for him, and for what reason. Presently the light dawned and he stood with the bouquet in his hand, embarrassed and bowing and smiling, like an elderly bride.

It was with the utmost delight that I was wont to make my way each evening from the dull routine of the office to those studious bowers. The teaching staff consisted of men who almost all subsequently attained to high places in the Church. Foremost of them was the Principal, who lectured on Dogmatic Theology. The subject, as handled by him, was not that arid waste suggested by its cacophonous and un-inviting superscription. The professor was a conservative theologian, but a man of broad and enlightened views, and he succeeded in extracting from the controversies of which the subject seemed principally to be made up a considerable amount of mental stimulus for those who were privileged to listen to him. No doubt it is necessary for those intending to become ministers of the Church to have some acquaint-ance with Dogmatic Theology, but, apart from the intellectual satisfaction of following the arguments of acute minds, I obtained but little mental food from this subject. Nevertheless, I saw that, granted the premises on which the arguments were based, the superstructure imposed by the great theologians was as impressive an example of what human thought can achieve as it is possible to imagine.

But where was the rock foundation? The whole thing appeared ultimately to rest upon authority only. What was the truth on a certain matter? St Augustine had said this; St Cyprian that. Did you desire to probe yet deeper, St Paul had uttered his mind on the subject, and his testimony is part of Holy Scripture. There we touch bottom. There is infallible truth. In those days I asked no more, but subconsciously, I think, I was not satisfied. However, it was matter to be got up for examinations, and at the end of each term I duly repeated what I had been told, not seriously concerned as to whether or no all this bore any real re semblance to the facts of existence.

The New Testament was expounded by a very painstaking scholar of the Traditionalist School. He regarded his function as that of counsel for the defence; the authenticity and inerrancy of the books of the New Testament was his brief, and he stated his case with impressive conviction. Under his guidance I conceived of the higher critics as persons intellectually negligible and morally to be suspected. He gave to his pupils a good working knowledge of the text of the New Testament, and did not countenance overmuch the symbolical interpretation of Scripture. It is true that he told us that in the Parable of the Good Samaritan we might conceive of the "Inn" as figuring the Church and the "two

93

pence" as mystically representing the two Sacraments, but to an ingenuous youth who suggested that the shipwrecked persons who escaped safe to land, "some on boards, and some on broken pieces of the ship" (as narrated in the twenty-seventh chapter of the Acts), might be regarded as typifying heretics, who got to heaven on mere fragments of the true faith, he was non-committal. "It may possibly be so, but I should not press the point!"

The Old Testament professor was one of the less conservative members of the staff. He took, indeed, the modern or liberal standpoint, but I suppose that in those days he felt himself restricted by his position from urging his views upon us. It is quite possible, however, that my indifference to the subject prevented my appreciating the force and tendency of his teaching. A fact which experience has impressed upon me is that fresh thoughts cannot find a lodgment in minds whose constitution has no point of contact with the unfamiliar matter. For this reason a convinced Catholic is impervious to the arguments of the Protestant, and *vice versa*. The protagonists are moving in two different planes of thought. Like parallel straight lines, they go on indefinitely without ever establishing contact.

The full significance of modern Biblical Criticism, however ably expounded, could not impress itself on me, since there was no point of contact with it in my mental furnishing at that time. I had not studied the Bible with any remarkable carefulness; I accepted it as "the Word of God". That which did impress me in these lectures was the illustrations and analogies from ancient and modern literature with which the professor's cultured mind and wide reading

94

enabled him to elucidate and adorn his teaching. I was thrilled by beautiful thoughts from the poets of Greece and Rome, and the great masters in English literature, and stimulated to persevere in attaining to a position in life in which I could indulge my ardour for browsing in these golden fields.

Pastoral Theology, the subject which deals with the practical details of the priest's life and work, was entrusted to a professor who was known chiefly for his exquisite literary gifts. I believe he had had a brief experience as a country clergyman, but I think that he was not qualified in any extraordinary way for imparting wisdom concerning the practice of the pastoral art. On more than one occasion he entertained us all at supper at his house, and, in addition to an excellent meal (which to most of us in those days was a godsend), he gave us intellectual fare in the shape of disquisitions on things in general, and on books in particular, ample subject-matter being provided by the truly glorious array of volumes that adorned his shelves. It is a vain wish (for untimely death has long since claimed him), but I would that I could listen now to that rare talk, so much of which the raw and uncultivated youth of those days was totally unable to appreciate, though he attended with adoring reverence.

The professor was a truly conscientious teacher and included in his curriculum whatever he thought likely to be of use to us in our future work. He was an enthusiast on the subject of voice-production, and at his bidding the lecture room re-echoed with bovine lowings, and cluckings as of the hen rejoicing over her safe delivery, all of which were

95

part of the exercises with which we developed our vocal chords.

It fell to his lot also to endeavour to fit us out as pulpit orators. For this purpose we had to compose sermons which were submitted first in manuscript and afterwards preached in the pulpit of the college chapel in the presence of the students and such of the staff as sought enlightenment from the spoken word.

Afterwards we adjourned to the lecture room where the discourse was discussed and criticized, first by those of the students who desired to speak, and last of all by the professor himself.

Some of his criticisms dwell in my memory. They were of the character of *bons mots*. He hit off the situation in the fewest possible words, delivered with a slight stammer which contributed to their piquancy. "Mr A.'s sermon was the sermon of a very young man", he said at the conclusion of a discourse during which, in a series of questions and answers, one rash youth had summed up and disposed of the entire subject of Christian Faith and Morals.

"Mr B.'s sermon reminded me of beef tea. It contained, no doubt, plenty of nourishment, but there was nothing to bite."

"Mr C.'s sermon was all introduction—a house consisting of a porch only."

His comment on my effort was: "When I read MrWolfe's sermon I was delighted. When I heard him preach it I was not. I was reminded of what was said of Goldsmith, 'who wrote like an angel but talked like poor Poll'".

I admit the justice of the indictment. Extreme nervous-

ness, necessitating a convulsive swallow between every
five words, is not conducive to pleasing and impressive
speech.

My fellow-students represented every shade of theological
opinion, from him who caused the chapel to ring with denunciations of the Confessional, to him who thus concluded
a panegyric on the Blessed Virgin Mary: "Of this, brethren,
we are sure, that as certainly as, one day, we shall see our
Lord sitting on the right hand of God the Father, so we
shall see our Lady enthroned upon His left".

It must not, however, be supposed that our minds were
always austerely pre-occupied. There were swashing blades
amongst us. It was rumoured that our Lady's panegyrist
had taken a waitress for a trip to Clacton on her day off. It
would have been a joyous experience to have heard this
somewhat aristocratic person dilate on the glories of Mary
to the admiring but bewildered little cockney.

What mischievous sprite was it who one day suggested to
two or three of the future pillars of the Church, who were
sitting at an open window on an upper story of the college,
that it would be a joyful and pleasant thing to fill paper bags
with water and drop them with cautious aim on the heads of
certain members of the medical faculty, who, all unconscious of their doom, stood holding serious discourse below?
Why were the labours of certain earnest students of Natural
History, who performed their useful tasks in a lecture room
adjoining ours, not infrequently brought to a standstill by
sounds of violent disorder in the passage outside? And why
did the professor who superintended their harmless studies

fling open the door, inspect the occupants of the passage, and return to his flock with the news, "Theological students, of course!"

During our last year a doctor gave us a course of lectures on Hygiene. He used, for demonstration purposes, the skeletons of a man and a woman suspended on a kind of gibbet. These were familiarly known as Percy and Emmeline. I think of Emmeline as she appeared one day, chastely garbed in a bowler hat, whilst Percy despised the proprieties, a cigarette between his teeth.

But these were merely the occasional relaxations that brightened lives of toil. A picture more in our accustomed manner is that of a top-story room at the college, from the windows of which we could see the long string of lights on the Embankment, and the greens and reds of shipping on the Thames, and where, shepherded by our kindly chaplain, we met of an evening to discuss questions of serious import. We approached the higher reaches of thought by gradual degrees. First we had music, vocal and otherwise, most appreciated of all of which were the imitations of the illustrious Dan Leno (then in the full blaze of his glory), given by a youth who now shuns delights and lives laborious days as the incumbent of an important London church. Then, braced with coffee, and fortified with cake, we fell to discourse, our host leading us thereto by some guileless opening: "Mr A., what are your views as to the part the Church should take in social questions?"

Men came to this college from every walk in life; and each in his own way felt a real call to the work of a priest. One had been a schoolmaster; his stock of stories of the class of humour usually termed broad was inexhaustible, but his whole soul was in his future work. Another had been a journalist, and he still wrote for the papers. A mild-looking man, spectacled and prematurely bald, it amazed me to hear that he wrote pot-boilers for the *Family Herald*, that weekly instalment of sentimental fiction beloved by young ladies of a past generation. I have it on credible authority that *Lady Ermyntrude's Wooing* paid his fees for a whole term. I wonder whether, a missionary in South Africa, he still remembers those wild days when as "Rosalind Clifford" he swayed susceptible hearts at his will.

My part in all these gallant doings was that of the benevolent onlooker. I had not the spirit to initiate, or even share, in the stirring events that went on around me. It was not always easy for my tired brain to concentrate on the necessary tasks, but I benefited immensely by the assistance of tutors who, with the most generous kindness, were willing to try to answer every question and smooth out each difficulty. It was a great help, too, to be working no longer alone but with friendly companions with whom one could read over and discuss the notes we had made at lectures.

And so two years passed not unpleasantly by. It was now necessary for me to give up my work at the office in order to attend morning lectures during my third year.

The day had indeed come upon which, after twelve years of servitude (as I conceived it), I was at length to go free. To my profound surprise, a collection had been made amongst my fellow-clerks, and the chief cashier presented me on their behalf with a set of books. To this "the Firm"

99   7-2

ALMA MATER

added a money gift with words of kindly appreciation and
goodwill. My conscience pricked me for those past hours
during which I had furtively jotted down verses in the
Spenserian stanza when I ought to have been "totting up"
columns of figures. But what I had written I had written,
during that long chapter in my life.

My next-door neighbour at the office, that unsatisfied
aspirant for histrionic glory, took leave of me in characteristic fashion.

"Mr Wolfe," said he, grasping my hand, "Farewell! In
this sordid abode of Mammon your gifts were wasted, but
at least your companionship has cheered one compelled to
drudge amid a soulless herd. You go to high tasks, and I
doubt not your career will be brilliant. In future years,
when in your comfortable Deanery, or (shall we say?) the
Episcopal Palace, you ruminate on other days, perchance
you may recall an unhappy wretch destined (it would seem)
to drag out in servile toil the remnants of a wasted life. Then,
sir, have the kindness to breathe a prayer for your humble
well-wisher. And now, as the young gentleman who
addresses the envelopes appears to be growing impatient
for the letters I ought to have written, once more,
Farewell!"

The doors which had opened twelve years before on the
timid, ignorant boy, closed now on the man. It was seven
years before I plucked up courage to enter them again, so
seared was my mind by the memory of that exile from the
things that were most dear to me. Even now, at intervals,
I dream that my present life itself is but a dream, and find
myself back on the office stool overcome with misery

by the conviction that my imagined freedom is purely
visionary.

Released now from my commercial duties, I was able to
give all my time and attention to the work of my last year at
college. The results of my terminal examinations had been
satisfactory, and I had hopes that my place in "the Final"
(which depended largely on one's achievements in the
examinations held at the end of every term) might be a
good one.

And so it fell out. The last ditch was a much dreaded
viva voce examination in certain selected books of the Greek
Testament. The victim sat at a table surrounded by the
entire professorial staff, the Principal acting as president.

Terribly alarmed beforehand, now that the dreaded
moment had come, I felt perfectly calm and collected. I had
worked hard at the prescribed matter, and a hasty prayer for
help was at once followed by a sense that all would be well.

Very suavely and courteously the Principal directed my
attention to a passage in one of the Pauline Epistles, request-
ing me to read it in Greek. Then, apparently as an after-
thought, he desired to know how I would render the passage in English. I complied; and he next suggested (a kindly
concession to the humour of the company, as it were) that
I should favour them with my view of how a passage in the
Acts should be translated. At length came the words that
granted release: "Thank you, Mr Wolfe; that will do".

I sat in the college restaurant consuming a modest lunch
and pondering deeply on what was to be my fate. The door
burst open and an excited friend rushed in. "Congratula-

tions, old man! You have got a 'First'—the only one given this year." I continued my meal mechanically, as in a dream.

I had put up a hard fight and had succeeded beyond my hopes. My mother kissed me with affectionate pride when I told her the news. "How good God has been to you", she said. And I agreed.

V

"A POORË PARSON OF A TOWN"

There is, I suppose, no body of Christian ministers the members of which enjoy a larger amount of liberty to please themselves than do the clergy of the Church of England. This freedom commences at the very outset, when one chooses one's first curacy. Independent both of the "Call" from the congregation that is essential in most Nonconformist bodies, and of the fiat of the bishop which settles the matter amongst Roman Catholics, the duly qualified candidate for Holy Orders in the English Church has but to consider the varied possibilities of the many curacies so attractively set forth in the advertisement columns of the Church papers, and make his own choice. For me, however, the choice was limited by the fact that a fellow-student and I had resolved to seek curacies together in the same parish. He showed me an advertisement which offered two "titles" in a great seaport town on the south coast, and we decided to spy out the land.

It fits in with the apparent unaccountability of much of human conduct that I, who for years had pined for a retired country life, as soon as the opportunity for indulging the wish was within my reach, should have failed to avail myself of it. But I had certain reasons, one of which was the desire to prolong the enjoyment of the thought that what I

so earnestly desired now lay within my power and could at
any time I liked be attained,

> A temper known to those who, after long
> And weary expectation, have been blest
> With sudden happiness beyond all hope.

I would not yet rob myself of a golden possibility by laying upon it the destroying hand of achievement. As a curate,
to a large extent under orders, I would serve my apprenticeship in a town. When I had taken my due part in the harsh
rudiments of the Church's warfare, then I could rightly lay
claim to enjoy the ease and leisure of a less onerous charge
in a parish of my own in some pleasant sequestered vale
of life.

My friend and I found ourselves sitting in the study of
our prospective superior. It was autumn, and the little
garden behind the house was a litter of leaves of crimson
and gold, a battlefield strewn with small dead fairies once
brimming with ardent life. Beyond it towered the masts of
ships, and from the quays came the clank of chains and the
rhythmical beat of machinery.

The interview proving satisfactory to all concerned (an
incumbent who sees the chance of securing two suitable
curates at a blow is not to be outdone in urbanity), my
friend and I looked over the church and the parish. The
former was a vast building with galleries, the early Victorian
ugliness of which possessed for me a strange attraction; it
would have been forcefully handled by the pen of Dickens.
The parish consisted of a wilderness of streets, occupied

104

mostly by persons of the artisan class, almost all of whom were connected with the docks or with shipping.

My friend and I sat in a restaurant, exchanging impressions over the teacups.

"Well, guv'nor, what is it to be?" he asked, at length.

"How about trying it?" I said.

We shook hands. And upon that decision (one which might so easily have been otherwise made) has depended the whole course of my life and thought for upwards of twenty years. I have not the faith, the imagination, or the presumption (whichever be the right word) to be confident that this was definitely a case of Divine leading, yet, if I was destined to become what I am, I do not see how otherwise the event could have been so neatly accomplished. I hope, in Another World, to be given the opportunity of tracing out, in my own experience of it, the subtle interaction of free-will with external guidance of which the factors that control our lives appear to be composed.

The method of procedure in such matters ordains that, after being offered a title, the candidate must be accepted as suitable by the bishop in whose diocese the curacy is situated.

In due course I received a summons to wait upon his lordship, and an awe-inspiring rendezvous was appointed, no other than the Lollards' Tower in Lambeth Palace, a part of the London home of the Archbishops of Canterbury, which once served the purpose of incarcerating mediæval heretics but which is now allotted to the use of provincial bishops having occasion to be in London.

My nervousness was responsible for the gaucherie of thrusting out my hand to the Bishop upon being admitted to his presence. He took it limply and dropped it hastily.

I was motioned to a chair and my examination commenced. My credentials were in order, and the Bishop sat and looked at me in silence for a brief space. He was one who had always held dignified positions; a favourite at Court, an aristocrat. Before him was a pale, spectacled, awkward youth, obviously one of the people.

"What is your father?"

"A horse-dealer, my lord."

The overhanging grey eyebrows were slightly uplifted. "In taking Orders this young man stands to benefit by rising in the social scale", was, I imagined, his thought; for what seedy landlady does not obtain a patent of nobility, as it were, by being able to refer to "my cousin, the clergyman"?

"And what have you been?"

"A clerk in a City office."

"What salary were you receiving?"

"Thirty-five shillings a week."

"Under a hundred a year, and he stands to obtain considerably more than a hundred", appeared to be the unspoken thought.

Another pause. The Bishop was a good man. He fought down prejudice. "Your papers are all in order, Mr Wolfe. I have pleasure in accepting you as a candidate for the Advent Ordination, conditionally, of course, on your passing the examination for Deacons."

Pondering that interview now, I am bound to smile at its

oddity. Had I approached the Bishop as a scion of some important family, a finished product of Eton and Christchurch, he would have been perfectly at his ease. It was strange that he should have felt a little hesitation at the thought of ordaining one belonging to the humbler ranks of society, for the members of which his Master showed so marked a predilection.

As there was no Ordination earlier than just before Christmas, and the parish to which we hoped to go being without curates, it was arranged that my friend and I should take up our abode therein and render such help to the Rector as was possible for laymen to give.

Our mornings were given to study for the Deacons' Examination, and since the pleasant, grave days of autumn were prolonged that year to the very end of a perfect St Luke's Summer, we spent the earlier hours of the day on the beach, stretched at our ease, and getting up the text-books under conditions so delightful and so unaccustomed as to make the task merely an agreeable pastime.

For the examination we had to go to London. The two days' ordeal was conducted in one of the City's few remaining mediæval buildings, no less than the Grey Friars beloved of Thackeray. I had surmounted far more formidable obstacles, and thoroughly enjoyed answering the comparatively simple questions asked. At the mid-morning interval the Bishop's kindness provided us with sandwiches and sherry. I rejoice to have known something of the Church of England before the last vestiges of the laudable practices of an earlier day had disappeared. What bishop could or would dispense sherry under such circumstances to-day?

In the memory-haunted chapel of this illustrious foundation we were sent in turn to the lectern to read, the examiner sitting at the bottom of the building to mark our efforts. I blushed for my cockney upbringing when, at the conclusion of my lection, he gently chid me: "You pronounced a certain word 'chi-uld'. Should it not be 'chaeeld'?"

On my soul, I honour these men for their forbearance. The ministry of the English Church in those days was far more the preserve of the well-born and well-to-do than it is now, and it was an exercise of considerable forbearance to admit to it so unprepossessing a neophyte as I.

The closing days of the year found us on our way to the Bishop's Palace where, in accordance with custom, we were to spend in a sort of retreat the three days preceding our Ordination.

An omnibus from the Palace met the assembled youth at the station. We entered it and sat speechlessly surveying one another as is the manner of Englishmen of that station in life to which most of the company belonged.

The silence was at length broken by one who thus addressed us: "I suppose most of you fellows don't know what you are in for? I came up for my Deacon's last year, and I do. The Bishop will say these words to you this evening, 'I think, my brothers, you will all agree that at so solemn a time as this we should do what we can to mark our sense of the sacredness of the occasion. I suggest that one way in which we can do that is by refraining from smoking during these three days'".

A groan proceeded from nearly every one present.

This prophet of ill proved to be veracious. The fateful words were duly uttered that evening. Some heroic souls held out for two whole days, and then, on the third afternoon, when we were out walking, one daring spirit broke the spell. "Bishop or no Bishop, I must have a pipe."

Only the most lawless failed to confine their misdeeds to the seclusion of the quiet country lanes. These smoked up the chimneys of their bedrooms.

We reached the Palace as the twilight fell, and entered the great hall where a butler of episcopal appearance apportioned us our sleeping apartments.

We met in the dining hall for supper, where we were welcomed by the Bishop. A noble room it was, with a richly carved minstrels' gallery at one end, and the walls adorned with pictures of former bishops, from the austere, hollow-cheeked and indifferently shaven ecclesiastics in cope and mitre of pre-Reformation times to the ample bewigged prelates with enormous lawn sleeves of the opulent, easy days of the Georges.

We assembled for evensong in a delightful Jacobean chapel lighted by clustering tapers in brass candelabra. I was not unmindful of the deep meaning of what was going on, yet I could not help luxuriating in the wonderful experience through which I was passing. To one brought up in humble surroundings, the dignity, the beauty, the unfamiliarity of everything was impressive. I sat in a cushioned stall of carven oak. The prayer-book in front of me was a regal

109

volume stamped with a golden mitre and a coat-of-arms with many quarterings. The music was perfect. The chaplain, who played the organ, was an expert musician, and the improvised and ever-varying harmonies with which he accompanied the hymns ravished my soul.

The Bishop spoke to us in a way which was a revelation of an aspect of his character for which I had not been prepared. He dwelt on the solemnity of the occasion and reminded us of those experiences which had combined to bring us to this time, fraught with consequences so momentous. He showed us that it all went far back to the days when at our mother's knee we had uttered our childhood's first prayers and had listened to her as she told us of Samuel the little Levite, and of David the ruddy shepherd boy. From such beginnings God had gradually led us to these days when we were ourselves about to be commissioned to go out and tell of His love to others.

The Bishop spoke in that even tone which Englishmen assume when deeply moved, but the slight catch in the voice betrayed the emotion so carefully held in check. It was a great opportunity greatly used, and one heart, at least, was stirred with a desire to walk worthily of a high vocation.

The Eucharist which began each of the following three days will always live in my memory. The candles alternately burning feebly in the brilliant sunlight which shone through the east window, and then turning to gleaming sparks in the shadow thrown by the limb of a giant cedar swaying silently outside; the subdued voice of the celebrant; the profound stillness; the sense of a Presence.

Sunday at length came and, according to rule, we had

discarded lay attire and all appeared at breakfast in the customary suit of solemn black and the collar that fastens reversely, the only remnants of a distinctive everyday habiliment now generally in use by the English clergy.

As I marked the demure looks of those around me I was reminded of Evelyn's experience in Italy when, after the madness of the carnival on the night before, all appeared on the first day of Lent in penitential garb, with the folded hands and lowly regards of the devotee.

The bells of the parish church, in which the Ordination was to be held, were pealing out an ecstasy of unending variation as we left the Palace and passed into the clear sunlight of a noble winter's day. The building was crowded, the friends of the candidates sitting in front and presenting a truly representative gathering of the English upper classes—the grey head and upright form of the retired general; those proud and gracious mothers; the rosebud garden of glowing tremulous sisters.

The service proceeded to its central point when each candidate kneels separately to receive the laying-on of hands and the solemn commission, and rises the accredited minister of Christ and His Church. . . .

My friend and I walked silently through the country lanes in the afternoon, the sun pouring benediction, a Sabbatic calm within and around us. I felt an awed elation that, at long last, I had attained to that for which I had so strenuously toiled. As the mists gathered in the low-lying meadows and began to creep in filmy wisps towards the uplands, we returned to the Palace.

The last hour of the day we spent in the drawing-room, where the Bishop read to us from Tennyson's *Idylls of the King*. It was in the early years of the reign of Edward VII, but I felt transported to Victorian days. In just such a stately apartment would a Trollopean ecclesiastic of the better sort, with shapely gaitered limbs, recline in an easy chair declaiming sonorously the representative poet of the period. I feasted upon the scene.

The reading concluded. A canon, who had slept peacefully through the recital, awoke opportunely, and voiced our gratitude to his lordship, and we retired.

During the past three days none of our company had appeared more sensible of the solemnity of the occasion than one tall and silent youth. None had more often been seen kneeling in the chapel; none, on the day of the Ordination, had seemed more moved. Great, therefore, was our surprise when the door of our dormitory opened and this person appeared clad neatly and unpretentiously in pyjamas and a silk hat. Without a word, he proceeded to execute a *pas seul*, at the conclusion of which he raised his hat with a courteous bow and silently withdrew. I was apprehensive lest the events of the last few days had imposed a breaking strain upon him. He looked in again a little while afterwards, and, with an apology, explained that he had indeed felt so keyed up as to make some diversion essential, and had taken this odd way of relieving his feelings.

My friend Hallam and I returned to the scene of our future labours.

We lodged over a shop in a crowded thoroughfare, con-

signed to the care of a widow who, like most landladies, had
seen better days. She was a kindly, unmethodical person.
In clearing the table after meals it was her custom to
deposit the plates and dishes on the stairs outside our room,
and through them such visitors as called during the next few
hours had to thread their way. Occasionally she herself was
caught in the snare that she had laid privily for others, and,
approaching our room in the dark, her coming would be
announced by a crash, a heavy fall, and a piercing cry.
"Serves the old ass right", my companion would exclaim,
hastening to the rescue with a light.

The street in which we lived was a cheerful centre of
bustling life which approached a climax of obstreperousness
on Saturday nights. From our open window we were
privileged to enjoy the mutual badinage of rival tradesmen.

During a brief lull in the customary noise the voice of a
butcher would (for the benefit of his rival) be heard in-
structing an imaginary assistant to "bring up six more pigs"
as he had sold out. Promptly, across the street came the
appropriate retort: "Harry, don't shut up your shop yet.
You'll have one customer to-day. I'll come over presently
and buy some of your steak for our cat". A suitable reply to
this insult not readily presenting itself, his victim would have
recourse to unpleasant noises and unseemly gestures.

The profound peace of the early morning of Sundays
was in moving contrast to the confused noise of a few hours
before.

The first of many such days dwells in my memory. I
made my way to church through the rain-washed streets

which gleamed and sparkled in the clear sunlight; a stiff breeze blew in from the sea, brine-laden, and mingled with the odour of pitch as it passed across the docks.

A very small company was present in church for the Holy Communion. For the first time I read the Gospel for the day and administered the Chalice. Small as was the number of communicants, they represented the highly miscellaneous inhabitants of a great seaport town. A particularly clean and white-haired seafaring man knelt next to a negress. An elderly, wrinkled dame wearing a Salvation Army bonnet somewhat disconcerted me by saying, "Thank you, sir", as I concluded the Words of Administration. I got to know her well in after years. She liked the Gospel in strong and fiery doses and had therefore attached herself to the followers of General Booth, but she continued to attend Church services from time to time, and often in the course of my earlier preaching efforts I derived encouragement from the violent shaking of her ancient bonnet and the suppressed groan which, I knew, betokened approval.

Our work possessed the charm of variety. But St Paul's self-gratulation over the fewness of the number of persons he had baptized was not to be ours. Our church was a kind of baptismal Gretna Green. Infants were brought to us from all over the town, for we baptized twice every day. The inwardness of this somewhat unusual proceeding was borne in upon us when we reflected that joyful mothers who brought their children to be christened killed two birds with one stone by being "churched" at the same time, and the accustomed offerings made on such occasions are the perquisite of the incumbent.

114

At first I found it pleasant to admit these small pilgrims to the Ark of Salvation. But custom staled that which most certainly lacked infinite variety in that it was the continual performance of a ceremony regarded by parents and friends simply as that which had to be "done", a sort of spiritual vaccination.

A certain old monthly nurse, a staunch Methodist, boasted that she was godmother to two hundred children. She took on the obligation as part of her proper duty. I recall the genial complacency with which she reeled off the appointed responses, as one humouring a persistent child. She seldom tripped, but once, after I had enquired as to her belief, commencing with "God the Father", and so through the Apostles' Creed to "everlasting life after death", she answered comprehensively, "I renounce them all".

For experience, I was allowed, amongst other privileges, to administer spiritual truth and good advice in general to the Mothers' Meeting. Dear, dirty, toiling, patient souls, to whom it was the bright spot of the week to sit in a stuffy room and listen (amid the babel of infant voices) to a raw youth lecturing them on their duties, the proceedings reaching a climax of voluptuous delight when each received a bun and a cup of tea. I cannot now conceive how I had the effrontery to lay down the law to people so infinitely my superiors in wisdom and virtue. I expect I was as ponderously didactic as the average young clergyman, but, I am emboldened to think, not offensively so, for once, when I had been absent a week or two, one of the mothers remarked: "We are glad to see you back again, sir".

"Surely not," said I, "for I scolded you the last time I gave the address here."

"O, nothing to hurt", was the kindly judgment.

Amongst my other offices was that of superintendent of the Lads' Social Club, a society which met twice a week and provided an outlet for the exuberant spirits of some thirty biggish boys.

With the fearless courage of youth I started a Shakespeare class in connection with the club, and in the peaceful seclusion of a committee room we read one of the plays, each taking a part. For a time, at least, these classes were a vast success. *Macbeth* was my first choice, and we warmed to our work at the opening of the second scene when the young gentleman who enacted Duncan had to enquire (which he did two or three times with infinite satisfaction): "What bloody man is that?"

All envied the fortunate person to whose happy lot it fell to declaim: "The devil damn thee black, thou cream-faced loon". He himself earnestly pleaded that the scene might be repeated.

To my friend was entrusted the nominal superintendence of the Band of Hope, the real spade-work being accomplished by an energetic lady worker, while Hallam, intellectual, a dreamer of dreams, meandered about like a bewildered spirit, amid the din of battle.

With a groan he would drop into his seat at the supper table afterwards. "Push over the beer, guv'nor", was his first remark. "There will be wild work here to-night. I've spent the last half hour listening to old Mother Jones, with

116

her bonnet over one eye, teaching the two hundred little fiends to sing 'If I were a sunbeam'."

At intervals, as he sipped his beer, he would repeat, with bitter irony, scraps from the evening's feast of melody, such as:

> Give me water from the crystal spring;
> Water is the drink for me;

or that stirring ballad:

> There's a serpent in the glass!
> Dash it down! Dash it down!

Amidst innumerable interests of a social character, we had a certain amount of more definitely spiritual work to do.

I well remember the first time I was summoned to the bedside of a dying man. It was at a small public-house, and I was met at the door by the landlady, a stout rubicund person in black satin, adorned with much jewellery.

I was led through the taproom, redolent of sawdust, spirits and tobacco, its occupants rising respectfully as I entered. A profound reverence for the clergy is a well-marked stage in the process of spirituous mellowing, amongst the humbler ranks of society. I climbed many stairs to a top-floor attic where an old man in a semi-conscious condition dozed and writhed alternately on a little bed.

He had been a nondescript hanger-on at the public-house. He drove out its raw-boned horse and crazy cab on the rare occasions when it was required. He did odd jobs of various sorts and was rewarded by a lodging, meals, and the chance

117

of picking up drinks. By his side sat a consumptive young man, a cripple, who was a tailor by trade. This odd couple had struck up a warm friendship, and the young fellow had tended his old companion with womanly solicitude.

"Now, George," said the landlady, bustling in, "I've brought a clergyman to see you. You know you can't live much longer, and you must give in. It's no use your trying to hold out. You will really have to give in."

The words must have fallen like a knell on the old man's ears, supposing that he comprehended them, as in a dazed sort of way he appeared to do. What did they convey to him? I think it might be expressed thus: "George, your stay on earth is drawing inexorably to an end. You've had your ups and downs, but it hasn't been a bad world, on the whole. Haven't you been allowed to warm your old bones by the kitchen fire on wintry days, while, perchance, a tot of rum has sent an added glow right down to your finger-tips. In summer you have been permitted to prop yourself against the yard wall and doze in the pleasant sunlight. You have pottered about the stable, brushing down that knock-kneed horse, your companion for twenty years, or listening to his familiar whinny as you entered at night-time, lantern in hand, bearing his evening feed. The lame cur (like yourself a casual dependent on the landlady's bounty) has sat slobbering and worshipping you as you ate your broken victuals, throned on an inverted bucket. You were to him as a high god inhabiting Olympus, whence you dispensed ambrosia and nectar in the shape of bones and sweet lukewarm tea.

"But now, George, this is all about to end. Your time

118

is up. You have got to leave the old familiar spot and quest out into the Unknown.

"No more pipes and pots, and pleasant listless chatter for you.

"Moreover, George, there is a person called God. Him you have no doubt mortally offended, for, not only have you never donned Sunday clothes and attended church with the pious, but you have seldom uttered a prayer (except when your old horse was so ill that night). You know, you old reprobate, that all the connection you ever had with the church was that you enjoyed the sound of the bells as you sat in the stable doorway on Sunday mornings in summer, and vacantly watched the smoke from your pipe rolling in blue clouds across that shaft of light in which a whirl of golden gnats were dancing. You have never read the Bible, you have neglected God; and thought to go unpunished.

"But you were wrong, George. That Celestial Magistrate (you know what magistrates are, for one gave you fourteen days on a certain occasion, you remember) bides His time. He has been waiting long for you and now, it seems, He is about to get you.

"But, George, there is even yet a chance for you. Here is a clergyman. You have always sneaked out of the way of such, except when, hard put to it, you solicited alms. But now the parson is your only hope. It is his job to help lame dogs like you. Give diligent heed to what he tells you for he has the private ear of the Celestial Magistrate. He knows His likes and dislikes, and he can put you in the way of getting on His right side. If only you succeed in doing that, you may even yet escape the burning Pit, and find yourself in a white robe, an unaccustomed harp in your hand, engaged in a church service which will go on for ever and ever".

I started from the reverie into which I had fallen, to find myself seated by the bedside contemplating the dying man.

What must I do? Where could I begin? How could I help? My three years' theological training had not shown me that. The Catholic clergyman, Roman or Anglican, is, I know, in better case when dealing with an adherent in the position of my sick man. The two have common ground in certain thoroughly well-understood methods of procedure.

"You are, as you know, very ill—dying", the priest would say. "You will first want to make your confession. I am ready to hear it." Then, provided with a fairly good idea of the state of the patient's soul, he can offer useful advice and give real help, if he be an earnest, discerning person. The Viaticum and Unction complete the healing work.

But the label "Church of England", attached, as it is, to people of every variety of theological outlook, or of none, provides no starting-point, no common ground.

What could I do? I uttered some commonplaces of orthodox belief. I spoke of the alternatives of Heaven and Hell; the way of escape provided by the atoning Sacrifice of Christ, of which even the worst could avail himself by a saving faith in the Precious Blood.

The old man listened, uncomprehendingly, as I thought, but some hint of my meaning must have reached his bewildered mind. He raised himself a little and said fiercely:

"What's He going to interfere with me for? I ain't never done nothing to Him!"

I endeavoured to explain myself, but in vain; so, having prayed with him, I prepared to depart, considerably depressed.

The landlady was horrified at what she conceived to be his reckless obstinacy. "O George," she wailed, "why don't you give in? You know you ought to give in."

He made no reply, but his feeble hand moved, seeking something. It came to rest in the grasp of the consumptive tailor. He sighed gratefully and fell asleep.

The spiritual welfare of the great parish in which my friend and I found ourselves was in charge of an earnest and conscientious incumbent who was indefatigably supported by his wife.

It does not detract from the many virtues of our chief to say that he was hardly competent to be the spiritual leader of the hordes of people who swarmed in the mean streets of the parish. In a flight of poetic fancy he once pictured himself as "treading the slums of a great city with aching heart and bleeding feet". The lacerated feet were at any rate concealed by very shapely patent-leather shoes. He was not a "man's man", and the preparation of the few men and boys who presented themselves for Confirmation had generally been entrusted to a lady parish-worker.

In winter-time there was a considerable amount of poverty in the parish, and just at the beginning of the Christmas season, when altruistic emotions are at their zenith, the facile pen of the rector's wife would prepare an appeal for the local newspaper which invariably reaped a golden harvest. In preparation for this, the staff, clerical and lay, was bidden to produce the most harrowing cases discovered during parochial visitation, and these were worked up with telling effect.

The allocation of the means thus placed at our disposal would have driven the advocates of scientific charity to frenzy. Meat and grocery tickets were handed out in profusion, but not always wisely, I fear, since the tradesmen who exchanged the latter often reported a strange desire for pickles and tinned fruits on the part of the starving recipients.

The interior of the church on Sunday mornings afforded a grim comment on the designation of the Established Church as the Church of the English people. The building was designed to hold two thousand persons. An average of fifty adults would form the grown-up part of the congregation. The service was Matins followed by the Litany or the Holy Communion, in the middle of which latter service the bulk of the worshippers took their departure.

An Englishman feels cheated of the coin he contributes to the collection in church unless he gets a sermon. More often than not the sermon bores him; it is frequently uninteresting and even unintelligible, but it is part of the customary order and he resents its omission. I pity the unhappy folk who attended my early efforts. I spoke by the book, and said "what I ought to have said". I expounded passages of Scripture after the stereotyped pattern, and elucidated points of Church doctrine with the customary explanations. I was a spokesman of the Church and uttered

122

the Church's mind so far as I understood it, but I did not proclaim a Gospel fired with personal conviction and the result of personal experience. Possibly a young man could hardly be expected to do so. But the fact that intelligent people, people with experience of the hard realities of life, heard me so courteously and patiently inspires me with reverence for the truly Christian charity of the average church-goer. That he suffers so uncomplainingly the patronizing didacticism, the glib assurance, and the torturing mannerisms of our less competent pulpiteers (*quorum pars fui*) is a testimony to the grace of God worthy of all admiration.

There were two occasions in the year when the great church was actually full.

The Harvest Thanksgiving exercises an extraordinary attraction upon the average Englishman. If he is a countryman, he loves it because he knows what it means. It is the "happy ending" of a long story of sweat and toil in the blaze of the noonday summer sun, and of bowed endurance through many a biting wintry day. The townsman loves it since it brings tidings from far away of a visionary land of Arcadian simplicities.

The presence of fruits and flowers and sheaves of corn transformed our bare and ugly church, and a touch of exotic ritual (originated by the rector's wife) was supplied by the nosegays which clergy and choir carried, the stalks tucked into their hymn-books.

The other occasion each year in which the church held the congregation for which it was designed was on New Year's Eve. Crowds thronged every corner of the building,

and the opportune closing of the public-houses shortly before the time at which the service began always afforded us
a considerable number of worshippers in a state of tearful
devotion.

This sometimes resulted in incidents not provided for by
the rubrics. At a pause in his sermon, on one occasion, the
rector was thoughtfully heartened to proceed by the words:
"Go on, old cock".

At the close of the service I once had the task of per-
suading a sailor, who was stretched along a pew, wrapped
in profound slumber, that he was not snugly lying in his
bunk.

The rector revelled in these services, which afforded him
an opportunity for the exercise of a gift of somewhat sensa-
tional oratory. Death and Judgment were his favourite
themes, and unless his hearers slept off the effects of his
exhortations along with their potations, many a sinner must
have been at least temporarily awakened.

There is the valet's point of view of every hero's exploits,
and the sexton (a person of piratical appearance and
addicted to strong liquors) was not enthusiastic over these
functions. When once I remarked: "We must have taken
a big collection at last night's service?" he replied, "I took
up a good one this morning—two buckets full of orange-
peel and nutshells".

One evening when my friend and I were sitting in our
room talking over the doings of the day, he said, "Isn't it
odd that you and I should fetch up at this place, which one
would think that neither of us would have chosen? You, I

know, love the country, and here you are in a filthy crowded town. I am a Catholic and I find myself in a parish given over to the dullest, soul-destroying Protestantism".

"Amongst the other reasons that brought me here", I replied, "was a feeling that I ought to serve an apprenticeship in uncongenial surroundings before settling down in the land of heart's desire."

"My own chief reason, exactly", was his answer. "Before returning like the Prodigal to some Catholic home I resolved to fill my belly with the husks of a non-Catholic, or at any rate semi-Catholic, substitute for the Truth."

"My dear old chap," said I, "it has come upon me from time to time that my ways are not your ways, and therefore, probably, that your thoughts are other than mine, but I am such a poor theologian that I did not realize that you were so much out of sympathy with things here. As you know, I have some casual acquaintance with the allurements of Catholic worship, but I must confess to considerable ignorance of the nature of the attractions of Catholic doctrine. Expound, I pray you, this thing of which you speak, and as soon as I have refilled my pipe you shall enjoy our undivided attention."

He sat for a time in silence. Presently he said: "Old man, if you want an adequate and convincing statement of Catholic belief, you mustn't apply to me. What I can do and what I should like to do, is to tell you just a little of its appeal to myself".

"Exactly what I want to know", I replied. "I am in wandering mazes lost when I tackle thought in the abstract.

125

The only way in which I can get hold of ideas is through human response to them—my own and other people's."

"Well, to start at the beginning, I recollect that even as a child I was impressed by the existence of evil in the world. I once saw a shepherd whose dog had mistaken an order, call the offender to him. The old fellow came bounding up full of love and happiness. And then that devil kicked him with all his force. Damn him, the cursed swine!

"I felt sick for days; the look in that dog's eyes tortured me, and I kept saying: 'God can't be good to allow that'. It was the old dilemma—'either not good, or not almighty'. He can't be both.

"It was the doctrine of the Fall of Man which, as I grew older, showed me that He *could* be both. What I had previously thought of only as an abstract idea, became to me a terrific fact—God *is* good, but in giving man free-will—in making him a man, not a machine—He must suffer him to choose the wrong if he will. And man did choose it, deliberately, with his eyes open. My own experience and that of others demonstrated the inevitable consequences—the enfeebled will, the tendency to choose the wrong through the growing force of habit, the slow deterioration of character that follows. Heredity and environment are two of the determining factors in the formation of character; obviously, therefore, the children of such parents start with a bias to wrong. The evil spreads, and all nature seems to share the curse—the shepherd's dog did.

"To me, therefore, the doctrine of the Fall of Man, symbolized in the Genesis story, is fact. It is the only ex-

126

planation I know of which accounts satisfactorily for the moral chaos of human affairs otherwise than by forcing us to believe that the world owes its origin to a monster of fiendish cruelty.

"But that is common ground to us both, and in the next step in my belief you, as well as all other orthodox Christians, go with me.

"It is something to have light thrown on the problem of the existence of evil, but it is infinitely more to know that man's fall and its results could not baffle the loving purpose of God. The proof of that came to me personally after much thought on something which is found in almost all religions, the idea of sacrifice.

"I saw how the crude conceptions of previous ages from the earliest days of man's history were purified, and his blind gropings made explicit, in the sacrificial system of the Jews, and how this process went on side by side with the development in ethical and spiritual thought under the influence of the prophets.

"Thus, for centuries, the ground was prepared, and then, in the fulness of time, the wonder of all wonders occurred. God Himself, in the likeness of man, came, not only to carry the best thought of the prophets to its culmination in a life of absolute perfection actually lived, but also to give to the deepest cravings of men's hearts for union with Himself, which were so pathetically shadowed forth in the idea of sacrifice, a meaning and a fulfilment beyond our wildest dreams. The Life laid down on Calvary by the God-Man broke the horrible entail of sin and misery and opened up the way by which man and his Maker might, at

127

long last, become one, and all God's glorious purpose for the world enter upon the path of fulfilment.

"Words, words, words! I know this must all sound to you like an extract from a theological text-book. I can't express what I feel. I can only say that these thoughts gripped my soul. What was dark became as clear as daylight. What was formerly a mere idea became a vital fact.

"But you will be thinking that Catholicism cannot claim a monopoly in the dazzling truth which we degrade by calling it the Doctrine of Redemption. True! What Catholicism does, I think, is to draw the inevitable inferences, or, more correctly, rightly to enter into the results which flowed from the Incarnation, as they can be seen with convincing plainness in the course of the history of the Church.

"The Incarnation is not an idea left floating in space, so to speak. To be of any use to us there must be something by which we, as individuals, are brought into effectual union with it. That something is the Church.

"Almost all Christians agree that Christ founded a Church of some sort. Well, I believe that the Church He founded is the Catholic Church. He instituted Baptism as the means by which we become part of that Church, and the Eucharist as that by which we are actually incorporated into Himself, 'we in Him, and He in us', and share, for the salvation of body, mind and spirit, in that Sacrifice of His which makes us at one with the mind and heart of God.

"To me those are the most vital facts of human existence. Apart from them, the world appears a nightmare, a maze without a clue. In the light of those facts, all that is essential for us to know becomes clear.

"When once I grasped these facts, or rather, when once they grasped me, the rest of the Catholic system needed no argument. It all fitted together as essentially as limbs complete a body. The Real Presence in the Eucharist? Its only alternative is the unthinkable idea of the Real Absence! Apostolic Succession? Why, of course, there must be men duly appointed by those empowered to do so for the purpose of administering the gifts! Confession and Absolution? How otherwise can the Church assure her children of their own personal share in the divine forgiveness? The truth of these and of all the other subsidiary doctrines of the Church needed no demonstration. When the sun of truth rises upon the soul it illuminates not the mountain peaks only but floods light on the whole landscape.

"I found in Catholicism that which satisfied my mind and my heart. How could it do otherwise? Has it not inspired the world's greatest and humblest in all parts of the earth for nineteen hundred years? Has not the Church been the inspiration of the highest achievements in every sphere of human effort, in music, painting, poetry, and architecture?

"Its absolute universality is witnessed to by the abounding richness of Catholic life; mysticism and philosophy are not more characteristic of it than is the cheerful buffoonery of the mystery play. Its gaze is ever towards Heaven, but its feet are planted firmly on the solid brown earth.

"Compare this glorious family, every member sharing in the riot of its multitudinous life, all imbued with an unshakeable faith, all bound together by a common belief, with the botched fragments of religion that make up the systems of Protestantism—with the heart-numbing denials of unbelief, with the blank wastes of materialism.

"And this poor old Church of England of ours is a real part of the family! I know that the blight of Protestantism seems at times almost to have quenched the light. But where Catholic Orders and Sacraments are retained, life still exists, and the spark can be fanned into a flame. If the Faith in its rich fulness, its satisfying completeness, its winning beauty, can but be put before the English people with clear conviction, with burning passion, with undaunted perseverance, I am convinced that they will accept it; the night will pass, and day will dawn again."

He stopped suddenly, abashed, as any Englishman must be who finds that he has given way to emotion. For a time we both remained silent; I, at any rate, thinking of many things. "One loving heart sets another on fire", and I was moved by this personal confession of faith. What my friend had said was not unfamiliar to me as abstract doctrine. It appeared in quite another light as the whole-hearted conviction of a man I loved.

Might not this belief be the thing I had been ignorantly seeking? I realized the unsatisfactory nature of my own theological outlook, which was merely one department of my mental activity. I saw that a man's religion ought to be that which permeated all of his life, blending every interest into one harmonious whole, the crown and completion of being.

By this time the year of our Diaconate was drawing to a close, and the examination for Priest's Orders was upon us.

I faced the prospect with equanimity for I felt sure of my subjects.

The circumstances under which we had made our preparation were to me ideal. Used as I had been for many years to filch from my scanty leisure the time necessary for study, bringing to it, therefore, often enough, a mind already wearied by the occupations of the day, it was a sheer joy to take up my books after breakfast and to feel that the morning hours could be devoted to reading. Throughout the summer and autumn it was our custom to cycle to a quiet part of the beach and to prop ourselves against the sea wall and read in the pleasantest surroundings imaginable.

As often as my eyes left the book as I stopped to meditate some passage in it, I saw before me the wide stretch of ocean. Dreamily I watched the great ships making their way almost imperceptibly out to sea; the waves broke on the pebbled shore and the fresh breeze carried gusts of briny fragrance from the masses of seaweed that glistened in the sunshine. I thought of the years through which I had toiled in that suburban street, and rejoiced in the freedom I had won at a great price.

My books borrowed something from my surroundings, and even the Thirty-Nine Articles of Religion, studied under such conditions, took on a romantic tone, and as I recited them, the sentences flowed rhythmically with the surf that rushed and lapsed with the incoming tide.

With the approach of the later autumn days our visits to this pleasant spot were less frequent, but there were priceless hours when a warm mist overspread the water, and ships passed invisible, sounding at intervals low, mournful notes in the distance. The sea lay like a pond, and in the profound silence one's eyes closed involuntarily and the mind wavered on that delectable borderland where dream and reality meet.

I passed the examination satisfactorily, and reflected with delight that the last of a series of obstacles was surmounted, and also that in future I could browse at will in literary pastures, no longer confined to some narrow plot at the bidding of a remorseless examiner.

One result of my association with Hallam was that I approached my ordination as priest with a livelier sense of the solemn responsibility of the office I was seeking than I had experienced at the ordination of a year ago. It was impossible to be constantly in the society of one to whom admission to the priesthood was the greatest privilege possible for God to grant to a man without catching something of his feeling of exultant awe.

Unfortunately for myself, the heavy work in which I had been involved by my duties in the parish at the approach of winter, combined with the emotional strain of the occasion, had the effect of producing in me a state of nervous prostration. The long and stately service was almost more than I could bear. As the preacher leisurely pursued his way through the customary sermon, I felt that he would never stop and I had a strong desire to run away.

It was a feeble and dispirited creature that knelt for the solemn laying-on of hands. And then the curious and unexpected thing happened. As the hands of the officiant and his assistants rested on my head I felt an influence pass from them to me. Perhaps it was simply the effect of the contact of warm human hands tremulous with emotions of fatherly sympathy. Yet at the time I felt that I was indeed receiving power from on High. I myself was weak, uncertain, taught by experience how little strength or virtue was mine. Hampered, too, by an enfeebled nervous system which had often compelled me to realize that the higher part of man could be enslaved by the weakness of an overstrung mind and an ill-nourished body. To me, therefore, emptied of self-confidence, came a sense of being filled with something other than myself. I was to go forth to my life's work commissioned to deliver the message of a society infinitely wiser than I, and empowered to do so by an authority which could transmit to me a strength which was not mine.

The hands of an attendant-minister loosed the stole which hung deacon-wise over my left shoulder and passed an end of it over my right. The symbolic act betokened the new-made priest, and I rose from my knees glowing with the consciousness that the Divine strength had been, and would be, made perfect in my most human weakness.

It had often been my lot to realize how completely the activities of the higher centres of consciousness could be inhibited by mental and physical disability, but during the remainder of this service I had the delightful experience of the converse process. All nervous fear, all physical ill had vanished, and at the moment of Communion, which followed in due course, I felt that in my case the Prayer of Humble Access had been answered, and that I dwelt in Him and He in me.

The first occasion upon which I exercised my privilege of celebrating the Holy Communion was on the following

Christmas Day. I doubt whether this is ever a perfectly satisfactory experience. One is too much occupied with the unfamiliar task of properly reciting the ritual and performing correctly the prescribed ceremonial to allow the mind to concentrate on the thing signified. Yet I retain a recollection of solemnity and real heart satisfaction during that quiet midday service when a few simple souls, mostly old folk, knelt with such touching signs of devotion and recollection at the Altar of God.

The work of a priest in a parish of a theological complexion like that of the one in which I then ministered does not differ greatly from that of a deacon. During the two and a half years which followed my admission to the priesthood, therefore, I had much the same sort of duties to perform as in my first year. The parish was divided into districts, one of which was apportioned to each of the three members of the clerical staff. I attempted the customary, but impossible, task of endeavouring to get to know the individual members of my vast flock. I found that by strenuous house-to-house visitation I could encompass my district once in the course of a year. Before the next year came round, a considerable number of families had migrated and the work of making acquaintance had to begin afresh.

It was, however, exciting work. One never knew what surprise awaited the opening of the door at which, in those early days, one so tremulously knocked, appalled at the thought of invading the privacy of the Englishman's castle with no better excuse than, "I am the clergyman". One feared the natural response, "Well, what of it?"

But this was seldom given. If the preliminary reconnoitring through the front parlour window was unsatisfactory to the inmate of any house the door was not opened; that was all.

At times one got a cheering welcome. One kindly soul, on hospitable cares intent, whom I had found smoking by the kitchen fire greeted me warmly. "I'm glad to see you, sir. Sit down and light your pipe, and spit where you like."

These were the delights of the afternoon. We enjoyed them also in the evening when we had time to spare from the meetings of the various social organizations.

Altogether, a strenuous and not unpleasant period in my life. I try to sum it up. As a contribution to the spiritual, moral and social uplift of a portion of the English people, I realize that it was not a notable success. We made a few acquaintances, we wearied ourselves with clubs and guilds; we went through a large number of services which were attended by a small number of people. Meanwhile, the bulk of our population followed its duties and pleasures untouched and uninfluenced by the ministrations of the National Church.

In the morning the steady tramp of hundreds of feet as the men streamed towards the docks. In the evening the tide flowed homeward. An interval for tea, and then the throng, reinforced by wives and children, set out to promenade the streets, inspect the shops, and crowd the places of entertainment.

That was on weekdays. On Sundays the parish "lay in" until the morning was well advanced. At midday it devoured as ample and solid a meal as it could afford, the

savoury exhalations of which permeated entire streets. In
the afternoon it dozed over the Sunday paper, or philan-
thropically detailed the latest murder to seekers after knowledge who had not read the record. In the evening little
streams of humanity trickled into various places of worship,
one such diffusing itself in twos and threes throughout the
wide spaces of the parish church.

It was scarcely encouraging, but our chief had grown
accustomed to it in twenty years, and he no longer passed
restless nights in contriving means to lure his errant flock
into orthodox pastures. For myself, it was my first experience of Church work, and I vaguely supposed that our circumstances were normal and unalterable. Hallam alone of
the three of us was chafed.

One Sunday evening as we discussed the events of the
day he opened his grief: "A hundred people in church to-
night? Well, barely. But, upon my soul, I can't find it in
my heart to blame them. Why should they come? What do
we give them when they do? 'Dearly beloved brethren'
in the morning, and 'Dearly beloved brethren' in the
evening. Two or three psalms and two lessons, the greater
part of those we had to-day being detached fragments of
Jewish literature which could not possibly be intelligible to
any ordinary person without elaborate explanation. Further, we had two or three hymns, putrid stuff set to feeble
tunes. Last of all we had a sermon urging us to contribute
to a certain missionary society in order that the light of the
Gospel which shone upon us might penetrate the darkness
of heathendom. The whole of this wretched performance
being rounded off by an organ voluntary with every stop out.

136

"I tell you, Wolfe, that I doubt if I should attend church if I were a parishioner here. There is no life, no Gospel, no grip, nothing to get excited about. Everything as dead as mutton.

"Well, I told you before that I came here partly to discipline myself by forgoing for a time all the externals of Catholic worship. I came to see for myself exactly what manner of thing this vague Church-of-Englandism is. To make quite certain whether or not, beyond all question, I am a Catholic out-and-out. I have had the experience I sought. I have gained the assurance I desired. Nothing keeps me here now but yourself. If you went I should clear out at once.

"It isn't that I don't care for the people. I do. I love them. But I can't stand much longer being obliged to offer them stones when their wistful faces prove their hunger for bread. I am tied and bound in every address I give by a sense of loyalty to the chief. One can't, as a curate, run counter to the established methods. Even if I felt free to do so, one can't present the Catholic Faith as a set of abstract ideas. It must be interpreted and enforced by the whole system of Catholic ritual and ceremonial. It must be actualized in a common life, and brought home to the hearts of the people by all the means so amazingly well adapted to the purpose which Catholic custom provides.

"How on earth can we impress upon our people the glory and beauty of worship when all we offer them is Sung Matins? How can repentance and forgiveness be preached if Confession is a forbidden topic? How can you get people to believe in the sublime mystery of the Mass when they see

137

the choir and nine-tenths of the congregation clear out in the very middle of the service?

"Well, old man, I'll stick it a bit longer in the hope that when I do move you will be ready to move also to the kind of Church to which I intend to go."

"With a few words will you persuade me to be an Anglo-Catholic?" said I. "Yet, to be candid, Hallam, I admit that I do not stand where I did when I first came here. At least you have made Catholicism a possibility for me. And sometimes it seems more than a possibility when I reflect that no other religious system has impressed me more. Since I ceased to be a child I have always been attracted by Catholic worship. You know how I used to haunt those two city churches—mystified sometimes, a little alarmed occasionally, but always under a sort of spell that made me come again.

"I feel, too, that the religion we preach and practise here does not do for me what religion ought to do. I know I am not on fire with a Gospel. This moderate sort of religious belief doesn't mean a quarter as much to me as poetry does, or music.

"I can see that Catholicism takes account of the things that really move me; that for many it gives an added delight to these things by linking them to even greater things. I want to feel that my love of Nature, of poetry, of music, of humanity are all a part of my religion. At present, between them and it there is a great gulf fixed. I want something to give a unity to all the interests and activities of my life. Religion ought to be the golden thread upon which all the pearls are strung. But my religion isn't. If I were a con-

138

vinced Catholic I think it might be. But, so far, I can scarcely say I am convinced."

"My dear fellow," he replied, "if ever there was *anima naturaliter Catholica* it is yours. I have felt certain for some time that you will end up a whole-hearted Catholic. I would not hurry you for worlds, even if I could. But I know you are on the road, and I am certain you will arrive. Courage, *mon enfant*! I will hang on here with you until you give the word to strike tents and away."

VI

BUILDING JERUSALEM

HALLAM and I had now been in our first curacy for just over three and a half years when an unlooked-for event occurred which changed, in a way only possible in the Church of England, the entire state of affairs in the parish in which we were working.

Our chief, who had long since given up the hope of doing great deeds in his difficult charge, and who was now no longer young, was offered, and accepted, a country living. My friend and I talked the matter over and resolved to await the appointment of a new rector before deciding on our future course. The patronage of the living had changed hands since the last appointment, and the present patron, we learned, was an Anglo-Catholic nobleman who, Hallam informed me, with vast satisfaction, would be sure to appoint a keen Catholic.

Although we had come to Saint Martin's together Hallam had been made senior curate and was in charge, therefore, during the time the parish was without an incumbent. Anticipating the advent of one of his own way of thinking he felt it his duty to prepare the people for the changes that might be expected. It was a congenial task, and one Sunday he preached enthusiastically of the happy results which he believed would follow when the parish should be in Catholic hands.

Few people noticed that in the congregation was a shabbily dressed, undersized, pale young man with a mop of lank black hair and a straggling moustache, who listened with keen attention to the enthusiastic youth in the pulpit. This was no other than the patron of the living, and he perceived in Hallam a man after his own heart.

The shabby nobleman went away and made many enquiries, for he was a conscientious person, and the result was that when our letters arrived one morning Hallam turned pale as his eyes ran over the contents of one of his. He tossed it to me across the breakfast table. It offered the living to him. The Bishop, it appeared, had been consulted. At first he had demurred because of the youth of the suggested presentee, but it was pointed out to him that Hallam had been in Orders for the period required by law, and that his fitness for the post had been attested by all those to whom enquiries had been addressed. Then the Bishop had yielded with so good a grace as to add that he personally approved of the somewhat bold experiment. The letter concluded with an assurance of the writer's conviction that the acceptance of the offer would result in the parish becoming a great Catholic stronghold.

We shook hands in silence. "You must accept this", I said.

"I am a presumptuous fool," he replied, "for I am strongly tempted. My word, Wolfe, only just think of it! Poor old St Martin's to become a centre of light, and I am offered the job of kindling the flame! It's like a dream."

"A dream that must come true", I said. "Amongst other reasons for it, think of the effect upon myself of seeing what the Catholic Faith can do. For if you can put life into this poor old mummy I could not deny a miracle. But, there, you wouldn't want to be hampered in your work by such a Laodicean as I."

"My dear fellow, I couldn't have had a more faithful pal, and I know I should never have a more trusty helper if you and I took this job on."

"But you forget. You would hardly call me a Catholic, would you?"

"You are all I want anyhow. And I am sure that as soon as you see translated into facts what you now think of merely as ideas you will acknowledge that it is the Lord's doing."

"Well, you can sack me at any time if I am not satisfactory."

And so, in the half-jocular fashion in which self-respecting Englishmen settle matters upon which they feel deeply, it was decided that Hallam should accept the offer made him and that I should stay on as his curate.

The parish was mildly interested in the new appointment. My friend had won the affection of that small portion of its inhabitants with whom he had come into personal contact. Quite a respectable congregation witnessed the ceremonies of his Institution and Induction, and most of the people then present summoned up sufficient energy to attend church again on the first Sunday morning upon which he appeared as the new rector.

He outlined his future policy in his sermon. A certain method of presenting the Christian Faith had been tried in that parish for many years, and by an earnest and devoted man. It had had a fair trial. What was the result? Surely, a pitiable one. The bulk of the people—souls for whom Christ died—were uninfluenced, untouched. Was it not reasonable to take stock of their methods? If they were found inadequate, ought they not to be changed? He had no private fad to offer them. He had a method, a system, which had been in use now for over eighteen hundred years, in all parts of the world, amongst every kind of people. It had never failed yet. Was it not worth trying here?

What was the system, the method? The Catholic Faith taught and practised in its fulness—the Faith once for all delivered to the saints, without addition and without subtraction. But was this system alien to the Church of England? No! Look at the Prayer Book. It claimed to set forth, according to the use of the Church of England, the rites and ceremonies of the Catholic Church. Thus, the English Church made of obligation to its members belief in the Catholic Creeds. It dispensed the Catholic Sacraments; its ministers possessed Catholic Orders. Circumstances had at certain times and in certain places obscured its witness, but the Church of England had always claimed to be Catholic; had always intended to be so; and in these days, all over the country, earnest priests and devout lay folk were recovering the privileges which were their birthright.

He wanted their parish to share in the great movement which was giving new life to the National Church. For that purpose he would be obliged to make changes in several ways, especially in the services. Rather than keep them in a state of suspense, irritating them by frequent changes, he wanted to make the alterations he deemed essential within a fixed period, say, one year, during which time each change as it came would be explained most carefully beforehand.

There was one change he proposed to make at once, and that was the introduction of a celebration of Holy Communion each week as the principal service of Sunday. All would approve of that, for all there admitted its claim to be the highest act of worship, instituted, as it was, by Christ Himself. It was because that service should be marked in every way as unique that, in celebrating it, he would wear the particular robes which had been used for the purpose from the time of the Apostles. Lighted candles would be placed on the altar, a custom which had never entirely died out in the reformed Church of England, reminding us that Christ is the Light of the World.

But he had the warmest sympathy with any present who were attached to the ways to which they had been accustomed, and were unwilling to change them. They should have a monthly celebration conducted exactly in the manner to which they were used. They also should have their Morning Prayer and Sermon every Sunday as heretofore.

He concluded with a touching appeal for sympathy and help. He spoke of his own youth and inexperience, his sense of unworthiness for the great work which lay before him. He asked them to believe that his one object, the only purpose which lay behind every change he wanted to make, was the desire to bring every man, woman and child in the parish into touch with the Saviour of the World. The Lord had said, "I, if I be lifted up, will draw all men unto me". He believed that whenever the Lover of Souls was lifted up before the eyes of men, and His claims faithfully set before them, they responded.

There was a lump in my throat as I listened to these words, so unremarkable as they appear in a bare epitome, so moving when uttered with the earnestness, the disarming modesty and sympathy, the sincerity of this man whom I had learned to love. I vowed in my heart that I would help him in every way I could; I would set myself to care for the things that made so extraordinary an appeal to him.

Others appeared to share my feelings, and a group of people waited for him at the church door after the service to wish him well on his appointment and to assure him of their support. This readiness to trust and respond to anyone who appears to have a genuine conviction that he has an authentic message from the Beyond has always seemed to me a refutation of the theological idea of the natural depravity of man. It is only when long habit has staled the experience that a preacher can look unmoved on the wistful faces before him.

Looking back over Hallam's ten years as rector of St Martin's I am impressed by the conviction that there are times in some men's lives when the stars in their courses espouse their cause. Every leader of men achieves success because at the right moment he appears on the scene to give expression to ideas which so far had been inarticulate, to meet needs actually though vaguely felt. He makes progress which appears miraculously rapid until one reflects that the process has really been going on for a long time and did but come to a head when the man and the moment arrived.

Thus was it in the limited sphere in which my friend worked, as it is when great leaders sway the destinies of mankind.

Even in so relatively unimportant a matter as the appointments of the church, he possessed in two or three years what other clergymen spend half a lifetime in getting together. The patron of the living was rich and our church became for the time his particular hobby. He lavished money on the interior of the building. It was beyond the power of money or the wit of man to improve its outward appearance; but that was no great matter since it was surrounded on all sides by other buildings.

But within, the place was transformed. The mean table with its faded red covering gave place to a stately altar raised on marble steps so as to be visible from all parts of the church. It was backed by a lofty triptych filled with figures of saints in elaborately carved niches, the whole screen aflame with gold and colour.

The east ends of the north and south aisles were enclosed by light screens which converted them into chapels; one, that of our Lady; the other, a memorial to the patron's mother, for Masses for the Departed. The sombre colour-scheme of this chapel, its violet hangings and bronze candelabra, its black and white marbles, and its painfully realistic Pieta, were in striking contrast to the airy beauty of the other, with its blues and golds, and its statue of the Virgin, gloriously gracious with outstretched hands, banked round with a wealth of flowers and seldom without her tribute of little twinkling tapers on the votive-candle stand.

146

The church was blessed with an array of vestments which, being displayed to their wondering view by the beaming sacristan, stirred visiting altar servers to shrill amazement. No trumpery product of the ecclesiastical milliner were these, but Spanish copes with morse of dull gold powdered with dusky gems, and complete sets of High Mass vestments from seventeenth-century Italy, in splendid fabrics on which strange saints were depicted in needlework of divers colours. The censer, obtained from a Portuguese abbey fallen upon evil days, was modelled after the likeness of the conventual church and was of silver, as were the crucifix and candlesticks on the high altar.

But Hallam was not the sort of man to be unduly obsessed by the accessories of worship. Most of the value that these things possessed for him was that they contributed to form the appropriate material setting for the presentation of the sublime central mystery of the Catholic Religion, the Mass.

For this he valued music, although he had not even the untrained though deep delight in music which I possessed. The former organist of the church had soon found himself out of his depth amid the changes made by my friend, and had resigned. The liberality of the patron provided us with a new organist, a convinced Catholic, who entered into Hallam's plans with enthusiasm, and was, moreover, a skilled musician. His zeal and devotion very soon transformed the choir, and we became noted for the beauty of the musical rendering of our services.

While Fortune thus favoured us with those things upon which the external side of Catholic worship depends so largely for its appeal, she was busy in providing much more valuable material, to wit, a rapidly growing and enthusiastic congregation.

In the great town in which St Martin's was situated there was only one out of its many churches which was in Catholic hands. It was at the end of the town the farthest removed from our church, and its incumbent was a retired military officer who had taken Holy Orders somewhat late in life, and whose efforts to introduce the discipline of the barrack square into the ecclesiastical sphere had lost him most of his congregation. These malcontents descended upon us with delight, enchanted to find the privileges to which they were accustomed dispensed in an unwonted atmosphere of peace and goodwill. Moreover, from all parts of the town and the neighbouring countryside came Catholic-minded persons attracted by the growing fame of the new Catholic outpost.

To crown all, St Martin's got just what it needed in the shape of a little salutary persecution. A local Protestant Society which had languished of late years for lack of a grievance, scented, with almost incredulous delight, the prospect of a battle, and sounded the summons to war. Indignation meetings were held in the streets of the parish, at which the peaceful inhabitants who stood at their front doors silently smoking were exhorted to prevent the re-kindling, ere too late, of Smithfield fires.

But the days when the Protestant lion could be lashed to fury by oratorical arts appeared to be no more, and almost the only inconvenience we experienced was that the services were occasionally interrupted by timid persons who uttered scarcely audible remarks and, having discharged an obviously trying duty, hastened from the church.

148

The other and more serious inconvenience involved in this attack was due to our good Bishop becoming troubled in mind by the representations which were made to him. Like all wise rulers of the English Church, in days so difficult for a peace-loving episcopate, our Bishop let well alone whenever possible. But he could not continue to ignore complaints ever more violently reiterated. He summoned Hallam to his presence, at length, reluctantly enough, and did his best to discover the *via media* which would produce peace. But Hallam felt himself unable to give way to clamour from outside. The parish itself was not opposed to the changes. What had been done had not driven people away from the church. On the contrary, it was attended now as it had not been for years.

The Bishop agreed. Yes, it was a difficult case. But couldn't Hallam make some gesture of conciliation? Offer something that the Bishop could throw to the wolves?

No, he feared he could do nothing. Moderate churchfolk still came to Saint Martin's since their needs were met by the provision of the services to which they had been accustomed. The changes made had been the addition of other services which none need attend but those who found them helpful.

Again the Bishop was entirely sympathetic; but he was obliged to do something. "I am afraid", he said, "that I must take against you the one or two disciplinary measures in my power. I cannot visit your church, nor can I license a clergyman to your vacant curacy."

The serious difficulty of attempting to work such a church

and parish as Saint Martin's with but two priests was the one ill-result of the agitation.

On the credit side must be reckoned the fact that the church got a free advertisement and thus its membership increased more rapidly than it would otherwise have done. Dozens of cheerful young men offered themselves as altar servers, being attracted by our services, by Hallam's forceful preaching, and also, no doubt, by the prospect of "a row".

I used to wonder why young people who liked ornate services and were, perhaps, also attracted to Catholic beliefs and practice were content with such relatively meagre privileges in these directions as may be had in the Church of England, whilst they had only to join the Roman Church to obtain in full measure all that they desired. I had forgotten the natural human delight in struggle and effort. What one can get easily and respectably does not appeal. What one wins in the teeth of opposition and after a tussle is worth having. In the Roman Church, Catholic belief and practice is, of course, the rule. No one objects; bishops take part in it; this is not attractive to the combative instincts of youth. What these keen young spirits loved was that upon which authority frowned. They liked to join in services which might be interrupted at any moment by a stir in the congregation, and the sound of a voice saying, "In the name of Truth I protest against this blasphemy".

Some enterprising souls amongst them one day placed a bath near the church porch, which they filled with water smelling strongly of disinfectant. They vowed that the next objector who disturbed the services should undergo (at any rate external) purification. By Hallam's stern order the accomplishment of this design was prevented.

Later on, the same young gentlemen approached me with the request that I should form, and be the chaplain of a guild which they desired to see established. They explained that some of them used the Devotion of the Rosary in private and they all wished to say it together.

I consulted Hallam, anxious to spare him the additional work which I foresaw would fall upon him if I refused.

"I shall be delighted if you will carry on", he said.

"But I am not sure I approve of the Rosary", I replied. "I don't even know whether I believe in the Invocation of Saints."

"Solvitur ambulando!" he said. "The only way to become convinced of the value of Catholic customs is to practise them."

And so, week by week, at nine o'clock in the evening (the earliest convenient hour at which the church was available) a stream of persons, mostly young men, made their way through the darkened building to the little oasis of light in the Lady Chapel. There we would say the Office before the Mother's image where, with mild regarding eyes, she stood amid clusters of fragrant blossoms and a hundred starry points of light.

Strange and uncongenial I found the Devotion, at first. But, as time went on, one began to see why it has so strong a hold on the affections of simple folk. It translates theological mysteries into the intelligible terms of human acts and emotions—the joy of our Lady and Saint Elisabeth; the detailed sufferings of our Lord's Passion; the delight which ravished the Mother's soul at the Resurrection of her Son. One concentrated on each event for a brief space, while the murmur of the oft-repeated prayer calmed and steadied the mind. The simple arrangement of the beads, as they slipped through the fingers, just suggested, without disturbance, when the appointed tale of prayers had been said. It brought religion very near, to come out of the noisy, crowded, sordid streets into that quiet place where scene after scene of the sacred story passed before the mind to the soft murmuring refrain of prayer or the hush of a throbbing silence. I still see those young men kneeling in awed meditation, and the momentary glimpse of a girl with flushed cheek resting against folded hands, and a far-off look in her dreaming eyes, is with me yet.

In such an atmosphere Heaven and Earth were one, and it was entirely natural for the earthly members of the one Family to invoke the help of those that stood nearer the Throne of God.

The manner in which I drifted, so to speak, into a practical appreciation of the doctrine of the Invocation of Saints is characteristic also of the way in which I was led to accept the whole Catholic system of belief and practice.

It was impossible, for instance, not to be moved by Hallam's whole-souled belief in the Sacrifice of the Mass with, of course, its implication of the Real Presence of Christ in the Holy Sacrament. His manner at the Altar was that of one caught up into spheres altogether beyond the attainment of such a pedestrian religion as mine. Already he moved freely in Heavenly Places, transfigured by adoring love. Nor could one's glance rest on the faces of those who knelt at the Altar during the moments of Communion without being touched. Intense conviction, fervent devotion, the deepest awe, were mirrored in all those faces as, now dainty jewelled fingers, and now hands seamed and scarred, were lifted to receive the Bread of Life.

At length, conviction came on a sudden as I knelt before the Sacrament I had just consecrated. "This *is* my Body. This *is* my Blood." So spake the lips which uttered naught but Truth. So had the Church believed from earliest days till now. So were convinced that great body of people kneeling behind me, the solemn murmur of whose Amen at the end of the Prayer of Consecration had just fallen on my ears. And so, at that moment, illumination came to me.

The feeling was that of a sharp change from conjecture to conviction, from reflection on a doctrine to experience of a fact. "It is the Lord. O my God, Thou art true! O my soul, thou art happy!"

The belief that Christ Himself was really present in the Sacrament He ordained carried with it naturally the further conviction that in the Mass we had the unspeakable privilege of sharing in the Lord's mediatorial work. On His Heavenly Throne and on our earthly altars He is "this same Jesus" exercising in all places alike His High Priestly office. I knew, therefore, that in the Mass was offered a real, true and propitiatory sacrifice both for the living and the dead.

My initiation was completed by a practical acceptance of Catholic teaching concerning Confession and Absolution.

As soon as Hallam's labours began to bear fruit, an ever-increasing number of persons desired to make their con-

153

fessions at St Martin's. Except for occasional help, the task
of hearing them fell upon my friend, for he, with the utmost
delicacy, invariably refrained from suggesting my doing
anything which he thought might be distasteful to me.

One evening, during Lent, when he appeared to be quite
worn out with this work, I said: "This cannot go on, beloved. You must have regular help, and I must be the one
to give it. But you will have to coach me, for I am absolutely ignorant of the whole business. One thing I must do
for myself. I can't hear anyone's confession until I have
made my own. Then I must go ahead, and learn by experience, hoping, meanwhile, that a merciful Providence will
not allow people to suffer too greatly by my mistakes".

"Spoken like a man!" said Hallam. "I am afraid my
own training consisted chiefly in unlearning my errors, but
I have made my confession for years now and that was my
principal asset, combined with a small amount of commonsense and an enormous draft on the goodness of God."

To make a first confession is a fairly good proof, under
our Anglican conditions, of a real acceptance of Catholic
teaching. A great number of persons attending our ritualistic
churches account themselves Catholic mainly on the strength
of a keen enjoyment of ceremonial and good music. Any
person, therefore, who relinquishes the Englishman's cherished privilege of keeping his sins as a private concern between himself and God gives evidence of some sincerity of
conviction in regard to the Catholic Religion. I suppose I
may claim that distinction, since this was a task calling for a
greater sacrifice of my personal inclinations than any which
Catholicism had yet proposed to me.

With extreme reluctance I made my way to a distant village where lived a priest of some note in his day as a protagonist in the literary battles waged by his party against Protestantism. With beating heart and an urgent desire for flight, I heard his door-bell reverberate with unnecessary clamour in answer to my touch.

I gave the maid my card, and was presently informed that the rector would see me if I would come upstairs to his bedroom.

The good man was in bed—phlebitis—or he would have come down to me. Would I take a chair and tell him what he could do for me?

I explained my errand, and he waived aside my proposal to come again when he was in better health. "I am thankful", he said, "if I can be of any use, laid aside for the time as I am."

And so, kneeling by his bedside, I made my confession, reading from the notes I had prepared. My voice sounded to me like that of someone other than myself, as I repeated aloud the long catalogue of the faults and failings of a life.

When I had finished I thought that stern denunciations would follow. What right had I—selfish, worldly, full of faults—to have entered the priesthood at all? How lamentably had I failed to live up to my high calling. But, instead of the scathing rebukes I anticipated, I heard nothing but words of sympathy and encouragement, and, at the end, the solemn form of Absolution, with the gracious "Go in peace. The Lord hath put away thy sin".

I left my kind friend with expressions of heartfelt thanks, and started on my homeward journey another man. There was, of course, the glow of satisfaction that warms the heart when one has faithfully performed a thoroughly distasteful duty. But, far more than this, there was the conviction that a cloud had been rolled away from my soul and that, at last, there was nothing to hinder a full and free communion between myself and my God. I walked now with buoyant step instead of at the laggard pace with which I had come. No longer absorbed in gloomy introspection I looked about me, and surely the world never seemed so fair. The woods freshly misted with delicate green, the tufts of primroses, the clear azure of the sky, the purity of breeze-blown clouds. All were there in their unstained innocence, and I, redeemed, restored, forgiven, was one with them. I knew then that it is impossible to be in harmony with the surpassing purity of Nature, or to enter into full fellowship with her mysteries, except the soul be freed from earthly dross.

I made my confession many times subsequently, but I never found it possible to recapture the first freshness. My experience in hearing confessions confirms the impression I received from making my own. For all but the least emotional persons a genuine first confession is a profoundly affecting occasion. I have often been made to feel the extraordinary power of the desire for righteousness in human souls when I have listened to the tale of sins long past, and of a kind to make every impulse of one's nature protest passionately against imparting them to another; the utterance choked by the fiercely beating heart; the agonized silence while the effort is made to force the dry lips to utter the shameful fact.

Such moments, to a priest who has any love for humanity,

156

are perhaps the most sacred of all his ministry. One is inspired by this glorious urge towards holiness which flows, a
resistless tide, over every barrier of human pride and self-
love. The privilege of speaking the words which fall like
healing balm upon the troubled conscience is felt to be of
unspeakable greatness.

But custom stales these exalted feelings. What was once a
vital experience, stirring the soul to its depths, tends to become, by repetition, little more than a form. The dreadful
customary description of the act of confession is "going to
one's duties". It is just that. A duty which must be performed at certain intervals if one is to support one's reputation as a good Catholic. The memory must be ransacked for
a list of faults sufficiently ample to prevent the confessor from
feeling that his time is being wasted. How often have I
listened to such lists gabbled through with almost the appearance of self-satisfaction; serious moral offences jumbled
together with trivial omissions in ceremonial observance;
with no consciousness, apparently, of the essential difference
between sins against the spirit of Christ's teaching and
infractions of petty ecclesiastical regulations.

Gravest of all is the profound misconception engendered
by confessions of a perfunctory character, that the past can
be blotted out by what has become merely a ceremonial act.

However, *abusus non tollit usum*, and experience leads
me to believe that most adults would profit by making
one "good" confession. Did not that staunch Protestant
Charlotte Brontë, impelled by some strange impulse, once
find herself in a Belgian confessional?

The making of my first confession swept away the last barrier which separated me from a sincere and whole-hearted acceptance of the full Catholic system of belief and practice as it exists within the Church of England. I never at any time felt a desire to change my allegiance from England to Rome, because the problem of authority was not one which ever disturbed me. The English Church is able to show precisely the same fruits of the Catholic system as those which are found in the Church of Rome. In arguing the invalidity of English Orders and Sacraments, Roman controversialists appeared to me to cut the ground under their own feet by proving (if they establish their case) that the same results can be obtained without valid sacraments as with them.

But the bent of my mind was not towards abstract speculation. Circumstances had placed me in Catholic surroundings; loyalty and devotion to my chief, the sense of *esprit de corps*, and the daily experience of the many happy effects upon my own life and upon that of others of Catholic belief, completed the process of my conversion.

During the ten years of his incumbency of St Martin's Hallam developed remarkable powers. Whilst in a subordinate position, and amid uncongenial surroundings, his gifts had largely lain dormant. I, who lived in the closest daily intimacy with him, had not suspected their existence. I had recognized him as a man of utter unworldliness and of deep spirituality who made staunch friends of all who knew him intimately. But that was all. Probably at that time I had not eyes to see remarkable gifts of the kind he possessed. Also, the impression a man produces on others is

158

often the combined product of his natural gifts and the
position he occupies. The village Milton may be in himself
the great poet but he remains mute and inglorious as far as
the generality of his fellow-men is concerned. Moreover,
capacity ripens when natural ability is fortunate enough to
meet with its appropriate sphere of action.

So was it with my friend. Within a very few years he
developed to the full his natural gifts as a leader of men. He
had the true leader's eye for the human instruments best
fitted for the accomplishment of his purpose. There were
no drones in St Martin's busy hive. To receive and not to
confer benefits was the unpardonable sin. All were set to
work at the tasks for which they were best adapted. On the
rare occasions when incumbents receive offers of personal
service most of them are wont to reply, "You had better
take a class in the Sunday School". The result is, that the
average parochial organization for the spiritual uplift of
youth is staffed by the hopelessly incompetent. It was not
so with us. The rector invariably made choice of fit persons
to serve in this sacred ministry.

All our old inefficient amateurish arrangements were
swept away, and sound institutions, admirably staffed and
equipped, each with a clear objective before it, took their
place. Our literature was printed and our books excellently
bound by erstwhile turbulent youth which now toiled manfully of an evening under the direction of skilled instructors.

My friend had come under the influence of Christian
Socialist ideas, and insisted upon the practical expression of
brotherhood between the varied social elements of which
our congregation was composed. A system of the interchange

159

of Sunday visits was put in operation. Our wealthy adherents invited the poorest to their homes for the day. I recollect the account given me by a poor woman, the mother
of twelve, of a day spent in the company of one of the "West
End" members of our flock. She had dined upon many
courses; the adornments of her hostess's boudoir were such
as she had not conceived to exist this side of Paradise; she
had been taken upstairs in a lift, and "treated like a lady".
No resentment at the disproportionate allocation of life's
good things appears to have been felt by these poor guests.
They were, rather, like such as had been caught up into the
Third Heaven and live henceforth on enchanted memories.

Nor were the rich less happy in this arrangement. They
spent wonderful days in mean streets and experienced something of that courtesy which is the natural birthright of the
better sort of the English poor.

Hallam's influence in the parish itself grew rapidly, and
culminated, in his esteem, when he was welcomed by both
parties as arbiter in a dispute between the employers and
workers of a great paper factory within our borders who
were at variance, and who, marvellous to relate, whole-
heartedly accepted his ruling.

The services of the church were an inspiration. Even
when the building was empty, strangers who entered it
spoke of feeling instantly an atmosphere of prayer; but
seldom did one fail to find some kneeling before the Blessed
Sacrament. There was an unusual sense of fellowship
amongst all who frequented the church. They were a
family, and the services partook of the nature of a family
gathering. The music was exquisitely rendered, but was

160

never of such a kind as to prevent anyone from taking a share in the greater part of what was sung.

I have since felt that the highest point of my attachment to Catholicism was reached on the last Christmas of Hallam's incumbency.

I had spent a week full to the brim with happy work. On Christmas Eve, having heard the last of a great number of confessions, and with nothing else to do before the midnight Mass, I set out alone for the sea shore. I walked along the deserted beach, refreshed by the cold, salt breeze. The stars shone in myriad clusters in the clear sky. "Thus", I thought, "they looked down, these same stars, on those two who made their weary way to the inn at Bethlehem. Already the appointed squadrons of the heavenly host are winging their flight earthward, and soon the shepherds will have set forth upon their happy quest."

It was all so real, so splendid in its humility; so dazzling a light had been shed upon this dark world of ours. And it all seemed so near. It might be going on now. Indeed, it would soon be happening again when once more the Heavenly Child would come to earth and be present with His brethren at the Altar, His delight ever to be with the sons of men.

I returned through the busy crowded streets, past the multitude of shops with their glaring lights, and entered the great church, which was rapidly filling. The air throbbed with the subdued and solemn tones of the organ. The servers were lighting a multitude of tapers on and around the high altar.

I vested for my duties as deacon at the approaching service, a lay reader whom (for want of a third priest) we had taken upon ourselves to invest with the parish clerk's ancient privilege of reading the Epistle, acting as subdeacon.

The procession started upon its stately progress, the jewelled crucifix before, the waving banners wreathed with incense clouds. Reaching the lower end of the church we turned to enter the centre alley by which we were to proceed back to the high altar. I shall never forget the impressions of that moment. The vast congregation in place of the scattered handful which attended but ten years ago, the uplift of a great throng united in a common impulse and possessed by one glorious conviction of the nearness of God and the unseen spirit-world. The organ thundered and hundreds of voices offered adoring worship in the hymn, *Corde natus ex parentis*:

> Then let old men, then let young men,
>   Then let boys in chorus sing;
> Matrons, virgins, little maidens,
>   With glad voices answering;
> Let their guileless songs re-echo,
>   And the heart its praises bring
>   Evermore and evermore.

As I turned I caught a momentary glimpse of Hallam. His face was transfigured by an almost physical radiance and an entirely celestial beauty. The service proceeded, my old love the *Missa de Angelis* being the appropriate music used.

I felt profoundly the pathos and beauty of the Gospel it was my privilege to read. "He was in the world, and the

162

world was made by Him, and the world knew Him not. He came unto His own, and His own received Him not. But as many as received Him, to them gave He power to become the sons of God, even to them that believe on His name." "Lord, I believe"—the words welled up in my heart—"Help Thou mine unbelief!"

The moment of Consecration had come. A hush fell upon all, and then the chime of the sanctus bell and the booming of the great bell in the turret proclaimed that the Lord whom we sought had suddenly come to His temple. I approached and received the sacred gifts.

"Blessed be Jesus Christ on His Throne of Glory and in the most Holy Sacrament of the Altar." "Lord, I am not worthy that Thou shouldest come under my roof but speak the word only and Thy servant shall be healed."

I shared in the long but glorious task of administering the Most Holy to His loved ones.

The service ended, a solemn procession was made to the Christmas Crib which had been set up outside the chapel of our Lady. And then, kneeling before a not unworthy representation of that moving scene, we chanted the Divine Praises:

> Blessed be God! Blessed be His Holy Name!
> Blessed be Jesus Christ, true God and true Man!
> Blessed be the great Mother of God, Mary most holy!
> Blessed be God in His Angels and in His Saints!
> Blessed, for ever blessed, be God!

It was in the early part of the following year that, as Hallam and I sat talking one Sunday night, he said: "I was not far out, was I, when I prophesied what Catholicism, fairly presented to the people, could do for this church?"

"The half", I replied, "was not told me. In these ten years it has achieved what I should have thought to be utterly impossible."

"And yet", said Hallam, "I am under no delusion as to the extent to which the parish itself has been influenced. Two-thirds, at least, of those who attend the church are outsiders. A great many of these were instructed Catholics long before they came to us. The rest are attracted for various reasons. Some, I hope and believe, by the Catholic Faith, others by our music or the ceremonial. But none of that two-thirds are the folk we were sent here to shepherd. I welcome their presence, of course, and for many reasons, but chiefly because they set the ball rolling. Many people are attracted to a church for no other reason than that it is popular and well attended. These outsiders, therefore, advertise us to our own people and have helped us to attract the one-third of the genuine article. But the thing to hope for is that Catholic privileges will be offered them in their own parishes, so that, in course of time, they will disappear from our midst, their place being taken by our own parishioners. And that is what I hope you will aim at."

"Yourself, also?" said I.

"No. I shall be gone", he said, jerking out the words.

"Why, what do you mean?"

"Simply, my dear old fellow, that I am going to resign."

For a few moments I was too surprised to speak. Then I said: "Whatever is the matter? What possible reason can you have for giving up a work which has been successful beyond all hope? When everything is still going so well, too?"

"That is one of the reasons for my decision. Things are going well—very well—too well! Haven't you ever heard of the millionaire's child who was found in his nursery, surrounded by expensive toys, and crying bitterly because he wanted to want something? I am like that. What more can a priest want than I have here? There is now no battle to be fought. The position is won, and only needs consolidating. That is a task for which the qualities you possess make you eminently fitted, just as my restless and belligerent disposition makes me lust for conflict."

"What do you propose to do?"

"I am going to offer myself to a missionary bishop who has a diocese as big as Great Britain, and filled for the most part with devil-worshippers. There is a job there which would be worth getting one's teeth into."

I was not deceived by his jesting manner. Knowing the man as I did, I felt quite certain that he had heard a call to follow the Master into the thickest of the conflict, and in his simple, unworldly fashion he had at once prepared to leave all and follow Him.

I was lost for a time in painful thought. I loved this man. For over thirteen years we had lived in daily intimacy, during which time no difference of any sort had arisen between us. I had for him the sincerest admiration and the truest affection. I owed to him the greater part of what religious experience I possessed.

At length he broke the silence. "I need not tell you, Wolfe, that one of the things that made it hardest for me to come to this decision is the fact that it would separate us. Who was it who said: 'I shall leave half myself behind when we part'?"

"But whatever will happen to this place and all the work you have set going?" said I, casting about, I am afraid, for arguments to dissuade him from his purpose.

"That", he replied, in his kind, boyish way, which brings a lump to my throat now as I think of it, "that will be quite all right, for no less a person than yourself must step into the breach. Don't interrupt! I have talked it all over with the duke. He is in perfect agreement with myself that you are exactly the person to carry on, and he proposes to offer you the living upon my resignation. I shall go off with an easy conscience, if not with a light heart, at the thought that you are captain of the ship."

"I would do most things to please you", said I. "But this is something I could not possibly agree to. Most of what you have told me has come too suddenly for me to grasp yet, but I am quite sure about this, that I could not, under any circumstances, take on this parish. Apart from my unfitness in other ways, I haven't the physical strength for it."

"That was my only fear", said Hallam. "I have watched you, old man, and I know you have been working to the utmost of your strength for some time. But I figured it out that the Bishop will almost certainly withdraw his embargo on the parish when I go, so that with two curates you would, I hoped, be able to manage it."

"I am quite certain", said I, "that it would be madness in me to attempt it. But, believe me, I should be sorry for my physical disability were it not that there are a great many other reasons, any one of which puts me out of the running."

"I am not going to start our first quarrel!" he answered. "Well, if you won't be skipper, will you be first-mate still? Will you stay on as curate, and be a connecting link between the old order and the new?"

"I should find it unbearable to be here without you", I said. "And how could I knuckle under to anyone after the independence I have had with you? No, sir; when you quit, so do I."

As soon as I had spoken I realized, and began to repent of my selfishness. Hallam's look of disappointment completed the change of heart.

"I was a beast", I said, "to refuse you anything in my power. Certainly, I will stay on. That is, if the new chief will keep me."

"I am asking a great deal," said Hallam, "but it is for the good of the place that I press the point. Everything is so recent here. We have laid foundations, but the mortar isn't dry yet. We don't want some impetuous master-builder to come along and upset things. You must be the steadying influence. If you will remain for, say, two years, you will have done all that is necessary."

The news of Hallam's impending departure was a shock to his people, as it had been to me. The whole of his amazingly successful work had been built up around his outstanding personality. Yet he had never been in the least masterful or self-assertive. His influence had been felt at all points, but not until he was about to go was it realized that the leader's brain and heart had supplied the motive-power which made the church of St Martin a centre of vigorous life.

His resignation was to take effect immediately after Easter, and during the intervening weeks it was, no doubt, the thought that we should soon lose him which spurred us all to redoubled earnestness and activity, whilst he was yet with us.

The Lent of that year was an unforgettable time. The call to self-sacrifice, which came with such persuasive force from the lips of one who himself was leading the way, was met with the response which they who know how to touch the chords can always win from the kindly hearts of men.

No one could say that our people frequented the church merely for æsthetic reasons had he seen the numbers who attended the daily Mass in the early hours of those dark and bitter mornings. Courses of addresses such as are usually given during the Lenten season were attended by hundreds, although they dealt only with the simple and elementary concerns of religion.

And so the days of Lent sped by, growing in solemnity as they approached the last week. None, I think, could fail to be moved by the deep feeling with which the service of the Stations of the Cross was offered. It was one which the poor and simple folk loved, and numbers of them made the circuit of the church, kneeling before each picture of that sorrowful way with affecting devotion.

Holy Week, with its sense of tragedy impending, brought, at length, the solemn offices of Good Friday. A large part of our time during the week had been occupied in hearing confessions and even after the last service of Good Friday many persons still waited in the church. One could never forget the earnestness, the deep contrition, the firm purpose of amendment inspired by the very presence, as it seemed, of the Crucified.

Easter Sunday brought its customary dramatic change. Springtime is an old experience of humanity but it never fails to come as an enchanting surprise, and the sight of a church in all its Easter array, last seen in the sombre trappings of Good Friday, gives a catch to the breath.

Grateful affection for the leader they loved had no doubt mingled with a higher allegiance, causing the church to appear as it had never done before. It was the last Easter he would be with them. His people would make it worthy to dwell in his memory. Loving hands had disposed a wealth of spring flowers throughout the building. The high altar was most fair with its masses of lilies, its gleaming silver, and its cluster of golden-canopied saints looking down with grave eyes from their niches in the great triptych.

The beauty of the surroundings, the perfection of the music, the consummate ordering of the stately services of that day were almost too poignantly moving for me, over-taxed with work, overstrained by deep feeling as I was. I took my part in it all, almost mechanically, resolved, at any rate, not to break down.

And so service followed service until Evensong and the final Procession and Solemn Te Deum before the high altar brought the day to its close in a climax of splendid praise; Easter rejoicing, for the time, banishing all other emotions. We were caught up into those heavenly spheres where no time nor distance can ever separate the brethren. We shared in anticipation unfading joys, the largesse of the Risen Lord.

Our leader turned westward to bless us. His voice was unsteady; it would not have been heard by many had not the intense stillness favoured it. The hushed, kneeling multitude seemed to drink in the tones of that well-loved voice, and I am glad to think that as Hallam looked upon that great company to whom his mere presence was a benediction he must have been one of those favoured beings who, even in this life, see the results of their soul's travail with feelings akin to complete satisfaction.

The days that followed were stale and flat; we drank the very dregs of reaction. On the Tuesday evening we forced ourselves into unsatisfactory efforts to be cheerful when we met for the formal leave-taking and the presentation of parting gifts. On Wednesday he was to go. He said Mass for the last time at St Martin's, a multitude of those who loved him being present. That was his final leave-taking, for he dissuaded from their purpose those who wished to see him off at the station.

I alone was to bid him the last farewell. We walked to and fro on the platform and talked as English people must, when under the influence of deep emotion, of the weather and the news.

Presently, though after delay which seemed interminable, the train steamed in. We stood at the carriage window, our hands locked. Neither cared to be the first to relax that grasp. So we stood, silent, until the train moved off. He waved as long as he could see me. Then he was gone, and I never looked upon that dear, loving face again.

VII

BY THE WATERS OF BABYLON

I RETURNED to the solitude of our lodging, everything in
the room we had shared for so many years bringing poignant memories, and I felt an almost unendurable tension at
my heart. Hallam had left behind nearly all he possessed.
"A missionary to devil-worshippers", he said, "won't want
to carry more than a couple of books and a tooth-brush."

Fortunately for me, I was to have a month's holiday.
Hallam, who cared for everyone's comfort but his own, had
arranged it all, and I had acquiesced indifferently.

I had been told, but was not at the time able to be greatly
interested, that the living had been offered to, and accepted
by a priest named Hildebrand, who was willing to take up
his duties at St Martin's at once, and, with the Bishop's
permission, he was doing so on Low Sunday, although he
had not yet been formally instituted. He was bringing with
him his assistant curate (for the Bishop had been only too
thankful to find in Hallam's departure an excuse for removing his ban on St Martin's), so that I could easily be
spared for a very much needed rest and change.

I packed a few necessaries, and a dozen of Hallam's
books, and departed for a quiet village in a delightful part
of Sussex. The month I spent there was so unlike any which
ever preceded or has ever followed it that I can hardly
realize that I was the being who tramped all day through

the countryside, during those noble weeks of spring, with unseeing eyes and inattentive ears.

I was overstrained by years of strenuous work which had engrossed all my thoughts, to the neglect of the warnings I should have heeded. The emotional stress of Lent and Easter, combined with my grief for the loss of my friend, had brought me very near to a breakdown. The exercise in the pure country air saved me, no doubt, from collapse, but I brooded over my loss the more because of my weakened powers of resistance, and the mental tension, in a vicious circle, increased the debility.

Thus it was that the rooks tumbled and wheeled in an ecstasy of delirious joy above the windy downs; larks shot up, a multitude of little vocal rockets; primroses were massed in every sheltered spot; and I looked at them almost without seeing, quite unmoved.

In the evenings I read the books I had brought, because they were Hallam's, and, since they were his, I forced my mind to attention. They were all volumes of Anglo-Catholic theology, and, because he would have approved, I read on and on doggedly until at a certain passage in which the author described with deep feeling the wonder and beauty of the Catholic life I became interested. He spoke of the privilege of bringing others to see and know the truth.

This was a familiar story, of course, but it was the call I needed to rouse me from my aching misery. I put the book down. "That is my task," I said, "that must be my life's work. No leisured ease, no selfish indulgence for me. I must go back to the post of duty, and give my life to the work that was everything to my friend."

I was irritated that several days must pass before I could put this resolution into practice. The country's placid beauty became irksome to me. I longed for the ceaseless activities, the busy stirring life of the great parish.

My Sundays were even more distasteful than the week-days. I made a pilgrimage of the neighbouring village churches, but could find none to my liking. Morning Prayer baldly rendered, the music mostly of unspeakable badness, fretted and irritated me. I felt starved for want of our stately services, our solemn music.

With a sense of relief I entered the train for the return journey. I cannot recall a single regret at leaving all that loveliness which Nature so lavishly displayed, but which, unheeded, she did not obtrude upon the notice of her recreant votary.

When I reached my lodgings, the sight of the empty, cheerless room was well-nigh intolerable. I sat down to a companionless meal, and was thankful that the duty of reporting myself to the new rector made it necessary to get up and go out.

I was shown into Mr Hildebrand's study, and, upon entering, I found two men garbed in cassock and biretta. One was a tall spare person, grey-haired, with an intellectual face and steely eyes, a determined chin, and thin hard mouth. He could have sat, I thought, for a picture of St Dominic. He introduced himself as the rector and his companion as Father Forsse. The latter was a stout young man with close-cropped hair and porcine eyes. His head gradually diminished in size from the bottom upward,

173

the cranial region as meagre as the jowl was well developed.

The rector extended cold fingers, which I shook. I performed the same office upon the fleshy, damp hand of his companion.

"I am extremely sorry", I said, "that I was unable to welcome you on your arrival. Hallam arranged my holiday, and, to tell you the truth, I needed it rather badly."

"It was certainly unfortunate", the rector replied, "that there was no member of the staff here when we came. We have had to find out everything for ourselves, and have lost a good deal of time in doing it."

"I can only repeat that I am sorry. Anyhow, I am here now and anxious to do anything I can to help you."

"Well, the most important matter about which I wished to question you is this. On the first Sunday after our arrival we noticed with considerable surprise that there were nearly thirty communicants at the midday Sung Mass. We supposed that this might be due to exceptional circumstances, but we have had the same thing repeated each Sunday since. This is objectionable, of course, for many reasons. Amongst others, it prolongs the service unduly since the Sung Mass is for worship and not for Communion, and there is the very serious objection that it is difficult to know whether those who communicate are fasting. What steps did Father Hallam take to assure himself that the Church's rule was being kept?"

"Hallam was accustomed on suitable occasions to put very clearly before the people the duty of observing the ancient rule, whenever possible. And there he left it. I remember his saying that he had no right to institute personal enquiries. It was a matter which must be left to people's consciences."

"I am not in agreement with Father Hallam. A rule of the Universal Church is of universal obligation; there are no exceptions, save, perhaps, the case of persons in articulo mortis."

"And yet", said I, "I think I have heard that dispensations from the obligation are granted by the Roman Church in certain other cases."

"I was not aware of the fact. But if it be true, I can only say that we do not belong to the Roman Church, and our duty is to imitate the Romans in their virtues, rather than follow them in their faults."

"But, consider this instance", I replied: "a nurse who was attending an extremely difficult mental case came to me and explained that her weekly Communion was the one thing that gave her the moral courage and the spiritual strength to go on. Her duties prevented her attending any but the midday Celebration. If she fasted until after the service she was a physical wreck for two or three days after. What should she do? I consulted Hallam and we were in complete agreement that in her circumstances the custom could not be observed. To obey the Lord's command was of far greater importance than to observe a man-made rule, venerable as I know it to be."

"I disagree. It would have been far more spiritually profitable for her to have abstained from Communion, than to communicate in deliberate defiance of the express com-

175

mand of the society to whose rules she owed an unquestioning obedience."

"But take my own case", I rejoined. "When I had
collapsed after a late Celebration on two occasions, Hallam
called in a doctor. His decision was that in no circumstances must I celebrate late in the day without previously
taking food. Hallam then laid the facts before the Bishop
who enjoined me, upon the obedience I owed him, to
follow the doctor's instructions. He said it was showing
greater reverence to God if one approached Him with all
one's faculties on the alert than with quaking knees and a
swimming brain. At any rate, since obeying his orders I am
able to do my Sunday's work, which I was often unable to
get through before."

"Nerves, my dear fellow! Forsse and I can do it, and
why not yourself? And certainly you are under no obligation to obey orders given by a bishop in defiance of the un-
disputed right of the Church to rule otherwise. But why
are you smiling?"

"I beg your pardon," I replied, "but I recollected an
odd circumstance which once arose out of this matter. One
Saturday night Hallam put his head into my bedroom in a
state of great perturbation. 'I am so very sorry to disturb
you,' he said, 'but dear George' (a visiting priest, a friend
of his, who was to preach next morning) 'has been giving
me the gist of his sermon for to-morrow. In a word, his
thesis appears to be "Fasting Communion or damnation".
Now, my dear fellow, I hate to bother you, but since you
take the late Mass, would you, in the circumstances, and to
spare dear George's feelings, and as a great personal favour

176

to myself, have your tea and bread-and-butter in your bedroom.' Forgive my smiling, but there was something so whimsically pathetic in the recollection of Hallam's alarm lest either his friend or I should feel hurt that I couldn't help it. I assure you that I have no wish to be flippant."

"I fail to see the humour of a jest which turns on a deception practised by two priests on another. But to come to the point, unless I have your word that you will be fasting from midnight on all occasions when you say Mass I am afraid that I cannot accord you the privilege of taking your turn in celebrating at midday. Of course you are fasting at early Mass?"

"Certainly. I am able to do that without any ill effect. But I am sure that I should be wrong in attempting the longer fast, and, as I have the Bishop's orders not to do so, I must decline respectfully to give you the undertaking for which you ask. But will not this arrangement lay an unfair burden on yourself and Forsse?"

"That is often the price which one pays for doing one's duty", he replied.

As a matter of fact, the price was not unduly heavy since, under the new régime, the priest who celebrated late in the day was excused from taking any earlier duty. And so, on every other Sunday, my fellow-curate was able to repose in bed with a novel and a cigarette until just before the midday service, by which time I had accomplished no inconsiderable part of my day's work.

The rector was determined to bring to an end the irregularity of communicating several persons at the Sung Mass.

He preached a sermon in which he quoted from Councils and the Fathers, and, having established his case, he proceeded to make the practical application. Henceforward any who desired to communicate at the late service must first satisfy him that it was impossible for them to do so at any other time, and, further, must give a written assurance that they would be fasting. Such persons would be given a badge which they must wear at the altar rails, and only they would be communicated.

The plan was duly carried out, but, it so happened that, from time to time, persons unacquainted with the rule approached for Communion. Wearing no badge they were passed over, and in shame and bewilderment crept back to their seat.

Forsse possessed two voices, one for ordinary occasions, and one for use in church. The latter was of a nerve-torturing description, and extremely loud and high-pitched. Amongst other irritating mannerisms he had the habit of pronouncing certain syllables as "aw"; thus, the Lord's Prayer was addressed by him to "Our Fawthaw". He was a man of humble origin and, I suppose, affected what he conceived to be an aristocratic method of pronunciation. I found that it was his habit to dot the i's and cross the t's of his superior's sermons.

The next time he preached after the rector's discourse on Fasting Communion he took up the tale. The rector's style was logical, cold, dogmatic. That of his colleague was rhetorical and declamatory.

Thus he admonished us: "As you picture the scourging of our blessed Lord you watch the blows fall, and soon you

178

see the gashes cut in His sacred body. The blood streams
out! The fainting Victim reels beneath the rain of pitiless
strokes! You picture this and you beat your breasts and
weep and groan in pitying sorrow". (Being English folk,
of course they did nothing of the kind.) "Yes, you think
you are moved by His sorrows, but in reality you are indifferent. Nay, more than that, you approve of the action
of that brutal Roman soldier. You take the scourge from his
hand and yourselves apply the torture. How? you ask in
horror and amazement. I will show you. Are there not
many among you who deliberately do despite to the Lord's
Body? You are overwhelmed with confusion at the accusa-
tion, or you indignantly deny it. But I will prove it to you.
Is not that which you receive in Holy Mass the Body of
Christ? Yes! you cry. And His most Holy Church protects
that Body from insult by certain safeguards, one of which
is that no food should previously have passed the lips on the
day of Communion. But you spurn this solemn obligation.
Rather than forgo for a few brief hours the customary
pampering of your bodies you approach the altar gorged
with meats and once again subject that sacred Body to the
scourge of indifference and contempt."

Different as was the style of the rector's pulpit utterance
from that of his disciple, their sermons had this in common,
they assumed hostility and dislike to truth in their hearers.
The rector lectured them, therefore, and Forsse abused
them. It was natural that I should compare them both with
Hallam. He invariably assumed the entire goodwill of his
people. He took it for granted that they were truth-seekers,
and he presented to them the truth as he conceived it, so

modestly, so affectionately, and with such winning sincerity that few were unaffected.

He carried out to perfection the advice my mother once gave to me: "When preaching, my dear, always remember to hearten and uplift your hearers. Never scold them. They have quite enough to discourage them outside the Church. When within it their need is of help and cheer".

Not long after Mr Hildebrand's arrival at St Martin's a young married woman of conspicuous earnestness and devotion whom I was preparing for Confirmation approached me for advice on a difficulty.

"My mother", she explained, "had a large family; she ruined her health and died at a comparatively early age worn out by this constant drain on her physical powers. She was always too unwell to be either a companion to my father or as efficient a parent to her children as she was otherwise exceptionally well fitted to be.

"When I grew up I vowed that if ever I had husband and children I would never inflict upon them the misery we had suffered. Before becoming engaged to my husband I discussed this matter with him, and we were in perfect agreement. We have been married ten years and we have three children. We are quite unable to provide for more, and we do not want more.

"During all this time it had never occurred to either of us that we were doing anything wrong, but just recently I read that the Church condemns the use of any kind of means for the limitation of families. I still feel absolutely certain that what we have done has been right, and neither my husband nor I has any intention of acting otherwise. But I felt I could not be confirmed under false pretences. So I have told you the facts, and I should be grateful if you would advise me whether or not I should be confirmed, as I am most anxious to be."

"I admire your straightforwardness", I said, "and I am grateful for your confidence. I am unable to see that you have done wrong, but I must tell you candidly that I have not given any thought to this subject and am quite ignorant of what may be said for or against it. Will you allow me to consult the rector, and then come again in a day or two, and I will tell you what he says?" She agreed to this, and I stated the case to Mr Hildebrand.

"At least she had a sufficient sense of decency not to want to approach the sacrament of Confirmation while living in mortal sin", he said. "Your answer to her question must of course be, 'You will have to choose between the laws of God and your own sensual passions. There can be no compromise'."

"The point upon which I desired to consult you", I replied, "is just that: Is she really living in mortal sin?"

"Obviously", he said. "The divine command is, 'Be fruitful and multiply'. She disobeys it."

"But is the command of universal obligation?"

"Certainly. Give yourself the trouble of referring to the first chapter of Genesis: 'God created man in His own image, male and female, and God said: Be fruitful and multiply'."

"Well, if the command is laid upon all, you and I are living in disobedience to it."

"Oh, that is quite another matter. We are referring to those who have taken upon themselves the responsibilities of marriage. Holy Matrimony is not a licence for the indulgence of lust."

"Then married people ought to have as many children as possible? You don't, of course, know Mrs Tippins of Conquest Row? She has had thirteen children and she is not yet forty. (Most of her offspring have died, it is true.) Would you commend this as an example to all?"

"I am not proposing to discuss the matter in every detail. You have asked me what answer to give in a certain specific case. Tell your candidate that the chief purpose of the marital relation is the procreation of children. To separate the act from its primary object is to sin against God's laws both natural and revealed. If children are desired at intervals only, husband and wife must practise self-control."

"Yes, but a couple who cohabited but once in a year would be self-controlled people surely, and yet Mrs Tippins might have had her family even under such a self-denying ordinance."

"I am not interested in these details, but I believe that the moral theologians suggest that women who are advised, for urgent reasons, to cease to bear children may have recourse to that part of the month when the marital relation is less likely to have results. This the Church may allow, but she absolutely forbids all artificial methods of frustrating natural processes."

"But is not the motive that which makes an act a sin? In the case of this allowed exception of which you speak the means employed are different but the intention is the same '

"I thought you wanted information and guidance? I am not prepared to debate with you. The Church has spoken and the matter is decided."

"If the Church's decision suffices to settle the matter, reasons for or against are evidently superfluous. But, do not those who believe that play with loaded dice, for even if the argument goes against them they are bound to win?"

"You may be a Catholic in doctrine, but you are certainly not one as regards morals", was all the reply he vouchsafed me.

I can honestly assert that in what I had said I was seeking only to get at the truth. I was quite unconcerned about which side, in the question at issue, proved true, provided only that my reason and conscience were satisfied of its truth.

I duly handed on to my candidate an account of what had passed.

"For myself", I said, "I am at present undecided about the right course for you to take in this matter. I am quite unable to condemn you. On the other hand, I am not certain that I ought to advise you to proceed to Confirmation."

"Then it all seems pretty hopeless", she said, with a sad little smile that went to my heart. She thanked me warmly for trying to help her; we shook hands and she went away. I never saw her again.

I was very perplexed and deeply grieved. I did not know how he would have accomplished it, but I felt sure that if only Hallam had been there he would have solved this difficulty.

The rector discussed the subject at some length in a sermon preached soon after our conversation. I was impressed by his formidable quotations of medical and theological dicta on the matter. I did not then realize that, in all questions in which either of those faculties is concerned, pronouncements are made with a finality which would be convincing were it not that they are invariably met by equally positive assurances on the part of experts of similar standing, to precisely the contrary effect.

Father Forsse made up whatever was lacking in his superior's argument when he took up his parable in the pulpit shortly afterwards. It was my first experience of the luxuriance of imagination which professed celibates sometimes bring to the discussion of such matters, and of the freedom of expression which they permit themselves, as some compensation, one must suppose, for their customary self-control.

These utterances were highly approved by that part of the congregation which was beginning to proclaim that until the kindling of these new lights they had, all unknowingly, been walking in uncatholic darkness. For, unhappily, symptoms of division for the first time began to be seen in our hitherto entirely united family. A certain number, not distinguished above others either in mental capacity or by their moral and spiritual gifts, began to establish tests of true religion by which they were enabled to pronounce judgment on others. Those who failed to satisfy them in regard to the strict fast before Communion, habitual and frequent Confession, the conviction that priests must be celibate, and so on, were described as "High Church people"

184

in contradistinction to themselves who were "sound Catholics"

The pronouncements on contraception made by the rector and his friend were welcomed by these good people chiefly, I think, because of the fact that they were supported by the citation of Roman Catholic custom and teaching. For to them Rome was the source of light and leading in all such matters, and they paid to the Holy Father every possible deference except that of personal submission to his authority. I recall one of their number declaiming with emotion upon the grossness of the sin of "tampering with the well-springs of life". He may be assumed to have spoken with conviction against the idea of imposing any check upon the natural instincts of humanity since, after his death, it was discovered that he had lived for many years under the same roof with his wife and another woman, both of whom had presented him with a numerous progeny.

A famous analysis of religious experience has resolved it into the elements of the emotional, the institutional and the rational. Like most other ordinary persons, I had reached the position in religious matters to which I had then attained by way of the instincts and the emotions, my intuitive feelings being led into certain modes of expression, and satisfied by certain means, through the agency of an institution.

Circumstances had placed me under the influence of Hallam's powerful personality, and, guided by him, I had been led to consider the claims of Catholicism, as he understood it. But the process of my conversion had little of the purely rational element about it. Few conversions have, of course. Men's instincts and feelings and circumstances lead them to a certain position; afterwards they cast about for arguments to justify to themselves and others the *fait accompli*.

So it had been with myself. During the time that Hallam had been a curate at St Martin's I had heard from his lips an outline of Catholic belief. I was impressed by his sincerity and earnestness but I was not greatly affected by the substance of his discourse. The whole matter was in the air, so to speak, and could have been apprehended by myself only after the prolonged and earnest intellectual effort which I was not in the least desirous of bestowing upon it.

All was changed when he succeeded to the incumbency. I then saw the process at work. Its details came before me in practical shape. Loyalty to my friend disposed me to approach them in a teachable spirit. Experience of the efficacy of the system to meet my own religious needs and those of many others confirmed me in the belief that the thing was of God. Faith and enthusiasm were kept at a warm glow by the share I had in the common life of the church. There was a prevailing buoyancy and energy and keenness which swept one along with it. There was too much happy and varied and successful work to be done to allow of time being given to a careful scrutiny of the foundations and the implications of all we were doing.

With Hallam's departure, a change gradually revealed itself. One was able to feel it but not exactly to define it. The services were as beautiful æsthetically, and, for a time, as well attended as ever, but the atmosphere was different. One was conscious of precision and formality where all had been natural and spontaneous.

The loss of Hallam as a preacher partly accounted for this, no doubt. He was always at one with his congregation from the outset. He felt their difficulties almost before they themselves were fully conscious of them. He expressed them in a way that proved his comprehension. He solved them by suggestions so modestly offered that they could not have given offence even had their cogency not won for them the assent of heart and mind. He always assumed that those whom he addressed were as anxious as himself to know and do the right. He gave them credit for intelligence and good-will, and submitted what he said with a grace which is indescribable.

It was, therefore, no small troubling of the waters when the sermons of such a man were succeeded by the cold, authoritative pronouncements of the new rector and the self-confident, over-emphasized harangues of his colleague.

Nor was the difference less noticeable in their manner of conducting divine worship. The unique importance of the Mass was emphasized by the belittling of Morning and Evening Prayer. The daily offices were no longer recited in the atmosphere of dignified and thoughtful devotion which they need for their due rendering, but were gabbled through at high speed, the lessons from Scripture being read as one might deliver the contents of an auctioneer's catalogue.

Both my colleagues, I am convinced, had a profound veneration for the Eucharist, but their manner of celebrating it suggested that the essence of their duty was the puncti-liously exact performance of a long series of ceremonial acts. Forsse, whose natural instinct was towards exaggeration, performed his part with the dexterity of a conjurer.

187

All this was a fresh experience for the people of St Martin's who, when Hallam led their devotions, became so identified with him that they shared his deep spirituality and, with him, entered the Unseen.

Outside the church, too, things were no longer as they were. I soon found that my colleagues took little or no interest in the multitudinous activities of the parish, all of which had been so dear to Hallam's heart.

After a time I ventured to approach the rector on the subject. "I have no intention," he said, "at any rate for the present, of closing down any work inaugurated by my predecessor. I shall judge each by its fruits, and act accordingly. I may tell you, however, that I consider that a priest's time is wasted if it is frittered away upon objects which are no concern of his office."

"But Hallam always thought that whatever affected his people was his concern", I answered. "He believed that Catholicism should touch all life, and that its priests had a ministry to serve in sharing the toils and pleasures of men as much as in succouring them in their sins and sorrows."

"I do not agree that we are to be caterers of amusement, even if it conduced to any spiritual result, which it does not. To hobnob with men over a billiard table does not bring them to Mass or Confession."

"No, not necessarily, although that is the path by which some of our men have come to us. Hallam held that we entered into our people's pleasures and recreations without any ulterior motive whatever, and simply because it was the human and natural thing to do; the reason why our Lord so acted."

"I deny that absolutely. Do you suppose that God the Son mingled with publicans and sinners in their coarse festivities for any other reason than to teach them about Himself? And I will frequent your billiard room only when I am invited there to give a course of instructions on the Person of Christ. I do not anticipate any such invitation, and meanwhile I propose to give myself to the work for which I was ordained, the ministry of the Word and Sacraments."

The view they took of this duty dispensed my colleagues, apparently, from any obligation to visit their people except when they were asked to do so in cases of sickness. "I am always to be found by those who want me," said the rector, "in my study, or in the confessional. I cannot neglect my duties in order to tramp about the parish paying social calls."

Towards the latter part of the two years which I had promised Hallam to spend at St Martin's his successor's policy had begun to show saddening results. The social activities were the first to feel the effect of the studied lack of interest of the head of the parish. Keen workers at length grew discouraged as plan after plan for future effort was turned down by our chief. I did my best to keep enthusiasm alive but I worked against irresistible odds. The membership of once flourishing organizations dwindled to nothing and the club or guild flickered out. Even our convalescent home closed its doors. This was a house on the sea-front which we had rented and furnished for the use of our poor folk who needed good food and change and rest, after illness. It was presided over gratuitously by a lady whose efficiency amounted to genius, and it was the merriest household in the town. It was an expensive hobby, I know, but we had never experienced any difficulty in raising the necessary funds.

Now, however, with a dwindling congregation, our financial resources were becoming straitened, and the rector ruled that those organizations which did not perform a directly spiritual function must be the first to be sacrificed, and so that bright little house, which Hallam had opened and duly blessed with incense and holy water one summer's day four years ago, ceased to be.

As soon as we became conscious of the fact that a great deal of Hallam's work was about to be undone, the few of us who corresponded with him bound ourselves by a self-denying ordinance on no account to let him know how things were going. It was impossible for him to help in any way, and we felt that it would break his heart if he became acquainted with the facts. I was debarred, therefore, from pouring out my heart to my most understanding friend, and loyalty to my colleagues forbade my bestowing confidences on any of our people.

I had to face the situation alone, and thus it fell out that I was led to an acquaintance with the rational element in religious experience.

So far, I had given hardly any attention to the why and wherefore of the theological furnishing of my mind, and there is little doubt that if the rest of my life's work had been done in close association with Hallam I never should have troubled to use the rational processes to modify or supplement the beliefs which I held partly on authority and partly because I felt naturally attracted to them.

As soon as differences between my colleagues' point of view and my own in various matters made themselves manifest, I came to a parting of the ways. I could no longer accept statements on authority. Objections leaped to my mind, and I had to give them utterance. So far, however, there was not the least weakening of my absolute belief in Catholicism, as I understood it. But I was forced to realize that there were serious differences between the Catholicism of Hallam and that of his successor. Not that the two men would have differed in any way as to the content of Catholic faith and practice; but they were as far as possible asunder in the emphasis they laid on the various constituent factors of their belief and the methods by which they sought to propagate it.

Hallam's was a wide, sympathetic and entirely human outlook. He taught quite definitely, but it was impossible to be otherwise than attracted by his teaching. Catholicism embodied for him the principles of a happy, balanced, all-embracing charity founded upon the rock of solid fact. Catholic practices were not burdens grievous to be borne, but delightful privileges of which people were only too glad to avail themselves when once they were put before them. Yet he never censured those who did not. He credited them with reasons which appeared valid to them at the moment, and always believed that, given time, they would do the right thing.

Hildebrand's nature was strikingly dissimilar. He had an entirely logical mind. His conception of Catholic duty was clean-cut; he had no uncertainties and he admitted no exceptions. He never spared himself, but followed unflinchingly, and at any cost, what he believed to be the path of duty, and he expected everyone else to do the same. He was impatient of half-measures, and quite incapable of temporizing. He had a neat and orderly mind, finally made up on all matters affecting theology and morals, and the conclusions he had reached were to him the Will of God.

Profoundly attached to Hallam as I was, and by nature disposed to see things much as he did, I found it impossible not to be affected by Hildebrand. I was curiously fascinated by the strength of this man's clear convictions and forceful will. I did not agree with him, and I felt bound to challenge his point of view, but I could not help being impressed by it.

Which man, I would ask myself, this one or my friend, is really acting in accordance with that inscrutable thing, the Will of God? Hallam did a great work, and Hildebrand appears to be destroying it. With one man there was popularity and success; the other would be regarded by the world as a failure. Yes, by the world, but also by God? Is not the path to Heaven itself a strait and narrow one and found by but few?

Thus I was being prepared, it seems, for facing facts, for weighing evidence, for deciding, amid many difficulties, what is truth to myself personally.

The train was laid, and a very small incident applied the match. The rector had given me an unaccustomed invitation to supper to meet a visiting preacher who represented a great Church society. He was a well-known ecclesiastic, an elderly person of pleasant, courtly manners, knowing much of men and of human affairs. He was an admirable raconteur, and at supper related all sorts of amusing experiences with infinite humour.

One of his recollections was that of dining with a friend, a Roman priest, a wealthy person and a "good liver", who was also entertaining his bishop. The dinner, it seems, was perfect, the wine beyond praise, the bishop in happy mood. Confidences were exchanged between the host and his principal guest; even the most occult fragments of personal scandal were freely discussed by them, and duly absorbed, with an incredulous joy at his rare good fortune, by the Anglican witness of the unbuttoned ease of these unguarded watchmen of Rome. A bottle of port, of an age and vintage only to be referred to with reverent wonder, was opened at dessert and as often as the bishop looked the other way his host replenished his superior's glass. "No, not a drop more!" protested his lordship whenever he caught him at the trick. But the bishop's attention would wander and the wily priest would persevere.

The story was told with irresistible drollery; yet I was surprised to see Hildebrand amused at such a recital until I recollected that an occasion upon which members of the Anglican and Roman clergy met on equal terms could not but appear to him admirable in all respects.

"A genial old pagan!" was my mental summary of our guest's character, but he appeared in quite another light later.

By what devious path I cannot remember, the conversation had got round to theological matters, and the subject of the Kenosis was mentioned, that doctrine which concerns the nature and extent of the self-emptying of God the Son when He incarnated as Man.

"What are your views", I asked our guest, "on the limitations which the Eternal Son imposed upon Himself when He became Man? His knowledge, for instance, was not, I suppose, omniscience?"

"I recognize no such limitation", he replied. "He did not cease to be God when He became Man, and if at times He acted as though He were ignorant concerning any matter (as when He asked questions), it was merely an accommodation to the conditions of human life plainly necessary under the circumstances."

"But man's knowledge is limited; he cannot but be ignorant of a vast number of things. Our Lord, surely, could not be really Man if He were omniscient?"

"The facts are just these, as far as you and I are concerned", he said: "the doctrine of the Incarnation is the inner citadel of our religion. If that were demolished, orthodox Christianity would cease to be. Well, that doctrine is being attacked on all hands; the enemy is set on capturing the citadel. Are Christ's soldiers, at such a time, to make him a present of the outposts? Our assertion of the absolute infallibility of our Lord's utterances is just one of the results which necessarily follow from our belief that He is God. It is, therefore, an important outpost, one of the bulwarks of the central Christian verity. Shall we hand it over to Christ's enemies? A thousand times, no! We must yield nothing; concede nothing; admit nothing, in so vital a struggle."

"I take it, then, your idea is, that even if the facts suggest the possibility that, since our Lord was really Man, His knowledge was limited and He was liable, therefore, to be misinformed, yet you would not admit it, since to do so would be a concession to those who deny the doctrine of the Incarnation? But would such an attitude be consistent with loyalty to truth?"

"Entirely so, both in intention and in its practical result. The fundamental truth of the Catholic Faith is that God came to earth and lived as Man. Though He became Man He did not cease to be God. As God, He did not cease to be omniscient, although as Man His knowledge might have been defective had it stood alone. My own feeling is that any possible defect in His knowledge as Man would be remedied through the union which existed between His Godhead and His humanity. Surely, the former flooded His entire being with its divine attributes?

"But", he continued, "I leave to the theologians the solution of the subsidiary and technical questions that arise out of the fact of the Incarnation, and to the critical experts the discussion of the relevant passages in the Gospels. They are matters of technical or antiquarian interest which I am quite willing that duly qualified persons should discuss among themselves. I have a friend in the British Museum who is the greatest living authority on some abstruse branch of Eastern mythology. He told me he had written a book on the subject, and that there might be six people in all Europe who could understand it.

"Of such a class is this problem of yours. It has no practical bearing on life. Dismiss it from your mind."

"But surely", I persisted, "it is a practical matter of the very first importance to be sure whether or no all our Lord's recorded utterances are to be regarded as of equal authority. I assume that as Man He shared the ideas of His contem-

poraries in regard to scientific facts. Had He taught that
the sun moves round the earth you would not, I suppose,
have considered such teaching to be authoritative for your
mind as His moral teaching is for your conscience?"

"My young friend, if the Incarnate Son of God had
taught me that the sun moves round the earth I should have
believed Him in defiance of all the scientific evidence. As a
matter of fact He taught nothing which cannot be reconciled
with what we have gained from our other sources of knowledge, provided there is a sincere desire to seek such a
reconciliation.

"Let me warn you earnestly against the first approaches
of the devil in his attempts to undermine our faith. He baits
the trap with the pleasing idea that we are trying to keep
abreast with modern knowledge, and to square religion with
science. An impossible feat! Scientific ideas are in a state of
perpetual flux. It is a commonplace that a text-book on any
branch of science is out of date in ten years' time. Our
religion, on the contrary, is 'the Faith once for all delivered
to the saints', and like the laws of the Medes and Persians,
it 'altereth not'.

"The Science of Biblical Criticism, as it is pretentiously
called, is, of all so-called sciences, the least dependable as a
source of knowledge. Every theory advanced with such
plausible confidence invariably succumbs to a newer guess.
I am old enough to have observed the birth and death of a
dozen such attempts to overthrow the authority of God's
Word by a fresh theory as to the origin and nature of this or
that part of the Gospels. And is the Church, rich with the
accumulated evidence and experience of well-nigh nineteen

hundred years, to cease to feed her children with the Bread of Life, and, in its place, to give them the husks of ephemeral speculation?

"To come in a practical fashion to the question you have raised, are you to tell some lad in your congregation, who is fighting a deadly battle with impurity, and whose one chance of keeping straight is to believe that God the Son is with him in the struggle, that, after all, the Lord Christ sometimes made mistakes as to matters of fact? Do you not see that by so doing you would shatter his faith? I know a young actress, the life of whose soul depends upon her Communions. In them she meets her Lord, and He gives her the grace to live like a saint in the constant society of men who are devils. Am I to go to her and tell her that her divine Lord was so little like what she supposes that we can't be sure that what He said was true? Even 'This is my Body' may have been a delusion of His!

"I offer you one more example. Think of a missionary surrounded by hordes of creatures scarcely human in their bestial vices. He is almost beaten in the struggle. The languorous climate, the rich, sensuous, teeming country, the hot breath of the devils of impurity that bear sway all around —these things seem to close in upon him. With despairing fingers he clasps to his heart the image of the Crucified, and is saved 'so as by fire'. Am I to send word to that lonely outpost that God in Christ is now, at length, found to be a myth? That though 'never man spake like this Man' yet this Man's voice did not always utter truth?"

As I sat pondering the conversation afterwards in the

solitude of my own room, I felt towards the guest of the evening much as I felt towards Hildebrand. The man had a strong case. His was the practical outlook of the ecclesiastical statesman. Such men are not primarily concerned with abstract truth. They are confronted daily with questions of an urgent and practical kind; they have neither time nor inclination for the leisurely and scholarly consideration of matters which appear to them simply as intellectual niceties. They are the leaders to whom men and women in every variety of difficulty and trouble and sorrow look for simple straightforward guidance in the affairs of daily life. Such people need clear-cut, authoritative statements, with none of the blurred edges which the scholar's scrupulous conscience, loyal to abstract truth, dares not round off neatly with glib assurances.

On the other hand, some chance reading of late had introduced me for the first time to the attitude of the scientific spirit. Compared with that calm, careful, unbiased study of the facts, that passionate desire to know the truth which is so intense that it produces an awful restraint in its methods and in its utterance, ecclesiastical opportunism, with its foregone conclusions, its reckless statements, its prejudice, its obsolete methods, seemed to me an unworthy thing.

And yet there were all these simple souls of whom my companion had spoken, souls for whom Christ died, whose bewilderment and misery I could so plainly foresee if their childlike trust were rudely disturbed by careless hands.

I felt utterly bewildered. I had not suffered the least loss of belief in Catholicism, I thought, and yet I had begun to see that there were difficulties ahead for me. Both Hildebrand and my other companion of the evening seemed to me to be at one in the idea that the Catholic system was to be accepted *en bloc* and unquestioningly. To admit any kind of doubt or difficulty was essentially disloyal. Whilst Hallam and I had been together it had never crossed my mind to question or deny. But under the régime of his successor I began to see that those who thought with him accepted on authority certain statements concerning which I was in honest doubt. I found myself unable to receive merely authoritative rulings. Where vital and fundamental matters were concerned I wished to know the why and the wherefore of what I was asked to believe.

It is, I suppose, a matter of temperament. A Roman Catholic convert, having been asked if he entertained any single objection to the Church he was about to join, replied that he had grave intellectual difficulties concerning some of the local Roman Catholic devotions to the Blessed Virgin which he had witnessed in Southern Europe, but so convinced was he that the Church was always right that he was quite sure his objections were entirely wrong.

To me such an attitude was impossible. As I sat and reflected I felt stealing across my mind, with the warm glow of an emotion, a pure and passionate desire for truth. I felt that I did not care, in comparison, what beliefs of mine might be destroyed, or even what ideals shattered, if, in the process, I might attain to some knowledge of the truth. I was conscious of the thought, which came to me now with the urgency of an inspiration, that truth was of God, and that to reach truth (as far as it was possible for me, by earnest study, to do so) was one way, and a very important way, of serving

God. I felt to the depths of my heart the force of the arguments to which I had listened that evening and yet I realized that there must be some fatal flaw in them, for the cause of the God of truth could not be served by concealment and evasion.

I had not the least idea whither this quest would lead me, but that night I became in intention, as never before, a truth-seeker.

VIII

SHAKEN FOUNDATIONS

DEEP-ROOTED in the natural heart of man is a thirst for knowledge. That which prompts the insistent "Why?" of childhood causes some who are but children of a larger growth to reckon all else as dross compared with the delight which is theirs who are conscious of a growing apprehension of, at least, some aspect of truth. I had conceived a rudimentary sense of this pure pleasure when a clergyman's easy and graceful rendering into English of a Latin epitaph had inspired me with a wish to possess the knowledge which would enable me to do likewise; and so there had been aroused in me a delight in the acquisition of knowledge, of facts and their meaning, which had lain almost entirely dormant during my school days.

This gusto for the perception of facts and their mutual relations had, in my student days, invested even algebra and geometry with something which gave me an emotional satisfaction.

The course of study prescribed by the college I attended for three years was a task to me only when enfeebled health sometimes made reading and thought a painful tax on mind and nerves; otherwise it was entirely pleasurable.

I continued to taste these delights until I had passed my last examination for Holy Orders, and then, duly priested, I shared the fate of so many conscientious and energetic young clergymen, I was borne along on a resistless tide of external activity which left me scant leisure for study and meditation.

With Hallam's departure from St Martin's and the consequent loss of his daily companionship, I was thrown much more upon my own resources, and being no longer dominated by that powerful personality which had swept me into the current of its enthusiasm, I had begun to think for myself. This process was accelerated by the clash of aims and methods between my new chief and myself which manifested itself so soon after his arrival. Moreover, the chance conversation with his guest when we spoke of the theological problem of the Kenosis had revealed to me that there is a great gulf fixed between the ecclesiastical outlook, which is essentially pragmatical, and minds (my own amongst them) which share something of the true scientist's conviction that truth is first and for ever to be sought and taught, be the consequences what they may.

But the imperative claims of duty to be done in the course of my daily work deprived me of the necessary leisure for reading and thought until the last two years which I spent at St Martin's. By that time the steady pressure of my colleagues' disapproval had gradually ousted me from the part I had so long taken in the multifarious activities of the parish, and I found myself, for the first time during many years, with the opportunity to read as I chose.

The exact direction of my preliminary studies was suggested by some words I chanced upon in a book of "Confessions" by a recent convert from Anglicanism to Rome. The author had delivered himself of the following artless and engaging confidence: "I regarded it as axiomatic that the Bible is an inspired and divinely safeguarded record of the facts of the Revelation of God given by Christianity".

But that, thought I, is precisely such a position as I must not assume to be axiomatic if I am in quest of truth. The statement may be true. I have always believed it to be so, but the grounds upon which I have held that belief were simply that it was presented for my acceptance by authority, and that I have had neither the leisure nor the desire to question it. I now have both, and I will face these problems: What is the Bible? And, Why do I believe in it?

In order to answer the former question I got together a number of books on the New Testament. The Old was of secondary importance; I would concentrate first on what I felt to be the essential part of the problem.

The books I used were written from various standpoints ranging from that of the convinced inspirationist to that of the most thorough-going "modern" critic. Books of the latter kind predominated in my collection, since I was fairly well informed as to the position of the former school of thinkers, and it was with the opposite point of view that I wished to make acquaintance. I should, perhaps, preface my account of this venture by saying that my attitude towards the New Testament had hitherto been that of the majority of clergymen of those days, as I suppose. I had accepted the New Testament books at their face value, and had never questioned the orthodox manner of interpreting them. I had regarded the New Testament as a book for devotional reading and as a quarry which provided sermon material. Thus furnished, I had pictured the origin and progress of Christianity as, on the whole, a dignified and ordered movement, checked, but not thwarted, by persecution from without, and hindered from within by the heretical and disintegrating tendencies of a small and relatively insignificant minority. I had supposed that the earliest Christian leaders were a happy and united band of amiable persons who propagated a complete and satisfactory body of doctrine and practice identical, mainly, with Catholic belief and custom in our own times. I did not exactly share the mental outlook of the young Anglican clergyman who thought that when St Paul besought his correspondent to bring him "the cloak which he left at Troas and the books" he was anxious to recover his cope, his missal and his breviary; and that "many lights" were burning on the occasion recorded in the "Acts" because the Apostle was celebrating Pontifical High Mass; but I fear I participated in his historical presuppositions. My course of reading during the next few months afforded me the opportunity of regarding the matter from another point of view.

I chanced to have secured certain standard works, the critical position of which lacked nothing in thoroughness. In place of the placid scene I had formerly imagined I became the spectator of an enthralling drama in which love and hate, fanaticism and formalism, high mystic insight and crazy speculation, profound thought and superficial guesswork strove together in a riot of events beneath the blazing Eastern skies.

All that (when afterwards I reflected on it) tended to be destructive of much that I had believed, but this was offset

204

by the thought of eternal truth emerging from the welter of mundane strife, not as a compact body of doctrine delivered in its entirety from Heaven, but as a Faith hammered out on the anvil of circumstance by dauntless human effort. However, reflection on the implications of what I had read followed later; for the present I was wholly absorbed in the subject itself.

The picture of the origin and nature of the New Testament writings which gradually formed itself in my mind was made up principally, of course, of material derived from the authors I had studied, but it was material selected with a kind of spontaneous apprehension of its significance. Thus, the convictions I acquired about the books of the New Testament differ from the vague views I had previously held in that they were not passively accepted at second-hand, but (such as they are) were formed out of material which I had personally assimilated. And, further, they are of a kind so essentially congruous with the rest of my mental furnishing that I should have to become another being before I could re-think myself back into the traditionalist outlook.

I see, then, in this literature an epic of the interaction of those forces, tendencies, and conflicting (or, rather, in a wider perspective, complementary) ideals which are universal wherever man is active in the moral and spiritual planes.

In the New Testament certain fundamental problems of all religious thinking are faced. But they are not argued philosophically; they are more arrestingly presented in the words and acts of striking personalities.

An outstanding figure in the drama was one who achieved

a synthesis between those universal and complementary constituents of all religious impulse, the outlook of the priest and the prophet, the institutionalist and the mystic, the traditionalist and the modernist, and, broadly speaking, the Jew and the Greek.

His was a scheme of things not elaborated in studious leisure and embodied in formal treatise, but beaten out in a life of incessant external activity and thrown off casually in chance letters prompted by temporary occasions; but it was the right understanding of these occasional letters that I found to be the key to the problems presented by the literature of the New Testament. The study of the life and work of Paul the Apostle, then, and of those letters which are generally accepted as his, was the gateway through which I passed to what I believed to be a view of the New Testament writings which is, in its main features, at any rate, true.

It appeared to me, with ever-growing conviction, that to the mind of Paul the Catholic Church was indebted for the fundamental concepts of its theology. The doctrines of the Person of Christ (the identification of Jesus of Nazareth with the eternal Son), of the atoning Sacrifice of the Cross, of Salvation by union with the Redeemer through a participation in His Spirit, of the initiatory Sacrament of Baptism, and of the Lord's Supper as a mystical partaking of His Body and Blood—most, indeed, of the great foundation doctrines of Catholicism appeared to owe their origin to him. It is, of course, a well-known conclusion of New Testament study that it was Paul who transformed what might otherwise have remained (if it lingered on at all) a sect of reformed Judaism into the Catholic Church. It was he who interpreted certain events (superficially local and temporal) of the Master's life as of cosmic significance, and gave them a world-wide appeal. Jesus of Nazareth, the Messiah of the Jews, the Saviour-God of the Greeks, lived, died, and rose again; dying for our sins, rising again for our justification, sanctifying us by the imparting of His Spirit through the prevailing power of His ascended life. These gifts, corresponding to the ultimate benefits sought, however dimly, in all ethical religions, are ours through an act of the entire personality yielding itself in faith to God's almighty power, by which we mystically participate in a death to sin, a rising again to righteousness and an ascension into the heavenly places of the spirit.

Thus, Paul seized upon the salient facts of the Master's life, saw in them an eternal significance, invested them with a universal appeal, and by a life which witnessed to the depths of his convictions and the saving grace of the truths he taught, secured for them the attention of the civilization of his day and affected, ultimately, the course of human history.

It seemed to me that there was no reason to suppose that St Paul possessed a detailed knowledge of Christ's ministry and teaching. One saying only of His does he quote, but his spiritual instinct fastened upon the foundation principle of the Master's doctrine, and in the sublime conception of Christian love he gathered up all that the Lord said and all He did, and all that His followers should be. This is the essential principle of the New Life. Love is to be the solvent of life's problems. Paul's greatest disciple, the Johannine

writer, sums it up: "God is Love, and he that loveth
dwelleth in God and God in him".

The next stage in my enquiry brought me to the consideration of the fact that, side by side with the rapidly
growing communities which owed their origin to the labours
of the Apostle to the Gentiles, there existed another Christian body differing in a remarkable manner from the
churches of Asia Minor. This was the Church which had
its centre at Jerusalem and over which presided James "the
Lord's brother". It was a Jewish community whose belief
in Jesus of Nazareth was as sincere and whole-hearted as
Paul's, but it was quite unable to think out (as he had done)
the implications of the Master's life and work. To these men
Jesus was the giver of a new and higher code of morals.
Their duty was to make disciples, teaching them to observe
and do whatsoever He had commanded them. Their faith
in Him as the Messiah, a belief temporarily overthrown by
the Crucifixion, had been revived by His Resurrection.
They expected that He would restore again the Kingdom
to Israel, and, using the customary and convenient vehicle
of apocalypse, they pictured Him as soon to appear upon
the clouds, taking vengeance on His enemies, whilst the
chosen Twelve, seated on thrones, exercised His delegated
authority. These simple beliefs were quite consistent with
the continued acceptance of the orthodox Jewish religious
system, and there appeared to be no doubt that, at first, the
Jewish Christian converts regarded themselves as still bound
to observe the full ceremonial law of the national Church
and to keep all those rules which helped to preserve the
distinction between Jew and Gentile. Thus informed, I

followed with fresh insight and with the liveliest interest the controversy which was bound to arise.

How could Paul, with his doctrine of God's free grace, accept the suggestion that any kind of ceremonial observance was a condition of His favour? How could he tolerate the setting up again of the barrier between Jew and Gentile which had once for all been thrown down in Christ? How he took up the challenge I knew from those letters in which he poured out his heart. From them, too, I saw that the victory rested with him, for the good men who at Jerusalem followed their Master in their simple way, were great-hearted enough to believe that to this strange enthusiast, with his incomprehensible ideas, God had also entrusted a message.

Before Paul's death this vital controversy had died down, and I found that it was with opposite tendencies that he was then called upon to deal. The thought of all religious pioneers invariably suffers deterioration at the hands of their followers. Always a right and a left wing is developed. The former tends to shrink from going to the full length of its leader's daring thought. It dwells upon the less revolutionary aspects of his teaching; and endeavours to formulate that which owes its vitality to the impossibility of its ever being confined within a dogma. This tendency is provoked and accelerated by the lengths to which the more daring spirits amongst the master's followers will press the unusual, the startling, the innovating side of his teaching. So it happened in the case of Paul. The restless minds of the Greek world into which his teaching had fallen gave the rein to the speculative faculty; being unable to grasp the balance and essential sanity of his scheme of thought, they luxuriated in the fancies of their teeming brains, pressing these to impossibly logical conclusions and involving themselves in a morass of crazy imaginings accompanied by a loosening of moral restraint.

The right wing of the Pauline churches, horrified by these excesses, felt the need of authority and disciplined thought. It fortified itself with apostolic precept, the Faith once for all delivered to the saints, the pattern of sound words. It was ripe, therefore, for an approach towards the more liberal members of the Church of Jerusalem. This group had not been uninfluenced by the thought of Paul, and would be favourably disposed to the more conservative element amongst his followers. Moreover, persecution from without made a united front an imperative necessity. And thus, as I saw it, a compromise was effected between what had once been two schools of radically diverse attitude of mind. The pure light of absolute truth needs dimming before the world's weak sight can make use of it. Yet, in the pages of the New Testament is given us by the hand of him with whom they originated some account of those ideas, which, accepted even in a form far removed from their original splendour and but half-heartedly embodied in conduct, have yet changed the course of the world's history.

Such was the fresh conception of the origin and early history of the Catholic Church which grew up in my mind as the result of earnest study, in which some apprehension of the truth was my sole object. The facts, of course, had been familiar to me long since, but I had not grasped their significance.

A matter of the utmost importance yet remained upon which I had to make up my mind. How would all this which I had learned affect my convictions about that divine Figure which stood behind the whole of the phenomena? To this I next directed my energies. It was apparent to me at the outset that the light I felt to have been thrown on the origin and early struggles of the Christian Church must affect my thought concerning the intentions of the Church's Founder towards the body of disciples He left behind Him to propagate the principles He had imparted to them by His life and teaching.

I was unable now to hold the view that He had given to His disciples anything in the nature of a codified system of belief, of however rudimentary a kind, nor could I accept the theory that during the forty days after His resurrection He had also given careful instructions on the details of ecclesiastical organization. It was obvious that His first followers enjoyed no such immunity from the task of using their own wits in endeavouring to apply to various circumstances, as they arose, the principles He had given them. But what had He given them, actually? Of what kind was their preparation for the task of leavening the world with His ideas? Yes, and further, what really were His ideals, what His teaching, what the character of His life, the nature of His personality?

The answer to these questions was plainly to be sought in the four Gospels. For a truth-seeker it was not enough to know what even the greatest of the Master's servants thought of Him. His faith in Christ must ultimately be based, I thought, mainly on what he could himself assimilate of the records of His life and teaching, in the light thrown upon them by half a century of research.

Thus began a serious critical study of the Gospel narratives on the part of one who pretended to no profound or exact scholarship, but who brought to bear on the subject sincerity, an open mind, and a zeal for the attainment of a knowledge of the facts. I did not handicap myself by the presupposition that my enquiries would be certain to confirm my orthodoxy. But I did assume that there is such a thing as truth, and that a less imperfect apprehension of it was possible for me if I followed the light into whatever unfamiliar and even uncongenial regions it might lead me.

To begin with, I saw that Paul definitely claimed to have received his gospel directly from the Master. His mighty Christology was evolved from mystical communings with Christ Himself; it owed nothing to man and could not conceivably be supplemented by men's halting and imperfect accounts of the external life of the Galilean rabbi. We have little reason to suppose that that which interests us so profoundly—what Jesus actually did and said during His earthly life—possessed any great attraction for Paul. His writings betray no knowledge of the parables, the miracles, the teaching (save for that one saying he quotes "It is more blessed to give than to receive"). So far as I could see, too, his followers shared his lack of interest in the details of Christ's life and ministry. Certainly, palates retaining the gusto of the heady wine of unfettered theological speculation would have found insipid those pure and limpid but homely and familiar streams. Thus I was introduced to the fact that great and growing Christian communities had come into existence by whom the details of Christ's life and teaching were probably but little regarded; to whom, possibly, they were almost unknown.

Fortunately for some of us, to whom a knowledge of what Jesus actually did and said is of more importance than the most exalted conjectures as to the meaning and implications of His life and teaching, the primitive Church was not so entirely preoccupied with speculation upon its Master's personality as completely to exclude an interest on the part of some concerning His earthly life.

The Church of Jerusalem had treasured the memory of His sayings, which embodied the commandments of the system of reformed Judaism it professed; but interest in the Master began, at length, to extend beyond this to the details of His life and actions. Our four Gospels appeared to represent four attempts to give an account of Jesus Christ which should contain a record of His life in such a form as would confirm the Church's teaching as to the meaning of His appearance among men and of His claims upon them.

Previously to that period of my life of which I speak my attitude towards the Gospels had been that of most Christians who accept without question and without much reflection the current orthodox attitude towards them. It did not occur to me to dispute the assertion that the Gospels are four accounts of Jesus which supplement one another. Where they appear to give contradictory accounts of the same matter the appearance is deceptive. If we knew all the facts, the apparent discrepancies would be resolved into a wider harmony. There might be small verbal inconsistencies between them but there was nothing in any of the four Gospels but what conveyed an historically accurate impression of the life and teaching of Jesus. It was obvious (as my Romanist author had implied) that in sending His Son into the world Almighty God would take care that the facts concerning His sojourn among men should be clearly and correctly recorded.

This point of view, whilst it had saved me from a vast amount of mental effort, now had its drawback for me in that one had but to accept an infallible record; there could be no intellectual conflict nor any of that delight which comes to one who feels that by honest and patient toil he has struggled upward toward a position from which truth can be, at any rate, a little less dimly apprehended.

My reading in this subject was to me a pure joy. I felt reverence and gratitude to that considerable body of scholars who, in the face of opposition so bitter, had applied their gifts of mind and heart to the elucidation of the real significance of the books that compose the supreme expression in literary form of man's efforts to understand the primary facts of existence and to put himself in the right relation toward them.

As literature, the New Testament gained incomparably for me when approached from the standpoint of the modern critical method. That which had been obscure or uninteresting became luminously clear and pregnant with significance. A sentence, a phrase, a word even, thus interpreted, flooded a whole chapter with meaning of absorbing interest.

One well-known conclusion of modern criticism is, of

course, that the Gospel according to St Mark is the earliest of the four, and that it, or the material that lies behind it, was used by the writers of the first and third Gospels as the framework into which they fitted additional matter to which they had access. This conclusion appeared to be supported by overwhelming evidence, and I was convinced of its validity.

With this simple but invaluable clue my study of the Synoptic Gospels became at times of almost breathless interest. With a finger between each of the three sets of pages, I turned from one account of an event to that given by the other authors, comparing differences, and noting the points upon which first one pair of writers, and then another, agreed with, or differed from, the third.

As is the case, I think, with most open-minded persons who have striven, in a humble fashion, to verify by their own efforts the main conclusions which have been reached by the modern critical method, I became assured of their substantial accuracy. I am well aware that this is a fact of no importance, but, as marking a complete revolution in my habits of thinking in those matters, it has a place in this record.

It is not easy to describe in a few words the changed standpoint from which I came to regard the Gospel narratives. Suffice it to say that I became very strongly convinced of the value (from the standpoint of the historical student who desires above all to know the facts) of the Gospel according to St Mark.

Tradition and modern scholarship are, in the main, agreed that this little book enshrines the reminiscences of

Peter, as collected by his disciple and interpreter John Mark. Its probable origin in Rome may account for the fact that the influence of Paul's great mind is seen in the presentation of the Master's life as leading up to and culminating in the Crucifixion and Resurrection. But, of all the four Gospels, it is that which is least affected by current ecclesiastical thought, and presents an honest, vivid, and relatively accurate account of the facts of the Lord's ministry and death.

I saw, however, the important bearing upon the value of the Gospels as historical records, of the indisputable fact that a long period (probably not less than thirty years) elapsed before the recollections of Peter were thus committed to writing. Remembering Boswell's frequent laments as to loss of fulness and accuracy in recording his hero's sayings and doings whenever he neglected to set them down on the very day upon which he witnessed them, I realized that even in the earliest and most historically trustworthy of our Gospels one might not look for anything approaching a meticulous accuracy of description. I found it a wholesome check to that rash dogmatism which attempts to settle questions by an offhand appeal to a text, to remember that the most reliable authority we possess for our knowledge of Christ's life is a record of reminiscences given at second-hand a quarter of a century after that life had ended.

The Gospel according to St Matthew I found to contain the framework of St Mark, freely amended, supplemented and corrected, into which were inserted blocks of the Master's teaching such as would be likely to be stored up in the retentive memory of a Christian scribe of the Church of Jerusalem.

I could not suppose that an actual eye-witness of most of the events of Christ's ministry would be obliged so considerably to avail himself of the work of someone else in making his record, and, consequently, I abandoned the idea that Matthew the Apostle was responsible for this Gospel, a conclusion confirmed by a study of the emendations made by the author in the Marcan material, emendations which consistently heighten the miraculous and predictive elements in the life and teaching of Jesus.

In the Gospel according to St Luke, the cultivated and attractive scholar, I saw a picture of the Master from the standpoint of one who had the skilled writer's eye for the picturesque and appropriate grouping of his material. The blocks of sayings inserted by the author of the first Gospel into the Marcan framework were by this writer broken up and disposed throughout his work to illustrate the actions to which they appeared to him appropriate.

Thus, Luke, even as Matthew, makes, I found, a very free use of his material. Neither Gospel is intended to be a bald, literal, historical narrative. Each was written, though from a different standpoint, to win men to Christ. Inconvenient facts, or inappropriate observations artlessly set down by Mark, are omitted or amended in accordance with the reviser's ideas of reverence, his presuppositions, or the class of persons he is trying to reach.

It is necessary for completeness, in this part of my narrative, to speak briefly of the attitude I came gradually to take up towards the Gospel according to St John. In a matter concerning which the greatest minds do not claim finality for their views it would ill become one so little qualified as I to propose a solution of the apparently insoluble.

It would, however, be shirking a plain issue if I did not confess to have approached a relative and tentative conclusion in regard to the last of the four Gospels, which provided me with a working basis for thought.

I became convinced of the probability that the Gospel according to St John is, in substance, an eirenicon offered, by one steeped in Pauline mysticism, to that mode of Christian thought which would feel itself insecure apart from the conviction that, in accepting the metaphysic of Paul, it was embracing no airy abstraction but something which was deep-rooted in the actual facts of the Master's earthly life. Thus, the author, saturated in Pauline thought, seeks to explicate his master's and his own profound conceptions by a selection of events such as he believed actually to have occurred or such as were likely to have happened, illustrated and elucidated by teaching, sometimes attributed to Jesus, but often shading off into the author's own comment, the two being conceived of as so substantially identical that a rigid distinction between them is unnecessary.

Someone has remarked that however great may be the difficulties in accepting this book as the work of John the Apostle, an actual eye-witness of most of what he records, they are as nothing to the sheer impossibility of supposing that the discourses of Jesus therein contained are, in point of fact, the work of the author. To me the case presented itself as of overwhelming cogency in favour of the opposite conclusion. I was so constituted mentally as to make it an impossibility for me, in the light of the available evidence, any longer to believe that the value of the fourth Gospel is inseparable from its claim to historical and literal accuracy. To me, this book reflected one of the most exalted spiritual interpretations of the Master's life of which it was possible to conceive. It made explicit (after a mystical sort, only to be apprehended by the purged eye and the love of an adoring heart) that which underlay the tender simplicities of the Galilean idyll, as well as what principalities and powers were interlocked in that last conflict at Jerusalem.

It is difficult adequately to express my sense of gratitude to those scholars whose writings were the means by which my conception of the origin, nature and function of the New Testament has been so completely changed. It is not merely for a mass of illuminating data that I am indebted to them, but much rather that they made me the better acquainted with, and imbued me with an increasing reverence for, the modern scientific attitude of mind, which, at its best, is the fearless and unfettered search for truth. I did not doubt the entire sincerity of the traditionalist scholar, but I felt that one who conducted the enquiry with the conviction that critical research could not but confirm the orthodox point of view must be biased, however unwillingly, by this presupposition, and, as a matter of fact, a study of the works of some of these authors strengthened that impression.

The course of reading and reflection, of which I have given this very brief account, afforded me, I am convinced, a clearer understanding of the proximate causes which produced the New Testament writings. It is scarcely necessary to add that I did not suppose myself to have obtained thereby an explanation of the ultimate causes which resulted in the world's enrichment with this choicest example of humanity's effort to picture in words a crucial period in its spiritual development. Thus, for example, I was given a detailed and intelligible account of the relative causes for the Matthean and Lucan variations from the original narrative of Mark. I saw clearly that these reflected the Church's developing conception of the Personality of its Master, but the ultimate question, why primitive Christian belief had developed along these particular lines, was still an enigma. Certain convictions, however, began to form themselves in my mind. I felt that the Christian religion, as pictured in the New Testament, is a revelation of God in that it exhibits human thought and action concerning Him on the highest plane of creative spiritual genius to which humanity has yet attained. This religion incorporates the essential data, but it is not a compact and infallible revelation, in the sense in which that word is customarily used in orthodox thought.

Of course, in a sense, all such human achievement is the result of a revelation from God, for "what hast thou that thou didst not receive?" But the divine influx is conditioned by and mediated through fallible human thought. "It pleased God", says Paul, "to reveal His Son in me." Consequently, whatever knowledge of that revelation he is able to impart is coloured, and indeed moulded, by his personal apprehension of the current thought of his day. The human and subjective element is an essential component of his teaching.

Thus, my conception of God gradually changed from the crude anthropomorphism of childhood, and the scarcely less naïve imaginings of my later years, to the thought of One in a sense at present unknowable, a Power behind the scenes. I could no longer permit myself those facile affirmations as to the details of His will and purpose which belonged to the more unthinking stages of my spiritual development. The undeniable contention that a crudely orthodox presentment of Christianity possesses an appeal which men fail to discover in the hesitations and half-lights of conceptions evolved largely in the study does not decide the question. I had to include in my thought of God His apparent willingness that mankind should profit greatly by beneficent illusions. The author of the Book of Job saw through the fallacy that prevails throughout a large part of the Old Testament, that material prosperity invariably attends those who conform to the Divine Will, yet, undoubtedly, this belief produced upright living in multitudes who would have been deaf to a purely spiritual appeal. In the New Testament the universal belief in the speedy second coming of Christ was entirely fallacious, but it is unquestionable that the illusion produced an other-worldliness which regarded suffering and death as negligible, and so gave to the primitive Church a power of resistance without which it would have been overwhelmed by the floods of recurring persecutions. Towards extensive spheres of thought upon the nature and will of God I held by what I trust was a reverent agnosticism. I reflected that it is not the least of the glorious qualities of the Apostle to the Gentiles that he professed a more limited knowledge of God and existence than do many who

221

invoke his authority. "Now we see through a glass, darkly."

But I thought I had a clue to the mystery. The mighty vistas opened by scientific discovery revealed a unity of purpose, unparalleled in its patient persistence, culminating in man divinely facultied. The process was continuous from the primal amoeba to the poet, the artist, the scientist, the saint; some of the details might be lacking, but the broad fact of this stupendous development was patent. It was that godlike man might be achieved that worlds were shattered and re-made, man who might progressively share in the counsels and co-operate with the purposes of his Maker. It seemed to me that in all ethical religions, in Christianity supremely, the instinct of the great creative thinker had leaped unerringly to certain of the conclusions which man's subsequent experience in every sphere of his thought and endeavour is progressively and painfully verifying. The unifying and illuminative principle, as I saw it, is Love—God's love to man and its response in love towards Him and to his fellows. This was the concept realized in the life of the Prophet of Nazareth (one saw it even in the imperfect memories of Him which we possess); it was worked out in the impassioned thought of Paul and John; it was the source of that pure stream which has constantly overflowed the barriers by which a rigid ecclesiasticism has striven to confine it. This was the conviction which has inspired the greatest and most fruitful part of all human endeavour.

But, while I held most firmly that the rational processes should be utilized fearlessly and to the utmost in the face of

222

every problem, and that there is no such thing as a sacred arcanum into which man's mind should not strive to penetrate, yet I felt that for the purpose of ascertaining truth man possesses something more than the sum-total of his reasoning faculties, and it was this something more in me which, doing no despite to the conclusions reached by ratiocination, enabled me to believe that God is Love.

An objection to modern Biblical Criticism once suggested to me was its lack of finality: one theory is rapidly displaced by another; the convincing hypothesis of to-day undermines that which seemed an equally unanswerable theory yesterday. But what was advanced as an objection was to me proof that modern methods of Bible study are in line with every other branch of scientific research. It is a commonplace that a scientific text-book of ten years ago is obsolete to-day. The book was once abreast with current knowledge, but growth in knowledge has superseded it; growth which the book helped to bring about.

I learned to realize that there is no such thing as utter finality in the results obtained in any branch of human effort and enquiry. The desire for such rounded and perfect completeness was to me a sign of that hunger for the Absolute which appeared to be implanted in us in order that we might never rest satisfied with limited and partial achievement. It seemed to be a betrayal of this ideal to suppose that one could ever attain a perfectly satisfactory foothold, in which further effort would be superfluous, if one found in either Church or Bible a final halting-place in the quest for truth rather than a lofty plateau from which one

could discern the nearer of those cloud-capped peaks that
still beckoned the dauntless explorer forward.

Thus, as I pondered the profound thought of a Paul or a
John I found myself compelled to say, "Poor feeble thing
as I am, I must yet be true to the best that is in me, and therefore, 'Nullius addictus iurare in verba magistri'". Nor, I
thought, would either writer have desired a blind homage
to his *ipse dixit*. They were truth-seekers who have enlightened humanity for all time by such account as they
could give of their mode of apprehension of the truth. We
of a later day cannot re-think ourselves into their mental
atmosphere in such a manner as to make it for ourselves
what it was to them. Our duty, rather, was to catch something of their spirit and clothe it in the forms appropriate to
the thought of our own times. That was the task of theology
which must, therefore, if it be a science true to its name,
constantly be obsolete and in need of perpetual renewal.

It would be as the effort to cage a mounting lark to try
to imprison the spirit of Paul in a fixed and rigid system of
dogma. For one thing, as his own writings abundantly
witness, his thought was constantly changing with the growth
of his apprehension of truth. Moreover, the setting of his
vital and fruitful thought was the material supplied by the
transitory, imperfect and even erroneous conceptions of his
day. Thus, it is indisputable that, in so far as this great
mystic could confine his lofty conceptions within the narrow
bounds of an ordered scheme, one of its foundation ideas
was that of the Fall of Man conceived of as an event in history as certain as that of the sacrifice of Calvary. To myself
that fragment of Semitic folk-lore was awe-inspiring in view

of its diagnosis of sin as conscious and deliberate disobedience to the authority of the higher self. But I could
not regard it, as Paul apparently did, as a historic event
which gave a satisfactory explanation of the existence of sin
and of physical death.

And it was obvious that the form in which the Pauline
doctrine of the Atonement is given is the necessary outcome
of the form in which he held the doctrine of the Fall. It is
expressed in terms of Jewish religious thought, and to become assimilable by us it must be divested of its transient
externals and re-clothed in the terms of our own modes of
thinking.

A process precisely similar appeared to me to be necessary also in considering the portraits of Jesus of Nazareth
given in the Synoptic Gospels. The artists who painted these
pictures made use of the only material available—the ideas
current in the times in which they lived. The differences
between the three pictures given us are traceable to developments in the conception of its Master held by the primitive
Church. At times we could wish that our authors had been
able and willing to give us the bare facts and had allowed us
to supply the interpretation. As it is, we have to try to get at
the facts behind the interpretations. One of the triumphs of
the critical method seemed to me to be the gradual emerg-
ence of a solid body of practically incontestable historical
fact as to the main outlines of the life and teaching of Jesus.
It was, perhaps, not too much to say that it had been the
privilege of the days in which we live to have rediscovered
the historical Figure which had been so long enwrapt in the
grave-clothes of abstract theorizing.

The result, as far as I was concerned, was the revelation to my soul of a Person of surpassing charm and attractiveness, the spirit of whose life and teaching shone even through the inadequate conception of His greatness which, we know, was held by those who were acquainted with Him, and to it my whole being responded as to the authentic voice of God.

The facts forbade me to seek in the Gospels a mass of infallible data, a quarry for the material from which to form a rounded system of dogma. One cannot thus, I became convinced, make one's own what Christ offers. That was something which could be felt but not adequately expressed. Yet it was that which the progressive experience of mankind was in course of verifying as illuminative of the purpose which underlies the whole creative process, and it was that which, in so far as it had become the lode-star of my own life, gave it the best of all the little of good it possessed.

"A truly unsatisfactory Christology!" would possibly be the verdict of Orthodoxy upon such a creed. Not much more unsatisfactory, I should have replied, than any attempt to formulate in words what has become intuitive and is the sum-total of a personal experience. Yet it serves me less inadequately than a conception expressed in the formulae of a purely technical theology. I could not now express satisfactorily my convictions about Jesus of Nazareth in the terms in which Orthodoxy endeavoured to make explicit its thought of Christ sixteen centuries ago. To me all such formulation became of the profoundest interest, but was no more mine than was the mental atmosphere out of which its terms were necessarily evolved.

I felt I could still say that to me Jesus Christ was the central fact of existence, and that growth in the knowledge and love of Him was to me identical with progress in the realization of man's godlike task of entering into and making his own the dimly-seen and far-off purpose towards which creation moves.

I now began to see that my attitude towards the orthodox Catholic system had undergone a change. The New Testament studies in which I had been engaged had given direction and impetus to the movement of my mind, but it was what appeared to me as the failure of Catholicism to establish its claims when tested by the facts of experience which began the process.

If it were possible to formulate the new conception of the place and function of Catholicism in the scheme of things which gradually possessed my mind, I might describe it as the conviction that the Catholic system was a method of approach to God of extraordinary attractiveness and of immense practical utility. If one could concede its premises, the superstructure which has been erected thereon was of an unanswerably logical consistence. But it was just those things which to Catholicism are axiomatic that appeared to me to run counter to the facts.

Thus, it is assumed that Jesus founded a Church, indicated the functions of its principal officers, arranged, at any rate, the outlines of its organization, and provided it with the material of which the Creeds are the necessary and inevitable outcome. The New Testament appeared to me to offer no support to any one of these contentions. It was an anachronism to attribute to the Jesus described by St Mark any intention of founding a Church in the strictly "ecclesiastical" sense. The functions of the officers and the details of the organization of the Church evolved gradually under the pressure of circumstance and at the dictates of expedience; the Creeds were a formulation of the wisest and most balanced thought of the times upon the essential facts of Christian belief as then understood.

This radical change in my outlook, due, as I believe, to a frank acceptance of the historical facts, did not diminish in the least degree my affection and reverence for Catholicism. Indeed, I continued to profess myself a Catholic, for I valued beyond my ability to express it that venerable system of belief and practice which has secured the allegiance of the majority of Christians through the centuries of the Church's history. I was convinced that, if anything like a complete reckoning could be taken of all that has contributed to make Christianity the supreme power for good in the world, the influence of those great ideas and noble ideals which are the heritage of Catholicism would be found to have been a factor of primary importance. I knew well, however, that such a belief just failed to concede those two of its claims which Catholicism regards as vital. For Catholicism considers itself as the sole depository of infallible truth and its system as the only logical outcome of the Life lived in Palestine nineteen centuries ago.

Freed by such study and reflection on the subject as I was capable of bestowing upon it, I dropped my provincial and exclusive attitude and assumed my true status as a unit in the brotherhood of humanity, a citizen of the world. I could now look with sympathy and an open and receptive mind upon any and all of my fellow-men who, in any way, however far removed from that to which I was accustomed, accepted Jesus as Lord.

I worshipped from time to time in the chapel of an abbey of exiled French Benedictines and never failed of a boisterous greeting from Brother Peter the doorkeeper. I suppose he took me for a secular priest of his own communion, and I had not the heart to deprive myself of his welcome by unasked-for explanations.

The brothers enter for the service two and two, he on the right dipping in the stoup and courteously offering Holy Water to his companion. All are oblivious of their surroundings; all are entirely absorbed in their devotions. Their heads are bowed as one at certain points in the service. At the tap of the Prior's ivory mallet all stand erect again.

The Benediction candles are lighted, the *Tantum Ergo* is sung to the haunting plainsong melody; the bell chimes, the Monstrance is uplifted. I, with the rest, bend low in the Divine Presence....

But what would England be like if deprived of its Plymouth Brethren? I see two of them whose acquaintance I made during a walk in the country. Two aged ploughmen, their round backs bobbing up and down on the skyline, are of that persuasion. They share the belief of their sect that they are of the number of those saints who, at the coming of the millennium, will return to earth to reign with Christ for a thousand years. Presently, sheltered from the wind under the lee of the willow copse, they will eat their "'levenses".

From the half-loaf and the lump of fat bacon pressed by gnarled thumb against that mighty cantle they will pare gargantuan mouthfuls, and as they slowly masticate, they will ponder the ordering of their satrapies when the golden day arrives. It thrills me thus to hear in our English countryside the last faint reverberation of the thunder and lightning and voices of that furious tempest of millennial speculation which swept over Asia Minor eighteen centuries ago. . . .

The same day, in a pouring storm of rain, I overtook an urchin plodding sturdily, supporting his steps by a huge staff. I greeted him, and though he was soaked and miserable, his blue knuckle instinctively sought his forehead and he "made his reverence", all personal discomfort forgotten at the imperative claim of his conception of the offices of courtesy.

"It is a cold day", I said. "Perhaps a penny would help to warm you. It is a very cold day; twopence would be better."

He pocketed the alms and sped forward to the village shop, in the window of which dainties of dazzling colours exercised silent fascination.

That also, I suppose, was a faint echo of words once uttered in a far-off land by One who had a kindness for children. Thus was the influence of Jesus mediated to me in countless ways: through that which connects it with its early days in Imperial Rome, through the bold imaginings of oriental speculation, and through that which owes nothing to ecclesiasticism but is a voice which, across the centuries, calls directly to human hearts, attuning them to harmony with One all love. . . .

So I had grown tolerant. *Homo sum; humani nihil a me*

alienum puto. Was it but a lazy dilettantism? The Gallio who is equally indifferent to the claims of each contending faction earns a cheap reputation for broad-mindedness. But converts, I knew, are not made by the feeble glimmer of a twilight faith. They are won by large certainties and un-qualified assertions, not by the conscientious scholar's nicely balanced hesitancies. Yet, thought I, to each his part, and perhaps that highly enigmatical matter, the Religion of To-morrow, may owe something to those who have tried not to be false to what light they possessed, dim though it may appear to those who walk in the full blaze of convictions that know no peradventures.

Meanwhile, though one who could find great store of spiritual good whether at High Mass or at a Quakers' meet-ing, I had in my heart the warmest place of all for the fruitful Mother from whom I had derived the greater part of the spiritual nourishment by which I lived. The English Church, with the decent solemnities of her normal modes of worship, her broad sympathies, her strong links with the past, yet prepared to welcome in her characteristically grave and cautious fashion all that the future may bring, this was the Church to which I was proud to belong. Her genius was that of the people to which she was still the principal mediator of things divine. Her faults and shortcomings were glaring and obvious; they could scarcely be otherwise since her sons and daughters proclaim them vociferously to the listening earth. But her contribution to the world's wel-fare had yet been the no mean gift of a succession of men and women, sober, peaceable and truly conscientious, who had been reared under the influence of her mild austerity, and who had taken, I thought, a not unworthy part in humanity's march towards the day when the kingdoms of the world will have become the Kingdom of our God and of His Christ.

The course of study I have described enabled me to reach conclusions such as are now becoming generally accepted by progressive clergymen, but were certainly not so even in quite recent years. I feel that by this personal (if undistinguished) effort I achieved intellectual emancipation and won my citizenship in the free democracy of modern thought.

But, owing to the fact that throughout my adult years I have played a part in the external world of business or profession, of social intercourse and all the multifarious duties and interests of daily life, and at the same time have been living, almost another person, in the inner world of the intellect, the emotions and the imagination, it has frequently happened that in one sphere I have found myself far ahead of the position I occupied in the other. Thus, by a combination of circumstances, I had been an assistant priest in an Anglo-Catholic church for some two or three years before I became inwardly a convinced Catholic. And, again, circumstances brought it about that I remained in Catholic surroundings for some months after I had inwardly rejected the Religion of Authority for that personal possession which is won by free and unfettered enquiry.

I did not at first realize how great a revolution had taken place in my inner life, and so I was for a time content with the working compromise which has just been outlined.

232

This cloud castle, however, was about to receive a rude shock from an event in the outer world; a shock which it, indeed, survived, but only after an impression had been made which was destined to lead me to a further stage in my inward pilgrimage.

It was in the opening days of autumn in the fourth year after Hallam's departure from St Martin's when, upon returning to my lodgings from the early Mass one weekday morning, I found on my breakfast table a letter bearing the postmark of the South African town from which my friend's correspondence was usually directed; but the letter was not addressed in his handwriting.

I opened it and read this:

Sir,

It is with profound sorrow that I write to tell you that our beloved Father Hallam passed away two days ago. He had been watching some natives who were cutting down a tree, which began to fall earlier than was anticipated. He ran forward to save the child of one of the workmen who was playing on the ground close by. He managed to fling the child out of the way, but was himself pinned beneath the tree when it fell, receiving injuries from which he died three days afterwards. During the all-too-short time he was with us our friend had won a remarkable position in the affections of the native people and had inaugurated a work of quite extraordinary promise.

I enclose a note to yourself which he dictated the day before he died, and which he asked me to forward. From the warm way in which he always spoke of you I can gather how much you were to each other. May God in His mercy soften the blow....

233

This was Hallam's letter:

Dear old man—I am finished. I cannot help some regrets, but God knows best. I was right in coming here. Could you but see those dusky upturned eyes, those pleading hands outstretched for the Bread of Life.... Saint Martin's.... God bless you all. We lighted a candle which will not easily be put out. The workers pass but the work goes on. Remember me at the altar. My dear love to you.   A. H.

I was numbed into a strange calm upon reading these letters. I read them again, deliberately, folded them and placed them in my pocket, and passed out into the busy street. This curious suppression of emotion enabled me to return the greetings of passers-by and even to converse for a few moments with one who stopped me. I entered the empty church and knelt before the Blessed Sacrament.

Then the arrested emotion broke suddenly like a flood upon my stricken spirit. "My friend, my more than brother, my dear, dear friend! I shall never, never look upon your face again...." I was overwhelmed with grief which cannot be expressed. Rising from my knees, exhausted by the tumult of my sorrow, I sat down to think.

There arose in me a dull feeling of rebellion. Why had God allowed this senseless thing? Why had He permitted a mass of inanimate matter to beat out so noble a spirit? I felt the full force of a thought which had haunted me from time to time in moments of depression: that material things constitute reality, opposed to which man's high hopes and splendid dreams are as ineffectual as spray blown against a granite coast.

I tried to put the nightmare from me. "There," I told myself as my eyes turned towards the Tabernacle, "there is the supreme Reality." And then there surged up in my memory a story I had once been told of a blind priest to whom, for his great sanctity, the Pope had granted a dispensation to say Mass at an altar in his own house. On one occasion he lay prostrate before the Sacrament, as was his wont, lost in adoring devotion. Meanwhile, a rat crept up on to the altar and consumed the consecrated Wafer....

I could stay in the church no longer. I passed out into the street, and made my way through the town to the open country.

It was an autumn day of rare beauty. Around the hill I had climbed lay spread on all sides a little bit of fair English land, radiantly lovely in the mellow sunlight. Beech woods dim and mysterious, the stubble fields, farmhouse and grange, the faint sound of far distant cock-crowing, the warm and scented air, the murmur of insect life, and southward on the horizon, dimly discerned, the sea.

For a moment I felt something of the old rapture. Surely the Lord is in this place....

Then the mood changed. What was this fair sight but an illusion? Our minds, for ever spinning airy webs of unsubstantial fancy, invest with an imaginary significance what is, in reality, but a material phenomenon, a non-moral and strictly utilitarian process of cause and effect, pursuing its relentless course in utter indifference to the hopes and fears of men. What cared all this happy-seeming world that far away in an African grave lay a mangled body once the tabernacle of a spirit burning with the love of God?

235

And where was that spirit now? O yes, I knew of the Christian hope of immortality, but might not this too be one of those fancies with which men strive to obscure the stark realities of inexorable fact?

The curtain falls, we know, but what happens behind it? Is there, indeed, another World, a land of far distances, a place where dreams come true? Many thoughtful people believe that no messenger has ever returned to assure us that this is so. Is man, indeed, an immortal spirit, or is the thinking, dreaming, worshipping part of him a mere by-product of his material organization and destined to share its extinction? The rapturous hopes, the golden visions of Christianity, could they withstand the cumulative testimony of all the facts that man shares the final annihilation which awaits all created things?

"Yet still," I mused, instinctively eager for some ray of comfort, "even if this world is all, yet life is a splendid gift. As Hallam says, 'the workers pass but the work goes on'." And then I recollected the state of affairs at St Martin's. All that my friend had built up with love and pains so great was being destroyed. The thing was crumbling to pieces before my eyes.

I could endure no more. I went to Hildebrand and desired him to accept the customary three months' notice of my intention to resign. He was kind about it, but was obviously relieved.

"The parish will miss you greatly," he said, "but you are, I think, acting wisely. It has been obvious for some time that you and I are not in agreement as to the methods which should be employed here."

236

IX

I, TOO, HAVE LIVED IN ARCADIA

In bitterness of spirit I had intimated my desire to leave St Martin's. Calm reflection revealed to me that I was thus shortly to become an out-of-work curate, nearing middle-age and singularly averse from learning fresh ways under a new master. If only I might be placed in a charge of my own! But I had never sought preferment. I had been shocked by a remark made to me in the early days of my ministry by an elderly incumbent. "What is it that a young clergyman is most desirous of obtaining?" he asked rhetoric-ally, nor waited for an answer. "Of course, it is a living."

"I am perfectly happy as a curate," I said, "and I should consider it disgraceful to make any effort to obtain promo-tion. If I am worthy of it, it will come to me."

"You will be wiser when you are older", commented the sage.

My brother, upon becoming acquainted with my situa-tion, expressed himself in somewhat similar terms. By this time his Anglo-Catholicism sat lightly upon him; indeed, he had become quite the man of the world. "It is a mistake", he told me, "to suppose that in the Church of England, as by law established, merit automatically meets its reward. It is necessary for merit to get up on a tub and draw atten-tion to itself with piercing cries. The Crown is patron of a

237

large number of livings. Place your name upon the waiting-list for anything suitable that may become vacant."

Unwillingly, and after much hesitation, I filled in the necessary forms and, as required, gave the names of three persons as references. Two of these wrote me kind letters which I enclosed with my application. The third, the Bishop, who had expressed himself as anxious to help me in the matter, would, I supposed, write direct to the Crown Patronage Office.

I received a printed acknowledgment of my humble petition which stated that the number of clergymen who applied for livings in the gift of the Crown was so large, and the qualifications necessary in the case of each of such livings so various, that my early appointment to one of them was improbable.

This, I realized, was the courteous official manner of telling me I had no chance, and I regretted that I had courted a rebuff. Our kindly Archdeacon, prudent counsellor, whom I consulted, concurred in this view of the situation, but indicated the correct counter-move: "You must watch the weekly clerical obituary," he explained, "and as each suitable Crown living falls vacant, you must apply for it and bring to bear all the influence you can command to back your endeavour".

I had neither the energy nor the inclination to join the clamorous throng which I pictured as falling upon the luckless Patronage Secretary immediately the death of each holder of Crown preferment was announced. (What must he think of his spiritual guides?)

I had, therefore, abandoned all hope of becoming one

238

whom the King delighted to honour, when a doubt occurred to me whether the Bishop had remembered to write on my behalf. It would not make any difference, I supposed, but I felt impelled to enquire.

I did so, and heard in reply that his lordship had supposed I only asked for his name as a reference. He had not understood that I wished him to write. Since, however, he found that I did, he had now had pleasure in addressing the Patronage Secretary, and only hoped that he himself would be able to forestall him in providing me with a suitable post.

Such kindly words from a great man fall as the gentle dew from heaven upon the arid souls of the undistinguished, even if it is but *vox et praeterea nihil*.

And the Bishop was a very great man, a member of a noble house who by his personal distinction added fresh laurels to the family honours. Within a week of the despatch of his letter I received a mighty envelope (for no self-respecting official commits his thoughts to a lesser medium than foolscap) in the corner of which appeared the magic words "Crown Office". My thoughts presaged some joyful news at hand. With trembling fingers I broke the seal and learned that it was His Majesty's pleasure that I should accept the living of Barnlands in the county of Suffolk, vacant by the retirement of the late incumbent thereof, the annual income of which living was £300 a year. God bless his kind heart, I would give His Majesty that satisfaction! Accompanying the official letter was a note from the Secretary saying that he assumed that I would wish to inspect the parish before giving my answer, but that an early reply should be sent. I was sufficiently respectful to my new

239

found dignity not to say what I felt, that it would have to be a very impossible parish if I did not accept it, seeing that it offered me the spacious independence enjoyed by an incumbent of the English Church, and an income sufficient for my needs.

I have since reflected upon how tenuous a thread of circumstance had depended the event which was to determine the whole course of my life during the years which followed. Had I not chanced upon the thought that perhaps the Bishop had not written on my behalf, I should have continued to assume that he had done so. And there the matter would have rested. Was it chance, or was this another instance of the intervention in my small affairs of some power or powers having my welfare sufficiently at heart to contrive these fine adjustments?

My brother, pluming himself upon the prosperous issue of his sagacious counsel, warmly approved what he considered the Bishop's perspicacity, and referred with awe to the extent of his influence. "He spake the word and it was done", he exclaimed in a pious rapture. "And let me tell you", he added, "that you are going to a particularly delightful county with a character of its own. It has no important manufactures; it is almost entirely rural; no tourists pass through it for it leads nowhere; and, finally, you will remember that in Suffolk the Warringtons had their home."

"You make me quite eager to see it", I said.

"You may well be so", he replied. "And, as a further inducement to settling there, I would point out that you will not be so very many miles from Newmarket, so that you may at the same time improve your health and materially assist me by rising early in the morning and watching the cantering on the Heath, whereby you will easily acquire a little inside knowledge which I hope I may rely on your kindness to transmit to me by the penny post."

I perceived that my brother's description of Suffolk as a county not yet sophisticated by the modern spirit was likely to be true when I found that my new parish was five miles from the nearest railway station.

I had a long journey thither and arrived in the afternoon of a wild, windy November day. As I got out on to the platform of the little station I inhaled with keen relish the frosty sweetness of the fresh country air. I resolved to cover the five miles on foot, and stepped forward eagerly and happily.

Oh, but those were great days! What cared I for the cold, grey skies, the sharp buffeting of the wind that rushed across the swaying tree tops! I was on my way to the haven where I had so long desired to be. I thought of all those weary years I had toiled in London in order to purchase this freedom, and of the time I had spent more happily but not less strenuously in the great town parish. I felt entitled, at last, to some remission of this unceasing labour. And mine now was to be the life that Herbert and Herrick had invested for me with the charm of their poetic fancy. I, too, was to live amid fortunate fields, and groves, and flowery vales.

As I approached what I thought must be somewhere near the end of my journey and was looking eagerly ahead for the first glimpse of my new parish (mine!), I saw a hamlet in the midst of which was a plain, square, modern red-brick building which my mind misgave me would be Barnlands Church. "A poor thing, but mine own", I said courageously.

With infinite relief I read the notice-board affixed to the wall which showed me that this was a district chapel of a neighbouring parish.

Presently I came upon a farmhouse which seemed as though it had remained untouched since the days of Elizabeth; its walls of dull red bricks laid herring-bone fashion amid mighty baulks of oak. I knocked to enquire my way, and half expected some kirtled dame with ruff and stomacher to beshrew me for disturbing her agelong repose.

I found I was near my journey's end, and soon a sign-post bearing the magic word "Barnlands" directed me along a lane at the end of which I saw a little village nestling in a hollow, above which, near the top of a gentle slope, stood sturdily amid the warring winds, as it had stood for six hundred years among its circling elms, a grey old church which, as I looked upon it, I loved. . . .

Opposite the churchyard gate I perceived a thatched farmhouse, its buff-coloured, pargetted walls almost covered with creepers. It dated but from the reign of Charles the Second and smacked therefore somewhat of upstart modernity amongst houses in Barnlands, where centuries are nothing accounted of. The owner of the house had lived there a bare sixteen years; he was, in consequence, "the new man up at Rosebank".

This worthy farmer was the rector's warden, and for almost as long as he had lived in Barnlands he had been nominated to that office each year by the rector himself. This was in accordance with respectable precedent, for later I discovered a memorandum in the handwriting of a Caroline predecessor stating that "such has been our custom since Queen Elizabeth's time".

As the short November day was now drawing to its close, the warden's wife lost no time in taking me to see the church and rectory. I had the impression of a large rambling house, built at various times. I noticed the vast carved beams supporting the kitchen ceiling, which, as I learned with awe, dated from the fifteenth century.

We passed into the shadowy, silent church and made our way to the east end, kneeling for a moment at the twisted Laudian altar rails, where my companion, I knew, offered kindly orisons for me, and I reflected, with grateful heart, that what I had coveted so long was at last within my reach. I made earnest resolve that, though my object in coming here was largely a desire for studious leisure, yet I would to the utmost of my power tend the little flock to be committed to my care.

I spent the evening with the kindly farmer and his wife. We dined upon pheasants shot, I was told, on my own glebe. It thrilled me to contemplate myself seised of a life-freehold of a hundred acres of English land, including a wood carpeted in spring with violets and anemones, and where the hunt not seldom put up a fox.

After supper my friends talked with even voices of country affairs which my eager fancy invested with Arcadian gleams, and whenever they considered that conversation languished they turned on a gramophone for which

243   16-2

they had provided an assortment of hymn tunes, an arrangement which they obviously regarded as of the happiest inspiration. But I felt so modern an invention an intruder in
that little parlour with its low-pitched, heavy-beamed ceiling, its spluttering wood fire, its fragrance of apples, the
subdued lamplight, the lazily floating wisps of smoke from
the farmer's pipe, and the ruddy, healthy faces and silvered
hair of my new-found friends.

I stood at my bedroom window, later, to take in the
brooding silence, now that the wind had dropped; for that
which so many town dwellers find almost unbearable is
delightful to me.

I awoke at dawn and lay dreamily enchanted with the
sounds that fell upon my ear: the antiphonal cock-crowing,
the trampling and voices of men, the slow heavy tread and
jingling harness of horses going afield. I looked from the
window, and there above the hedge rose the chancel of my
church with its cinquefoil canopied niches flanking the east
window, and its graceful tower soaring above the nave.

I breakfasted, with a townsman's enthusiasm, upon bacon
cut from a mighty ham whose fellow still depended from
the kitchen rafters; upon bread of pure wheaten flour ground
in the village mill which whirled its mighty arms above the
hill-top, bread baked by the heat of a wood fire in a brick
oven, and overlaid with butter which had made no longer
journey than that from the household dairy.

I had been instructed to make my absence from St
Martin's as brief as possible and so I was obliged to tear
myself away and hasten to catch an early train. It was over

a month before I should be free to return and I was seized with nervous fears that, even now, something might happen which would dash the cup from my lips. I might be ill, and the offer, on that ground, be withdrawn. Or perchance the offer itself was all a mistake, intended for another and misdirected to me. I was in an overwrought state and tormented myself with baseless fears.

I detest changes, and when I have one in contemplation I am sorely straitened until it be accomplished. My last days at St Martin's, therefore, were eagerly counted, and thankfully one by one dismissed.

I experienced a pang of shame at the anxiety I had felt to be off with the old love when I was summoned to attend a meeting of the people, who proposed to offer me a parting gift.

Hildebrand opened the proceedings with icy commendation, and at the conclusion of his speech desired that his further attendance might be excused as he was engaged elsewhere. Forsse took up the tale with homiletic intent. He hoped (but seemed to doubt it) that I would fearlessly uplift the Catholic banner where I was going. A time when the Faith was being betrayed by highly placed official infidelity, when faithful priests could not hope for recognition, when the love of many had grown cold, was no occasion for half measures dictated by mental confusion or the fear of men. He advised me to begin in my new parish as I meant to go on, and let people see plainly and from the outset what I stood for.

He practised his precepts, for I was told some time after that, being preferred to a small country parish with a century of Evangelical tradition, he introduced vestments and altar lights upon the first Sunday after his arrival and announced that next day, being the Feast of the Immaculate Conception of Our Lady, Mass would be said at nine o'clock, a notice which conveyed to his hearers as much information as would the repetition of the Hebrew alphabet. One of his new parishioners thus described him: "Our parson is a wonderful funny little old man. He don't wear a white gown like the others do, but a little short chemise trimmed round the bottom with lace, and every few minutes he spits on his hand and rubs it over his face". The last piece of information voiced the rustic interpretation of his repeatedly and rapidly making the sign of the cross.

In welcome contrast to my colleagues' hesitated dislikes were the stammering, broken utterances of love on the part of the people themselves. Surely in no other profession is an ordinary conscientious attempt to fulfil one's duties met with such rich appreciation as in that of a minister of religion.

"A clergyman", my brother once remarked, "has but to refrain from being insolent and offensive in order to have his people falling down and worshipping him."

It overwhelmed me with humiliation to realize how little I deserved the appreciation I received. A fairly good-hearted clergyman almost automatically says the kindly thing which means so much to the hearer, but costs the speaker so little. It amazed me that several hundred persons had bestowed upon me the final and authoritative proof of human goodwill by parting with hard cash to swell the amount of the cheque I received. I have the list of their

246

names still. A good many are those of people entirely unknown to me.

Dozens, even hundreds of hands held mine in friendly grasp, and, with emotions stirred at the thought of parting, kind eyes were dimmed as they looked perhaps for the last time into mine. I went on my way and saw most of them no more, but in another world, I trust, dear, toiling, patient, loving souls, we may meet again.

The last days of my sojourn at St Martin's had passed, and at the end I could have wished time to stand still, so ingrained is human reluctance to make the plunge into the unknown, however long and pleasantly it has been anticipated.

My clothing and books were packed, and the walls stripped of the photographs and pictures as I stood at the door to take a last look round the familiar room which I had inhabited for so many years—the room which Hallam and I so long had shared; where he had discussed his bright hopes and plans; where I had since read and thought alone; where I had twice undergone the experience of an intellectual uprooting: once when I was won by my friend to Catholicism and, again, when I began that process which was still going on, and which was to put me into another world of thought altogether.

I passed into the street and went for a moment of prayer and recollection into the church. What changes I had witnessed there! What deep experiences had I gained of the wayward, kindly hearts of men! I knelt, but with a mind too charged with emotion really to pray.

As I knelt, the bell was struck a few times and Hilde-

brand and Forsse entered to recite, without expecting any
assistant congregation, the office of some exotic sodality.
I crept silently out into the noisy street where the tide of
busy, eager humanity swept heedlessly past the church, conscious of no need, apparently, of its message or its aid.

I was ashamed of myself when I realized that I was per-
turbed at the thought that all this hurrying throng followed
its business entirely heedless of the fact that one who had
lived in its midst so long was even then on his way to depart.

As the train moved slowly from the station I looked for
the last time across the wilderness of roofs of the crowded
city, and passed out into a new life.

I was impressed by a sense of inexorable finality in the
period of my life which was now concluded. What ill I had
done could never be undone; what good I had wrought
could not be blotted out. I was able neither to add to nor
subtract from what I had accomplished. It was finished,
and the general community in which I had lived pursued
its way insensible to the absence of so insignificant a fragment of its life. So, thought I, in an access of weak self-pity,
at life's end. The last word written, the book is shut. The
day after my body is committed to earth, the world will
wake to sunshine and song, to sorrow and toil, oblivious of
Arthur Wolfe as though he had never existed. Deep down
in each man's heart is a sense of uneasy astonishment that
this should be so.

But will the world indeed be then as though one had
never been? I opened the book in which a neat school-
masterish hand had inscribed the names of those who had
presented me with my parting gift, and I found comfort in

248

the conviction that a few kindly hearts would still give an occasional thought to me. Life's greatest boon seemed then to be the certainty of a place in the memory of those whom one had loved and been privileged to help. That was a sure possession. *Quod scripsi scripsi.*

Hours, now, of comfortless travelling half across England, until again I reached the neighbourhood of my new home. Barnlands, in those days, boasted of but one conveyance for public use. It met me at the station and bore me along at the sober pace at which all things moved in those sequestered ways until, on reaching the top of a long hill, my driver stopped and pointed through the darkness towards a distant point of light and said, "Yon's your home". As he spoke there fell upon my ear the soft sound of far-off chimes. "What bells are those?" I asked. "Barnlands'",' he replied; "they are ringing because you have come."

Time had run back and fetched the age of gold.

My first Sunday at Barnlands was a fresh experience. I found myself, demurely clad in surplice, hood, and scarf, conducting Morning Prayer in a remote village church in the presence of some fifty people. But a week ago, at that very hour, I was taking part in High Mass.

Yet this simple, unadorned service soothed and healed my fretted spirit. There was a reality in the fervently uttered responses, and the loud and not particularly tuneful singing. My heart warmed towards these stolid folk with their impassive faces and the smell of the fields upon them. The Psalms were not sung, but were recited in alternate verses by priest and people. The *sortes liturgicae* were, as so often,

249

marvellously apt: "O what great troubles and adversities hast Thou showed me! and yet didst Thou turn and refresh me. Thou hast brought me to great honour and comforted me on every side...".

The day's duties ended with a service in the afternoon, as the custom then was in winter time, when days were dark and ways were foul. I drew my chair up to the fire and pondered the new life that opened before me. I thought of the long history of that grey old church; of the men who in the fourteenth century, at the period of the perfect blossoming of the mediæval builder's skill, had first raised its walls; of those who in the next century (after the leisurely manner of the times) had added porch and tower. I wondered how the village had received the first news of the Reformation. It seemed impossible to believe that the Suffolk peasantry had once been fervently Catholic. How had a later generation regarded the activities of the Puritans, evidenced in battered font and broken windows? What did the villagers of to-day think of the treasure set in their midst? The very sight of it, as I chanced at times suddenly to take notice of it, startled me—a piece of mediæval life which had not vanished with the dress and dialect of the middle ages, but still most miraculously survived, with its main features exactly as they had left the builders' hands. Later, I found that its outer walls took on the colours of the seasons. In winter they were a dark, slaty grey; in summer, at high noon, they were dazzling white; at sundown they flushed a rosy pink. At night-time, the tower, when I stood beneath it, assumed huge proportions as the wind-blown wisps of cloud raced across the stars that seemed to cluster around its summit.

The village, I thought, would not share my appreciation of its choicest possession, for had not the postmistress yesterday, in answer to my enquiry for photographs of the interior of the church, replied: "I am afraid we have none. I don't know why. For we have them of the chapel, and I am sure the church is just as pretty". The interior of the chapel needed to be seen to be believed.

Well, the forefathers of my people had been Catholic, and might not their children be led back to the old paths? Thus, curiously, I meditated, for, away now from the chilling influence of Hildebrand and Forsse, my mind reverted to Hallam's view of things Catholic and I pictured the enthusiasm with which he would have commended the patient, loving winning of these simple souls back to a fuller and richer faith. My intellectual difficulties seemed to fade away for the time in the presence of work to be done and responsibility to be shouldered. I would try to make this church a shrine not unworthy of its past.

I resolved upon the strange innovation of reciting Morning and Evening Prayer daily. To this the people made no objection when they realized that they were not to be pestered to attend.

I used to ring the bell myself and I delighted to think that its sound carried far and wide on wintry gales or through the stillness of a summer morning, reminding the men in the fields that their priest was at his task as they at theirs. The church was unwarmed on weekdays in the winter and I marvelled at the hardihood of our ancestors who endured this freezing cold during the prolonged offices of Sundays.

It seemed strange, at first, to go through alone services

251

intended to be shared by others, but I soon became accustomed to it and enjoyed the silence amid those solemn surroundings. I often lingered long and lovingly over one or another of the church's attractions. I would try to build up from what yet remained some conception of the wealth of glass which must once have stained with lost dyes the light that now stared in through the great Perpendicular windows. Here, surely, these uplifted hands, the wing-tips and the golden locks betokened announcing Gabriel, nor seemed he, in those glowing fifteenth-century fragments, less than archangel ruined. Anon, I would pore over strange birds and beasts carved on screen and bench-ends, and it was with a discoverer's joy that I made out, with the aid of field-glasses, the reliefs on the spandrels of the principal beams of the oak roof—Lazarus emerging from the tomb; Tobit with his dog (beloved of mediæval artists); and the legend of St George and the Dragon spread over several separate carvings. Here, the armoured warrior brandished his sword; on the next beam the dragon lashed his mighty tail and snorted defiance; whilst on the third, seated at the top of a turret, herself almost as large as it, was depicted a maiden with dishevelled hair and hands upraised, intent upon the impending encounter.

Sometimes I would clamber up the dark circular stone stairway into the ringing-chamber and peer about the walls for names and comments of seventeenth- and eighteenth-century ringers. Higher still, into the bell-chamber itself, to read again in that windy aery the inscriptions on the bells. Two were of the fifteenth century and bore, with the characteristic pious anonymity of the donors of the period,

252

the words: "Virginis egregie vocor campana Mariae", and the decorous punning: "Meritis Edmundi simus a crimine mundi". The seventeenth-century inscription revealed the change of thought: "Miles Graye made me 1652".

Climbing yet higher, I would emerge by the trap-door on to the roof of the tower and would lean well back from the embattled parapet (to spare my weak nerves the dizzy downward look), and gaze out over the countryside at houses and cottages in such harmony with their surroundings that they seemed to have sprung from the soil; some of these were coeval with the tower itself. Indeed, within view, was a small half-timbered building, the remains of a moated grange, by the side of which stood a barn containing four wooden posts supporting the roof, curiously carved and with the square abacus denoting Norman work. I gauged the capacity of Barnlands to leave well alone from the fact that the wooden framework of this barn was eight hundred years old. Thus, from my mediæval watch-tower I looked out on a scene very little altered from that which would have greeted the eyes of the builders six centuries ago, as they marked the train of pack-horses wind over the brow of yonder hill bearing squared stone for quoin and soffit.

Nor was there wanting evidence, in that sequestered place, of a yet earlier civilization for in the walls of the church were embedded blocks of concrete quarried, probably, from the hypocaust of some ruined villa dating from the days of the Roman occupation.

These things, of course, remain, but there was much in Barnlands when I first knew it, which even in the course of twenty years has gone for ever, and I realize now that I was privileged to live where traces of the old world still lingered in the habits and customs of the people. I wonder if, since the War, the new generation still speaks of "housen", and describes bread-and-milk as a "milk-mess". Do the men at work in the harvest fields demand "largesse" of visitors, employing the word their forefathers learned from their masters in those days when, as Doomsday records, with pregnant terseness, the old Saxon owners of Barnlands were dispossessed by the Norman conquerors: "Edricus tenuit ...tenet Gilbertus. In eadem tenuit Ulflet...Robertus tenet"?

O happy swains of a bygone age, albeit but twenty years ago, are your sons still allowed sixpence for ale each time they drive a wagon to the neighbouring town? Falls there still upon their ear (as in those halcyon days), every time they do the slightest bit of extra work, that sweet sound of the master's voice saying: "When you have done go round to the back door and ask for a pint of beer"? Not least of the devastating changes wrought by the Great War are to be reckoned, I fear, the final blotting out and utter extinction of those kindly usages.

> The times, too sage, perhaps too proud, have dropped
> These lighter graces.

Do your approaching old ladies, O Barnlands, still halt unexpectedly and drop a curtsy with a disconcerting suddenness suggesting the thought of their having received a blow behind the knees? Does the visiting parson (another than I, alas!) still hear such words of welcome as: "Betsy, make your reverence, and set a chair for the Rector"? Do the smaller children reply to one's greeting by rising on tip-toe and uttering the monosyllable "Miss", the title by which they are accustomed to address the schoolmistress and which they therefore conceive to be appropriate to all in authority?

Not long after I arrived at Barnlands my churchwarden one day handed me a substantial parcel, saying: "These are some old books and papers belonging to the church which I have kept over at the farm because the vestry-chest has no lock. You might care to look through them sometime".

That same evening, by my study fire, snugly sheltered from the wintry weather, I opened this magic bundle. It contained a number of deeds referring to various parish charities; several books in which had been kept the church-wardens' accounts during three centuries; and a collection of memoranda made by parsons who were interested in the past history of their cure. One had compiled from the Diocesan Registers a list of his predecessors with the dates of their appointment and the name of the patron who presented them. This list, and the various other documents contained in that truly wonderful packet, gave me occupation on many a lonely evening during my first winter in Barnlands, and by their means I became so completely transported into the days of which they treated that I feel myself (living, too, as I did, amid those old-world surroundings) really to have passed the months in a bygone age.

As one, hitherto of humble station, succeeding to a title of nobility, inherits the family honours, and, with the partiality of kinship, extols the prowess of his forbears; even so, I, a nameless plebeian, was now caught up into a great tradition and provided with an official ancestry extending through six centuries (a respectable pedigree). For the list of Rectors of Barnlands (that I may boast myself a little touching my ancestral dignities) commences in the year 1303 (in the days of Edward I and Bruce of Scotland) with the entry: "Thomas de Wycheford, ad praes. Rad: de Monte Hermeri". For at that time the living had not passed into the gift of the Crown. That happened in 1383 (the year before Wyclif died) when John Leefe was appointed "ad praes. dñi Regis rãone minoris aetatis comitis Marchiae". The Crown, having once got the advowson into its hands, of course never relinquished it, and so there followed a list of royal patrons which linked little Barnlands, together with my own self as being the present holder of the incumbency, with the most stirring events in English history. For does not Thomas Westhorp's appointment in 1426, "ad. pr. Dñi H. Rs" refer to the Henry who, five years afterwards, was crowned at Paris in the year of Joan of Arc's martyrdom?

I wonder what is the explanation of: "1521 Jul. 27 John Parker, ad pr. Katerinae Reginae Angliae"? Four years had yet to run before Henry would begin to tire of poor Katherine of Aragon and, in consequence, the whole course of the nation's history be profoundly influenced. On that summer day, four hundred years ago, when, perchance, the royal lady folded her white hands upon her jewelled *Horae* and prayed for him who by the bounty of her loving lord had been her choice, and who was then being instituted to his cure, how incredible would have seemed any premonition of the coming storm.

In 1547, Queen Katherine's nominee having died, her lord, now near his end, in his pious care for religion, appointed Henry Hamylton. Beneath his name, when later I hung up a list of rectors in Barnlands church, some visiting Papist scribbled (after the manner of obscene little boys): "Here the priesthood ended". Not so fast, my friend! Was not Mary a sound Catholic, and she appointed the parson who followed! It is remarkable how little, to all appearances, the Reformation changes affected the English parish clergy. At Barnlands the parson appointed by Henry VIII stayed quietly on through the introduction of the two Prayer Books of Edward VI and died, still Rector, in the days of Mary. Mary's nominee remained at his post despite the Elizabethan Settlement and was buried in the chancel of the church when Elizabeth had been six years on the throne.

He was followed by Robert Shawe, who became a living personality to me in virtue of my finding amongst other old documents his last will and testament made on May 18th, 1575, "in the eighteenth yeare of our most gratious Sovereigne Ladie Elizabeth by the grace of God, Queene of England, ffrance, and Ireland, defender of the faithe", and signed with his own hand. It is curious how an aggregation of petty details concerning a man will bring him to life before one's eyes, and as I sat and read his will, in the room in which Parson Shawe had himself so often rested over three hundred years ago, I could see him dictating his bequests to the attentive, obsequious scrivener: "Item, to Joane Evered, widow, and Ambrose her son, £14, which

Joane oues him, and 5 combs 2 bus. oats Sudbury measure, and one fat wether and 3/10 laid out for her suit at Norwich against William Hedgeman, on condition that they discharge the delapidations on the Parsonage and chancel of Barnlands. Item, to Maister Thomas Shackleton, clerk, his sarcenet tipet and two square caps. To Alice Hartelie, his sister, his posted bedstead, with the tester over it, one of his best feather beds with transsome and two pillows and one covering. Also 6 silver spoons and a maser to Alice Hartelie". He made his will betimes and was not buried in the chancel of the church until nine years later.

Stirring events were hinted in the seventeenth-century appointments. In 1643 Thomas Pakenham was instituted, "ad pr. Dñi Regis Caroli", but in the same year he was "teiz'd out of his Rectory by vexatious behaviour of his parishioners encouraged by the prevailing powers, and succeeded by one Samuel Boardman an Independent Army Chaplain". This happened but little over a hundred years after John Parker had been appointed by Katherine of Aragon in days before the English Reformation was dreamed of, and in that time Catholic Barnlands had become furiously Puritan. Yet Protestantism had not appeared to care much for its interests. Had not the Royal Commissioners dissolved the parish guild of our Lady, the niche for whose statue and the piscina of whose altar still stand in the south-east corner of the nave of our church? Had not I to pay yearly to His Majesty the sum of two pence as the rental of the Chantry House which still stood in the churchyard in 1686, though the chantries had long since been abolished to enrich a horde of greedy courtiers?

But Barnlands, despite the innate conservatism of the English rustic, had early become enthusiastic for the new order. No festival was more carefully observed, it seems, than November 5th, upon which day the ringers were annually supplied with copious libations at the charges of the parish, as the churchwardens' accounts bear faithful witness. The ancestors of my East Anglian peasants seem to have been swept along with the tide of Puritan fanaticism, and they were all for a godly, thorough reformation. They offered no opposition when the Parliamentary Commissioner, Colonel William Dowsing, and his men took Barnlands in one of their visitations of that black year for Suffolk churches 1643, and our Jacobean altar was contemptuously riddled with shot, as the pellets of lead still embedded in it testify. No hand was raised when the glorious glass in our great Perpendicular windows was smashed, the font sawn into a comely square, the upper part of the roodscreen demolished, and the statues of the saints tumbled out of their niches, while the grinning devils of the gargoyles remained untouched, watching still with bulging eyes and derisive protruding tongues.

To the militant Independent preacher succeeded, during the Commonwealth, one Clement Ray. He was not of the stuff of which martyrs are made, since in 1661 we get the entry "July 11 Clement Ray, ad pr. Dñi Regis". For King Charles had come to his own, and Black Bartholomew had claimed its confessors, but our intruded minister was not one of them. Undoubtedly he had conformed and been ordained. Alas, poor Clement, what can explain this lamentable fall from grace? Perhaps, these entries in the

Baptismal Register: "1651, Dec. 20, Maria; 1653, May 1, Joseph; 1654, June 20, Isaac; 1655, Nov. 17, Elizabeth; 1657, Dec. 2, George; and 1658, Dec. 16, Samuel; children of Clement Ray and Mary his wife".

Perchance, it was providentially ordered that the minds of the seventeenth-century inhabitants of Barnlands should, by Mr Ray's defection, be prepared gradually for the change from the fiery doctrine of the Cromwellian army chaplain to the orthodoxy of the staunch High Church loyalist Thomas Tyllot, who had been deprived of the living he held in 1643 and was now rewarded for his fidelity by Charles II. His successor, Henry Halstead, gave his flock time to settle their religious opinions by continuing in his incumbency for fifty-one years, and dying at the age of eighty-seven in the year 1728. "Hujus ecclesiae Rector dignissimus" says the record of his burial, departing from the customary curtness of such entries. He was born in the reign of Charles I, and lived on to that of George II. He was an energetic parson and his activities included the vigorous collection of money under the various briefs which appear to have been common at the time, and whereby so remote a place as Barnlands was drawn into active sympathy with stirring events in the great world. Milton himself would have been softened at the entry in our parson's rambling hand-writing: "1699 Vaudois and French Refugees £1. 18. 4". The sympathies of the people were even more strongly stirred by his eloquence in another cause: "Towards the redemption of English captives in Machanes in the kingdom of Fez and Morocco £2. 10. 0".

Halstead was a contemporary of Herrick, and as I

chanced upon a Perambulation Book which had belonged
to my predecessor, I chanted with joy the old poet's words:

> Dearest, bury me
> Under the Holy-Oke, or Gospel-tree;
> Where (though thou see'st not) thou may think upon
> Me, when thou yeerly go'st Procession.

But the ancient Rogation procession was now evidently
regarded more as an opportunity for securing the parish
boundaries than the occasion for prayer for the crops, or
soft thoughts of departed lovers, as this entry witnesseth:
"Taken upon an exact view and perambulation made by
Henry Halstead, Rector, and far the greater part of the
parishioners upon the 17th of May 1680:

"Stage the first: Walking from the Parsonage House
after a Competent Refreshment had and provided at the
charges of the Rector, we crossed the Churchyard and
Highway, etc."

And now upon that pleasant May day, two hundred and
fifty years ago, deep consternation and a wild surmise
suddenly struck "the whole company of Gangers or
Walkers", for they discovered that, "the interval betwixt
the two Oakes which was formerly a green slip with trees
Growing thereon had been plowed up, and, we fear by
the Direction of the Owner of that field who lived in the
next Parish with a design to erase the Antient Marks of our
Parish".

In further proof of the incontestability of our claim
"Goodman George Sargeant affirmed that a marked tree
stood formerly there, and he does believe it was a thorne,

261

and Goodman David Smith remembers it distinctly, and was formerly, as he there affirmed, taken up and bumped at it".

This indignity could not be tolerated, and at the next Summer Assizes, "the matter came to a hearing and the verdict was given for our parish".

Halstead, full of years and honour, looked for the last time upon his old home when the corn was ripening one early autumn day, and his body lies in the chancel beneath the ledger which tells that here "Pastoris officium cum pace et modestiâ exercuit: et postquam Dei Ministrorumque Ipsius Aedes pio animo decoraverat; immortalitatem adiit Augusti 8°, A.D. 1728°, aetat. 87°".

Barnlands now fell upon evil days, as to its spiritual pastors, since for the next hundred and twenty-five years its rectors were non-resident, the emoluments of the living serving as an addition to the already liberal stipends enjoyed by various court chaplains and magnates of the neighbouring university. Of the last named the most distinguished was the Senior Fellow of one of the oldest and richest colleges—a man famous in his day, who wrote a book praised by Dr Johnson on the occasion "when", says Boswell, "I took out my 'Ogden on Prayer' and read some of it to the company". I obtained a copy of the great man's portrait, and it bears out a contemporary description of him as possessing "a black, scowling figure, and a lowering visage, embrowned by the honours of a sable periwig". If he ever favoured the parishioners of Barnlands with a discourse I wonder what they made of it, for "his sermons were interspersed with remarks eminently brilliant and acute, but too epigrammatic in their close. His voice was growling and morose, and his sentences desultory, tart and snappish".

On October 11th, 1790, the college which had given us our first non-resident rector, provided as his successor its President, who, in addition to that office, and the care of another parish, now added to his princely income the stipend attached to the benefice of Barnlands. The Rev. George Ashby was instituted on the next day after that proposed (in a letter to his sister) for the return to England of a young undergraduate, who had passed the summer vacation wandering amongst strange scenes in France and Switzerland, and who was coming up to keep his last term at the college over which my predecessor presided. The great man and his unsatisfactory pupil have changed places in the world's estimation since, for the undergraduate was William Wordsworth. My predecessor is probably included in *The Prelude's* unflattering description of the Cambridge dons of the day: "Men whose sway and known authority of office served to set our minds on edge, and did no more".

But I am obliged to him for being a kind of link between myself and one to whom I am so great a debtor. Then, let him pass, a blessing on his head, and, for his epitaph, the encomium of a contemporary upon this Christian priest: "He was a very good antiquary, learned critic, and much conversant in medals and pictures".

The period of non-residence on the part of the rectors of Barnlands was completed by one who eclipsed all who had gone before him in the extent of the preferment he enjoyed.

He appears to have indulged a taste for collecting livings as others collect books or pictures. In addition to Barnlands he was incumbent of four other parishes as well as the holder of a rich canonry and a chaplaincy to the King.

But at length there was a stirring among the dry bones, and early in the reign of Victoria non-residence in Barnlands came to an end with the arrival of a fiery disciple of the newly launched Tractarian Movement, one who knew Pusey and Newman and corresponded with them on the burning Church questions of the day. His outward man is shown by his portrait which depicts him with shaggy eyebrows and bushy white beard. He is attired in a frock coat with a white bow at his throat, and a biretta (not correctly placed) upon his head. Something of his inward part was revealed to me by a "Catechism" which Joseph Masters published for him in 1867, and which I discovered in the churchwarden's magic bundle. New-fangled ideas in Biblical Criticism and Natural Science found no ally in him. "How long was God pleased to be in creating the world?" "Six days." "Who wrote the first five books of the Old Testament?" "They were written by Moses more than three thousand years ago and are the oldest books in the world." In this decisive fashion, throughout the little book, are the problems which have long agitated theologians and scientists briefly disposed of. A fine old fellow, he farmed his glebe himself and took his samples of corn to the neighbouring market, and got as good a price as any. After thirty strenuous years in our midst his body rests in the churchyard beneath the epitaph: "I have fought a good fight. I have kept the faith".

264

With him, this chronicle of men, great in themselves or linked to great events, who for six centuries presided over the spiritual destinies of my quiet rural parish came to an end. Undistinguished persons succeeded, none less dis tinguished than myself.

I was greatly moved as I pondered the story of the English people mirrored microcosmically in the history of the little plot of English ground in which I had been commissioned to minister. I traced in it the stream of broadening thought which had made me what I was. The lines had fallen unto me in a fair ground; I had a goodly heritage. I would tend it to the best of my power. I would try to make Barnlands church again a Catholic shrine (of a somewhat eclectic sort) and imbue its people with the spirit of ancient piety.

I wonder now how I could have determined upon this, seeing with what completeness the foundations of traditional Orthodoxy had been destroyed for me by the results of Biblical Criticism. Perhaps it was simply the associations of Catholicism that appealed to me. It certainly held me æsthetically. I viewed the havoc wrought in the old adornments of the village church and pictured its original loveliness. I would restore that, as far as I could. I dreamed that in years to come I would make my way along the churchyard, one Christmas morning, passing between the two lines of ancient snow-powdered yews. I would enter the church and inhale with satisfaction the warm, incenseladen air. A statue and altar of our Lady would stand once again, after nearly four hundred years, in their ancient places. A light should burn before the Rood, for the provision of which the rent of an adjoining meadow had been apportioned six centuries ago. My villagers would long since have grown accustomed to the restored use of copes and chasubles. They and their forefathers had seen many changes in past days and they had met them imperturbably, as their manner is. I smiled as I fancied how the ghosts of my pre-Reformation brethren would wander about the church, snuffing again the old familiar perfume, and singing "In exitu Israel" as they marked how far time had unthread the rude eye of rebellion and welcomed home again discarded faith.

Those were golden days for me which made up my first year at Barnlands. The freshness of the morning is upon them as they rise in my memory.

Aconite, earliest harbinger of better things to come, with frail strength had pushed its way through the imprisoning clods. Snowdrops next had quite carpeted the less frequented parts of my garden. Daffodils had danced and flaunted and were gone. And now it was a morning of sunny splendour in mid-May. With my faithful dog I would be abroad till nightfall. I passed through an avenue of beech trees which overhung a full mile of winding road felted with brown husks. These beechen giants are old enough to have sheltered Hob and Phyllis when English rustics still sang snatches of songs which sprang from the earth, even as they.

The road opened upon an extensive prospect of low rounded hills, sloping and folding into one another under a sky of liquid blue. In the foreground pale green lines of young wheat stretched marvellously straight across the brown fields. Peewits, jetty black and gleaming white, circled fluttering and crying in parental anxiety. High above them, larks, for the time oblivious of earthly cares, held ecstatic converse with the spirits of the upper air.

In the distance, cultivation had been extended to its extremest limit, as the yellowish stunted growth at the fringes of the fields which bordered the heathland showed. Beyond them the wind and sunshine were rolling light and shade across the close-cropped turf where a flock of sheep, stringing out through a gate, resembled a gigantic millepede with myriad twinkling black legs.

The heath was, in parts, a mass of golden gorse, and I knew what milky fragrance the sun was drawing from those countless buds....

The day had passed with all its splendour and as night fell I re-entered Barnlands, stopping from time to time to listen to the pleasant tones of human voices heard through the gathering shadows. And so, home....

Who could recount the glory of those first June mornings when I (freed from captivity) looked out of my window, clustered with a riot of roses and honeysuckle, over that soft and gracious landscape, a veritable garden of the Lord?

Each year the countryside underwent two astonishing transformations. When I came, all was field after field of brown clods, for ours is mostly arable land. In spring and early summer these became vested in freshest green. As summer advances the countryside turns to gold. In due time come the long, sultry days of harvest with its strenuous toil. These accomplished, bugles are blown lustily about

267

the village, according to immemorial custom. My fruit trees now bend beneath their wealth of Blenheims and Bons Chrétiens, and for the first time I behold medlars and quinces (those fragrant names!) dependent from their native trees.

The village policeman garners my honey for me, his official duties permitting him ample leisure. He comes after nightfall and sets fire to sulphur, which sheds a ghastly light upon our faces, and over the fumes he places the skep which has sheltered through the pleasant summer days those unwearied, unsuspecting toilers. Loud buzzings betoken their panic terrors. They rush to gorge themselves with honey, as is their manner when alarmed. But, as the stifling vapours do their cruel work, a hush succeeds. In the morning, behold, they are all dead corpses, and the policeman calculates, with cheerful loquacity, the weight of our golden spoils.

When all is safely gathered, we assemble in a church decked with corn and fruit and flowers, and sing our Harvest Thanksgivings as men sing them who have toiled through the bitter winter days and in the fierce rays of the summer sun....

At last Christmas draws near, and on the Eve the tinkle of bells breaks the frost-bound stillness as I dream beside my study fire. The handbell ringers are without, and very pleasingly they play the old traditional melodies. They are invited to the kitchen for cakes and ale, and pass out into the starry night with hearty words of goodwill. I listen as long as I can hear their footfall and until their voices grow faint in the distance....

Thus, the first year of my life in the country passed in a round of fresh and delightful experiences, realization not failing long and ardent expectation, and I enjoyed an interval of physical and spiritual refreshment ere called upon to face a renewal of mental strife.

X

A DARK NIGHT OF THE SOUL

Now that I was restored in mind and body by a period of sorely needed rest, conscience began to call "Lusisti satis", and I felt impelled to continue the effort which had originated so great a change in my outlook on life. I had accepted the results of modern Biblical Criticism, not grudgingly or of necessity, but with the eagerness and gratitude of a truth-seeker to whom light has been vouchsafed. I was, however, quite alive to the fact that the critic, be he never so liberal, is no more exempt than others from liability to presuppositions, prejudice, and an undue domination by plausible theory. Yet I was convinced that the generally accepted conclusions of modern scholars concerning the New Testament are established beyond reasonable doubt.

The studies which brought me to this position led me (about two years after I had taken up my country cure) to extend my enquiries in a direction having a very practical bearing. The modern critic's conclusions upon the origin and early history of the Christian religion being accepted as, at any rate, approximately accurate, this question gradually formed itself in my mind: In what ways was my belief in Christianity itself affected by my altered convictions about its first beginnings?

In seeking material for a clear understanding of the

matter I began my acquaintance with Modernist theology, and warmly acknowledge the debt I owe to several of its principal exponents. I had previously shared blindly the current orthodox conception of the Modernist as a person of perverted ingenuity who misused his gifts in an endeavour to undermine the faith by which his brother-men live. I had supposed that his theories were sophistical, the fruits of an unworthy diligence in opposing the established order.

Some knowledge of Modernist literature led me to reverse that judgment, if unthinking and ignorant prejudice can be so described. I discovered that the better sort of Modernist scholar was a man who, like myself, had, at any rate, an intense desire to know the truth. His work was largely of a destructive kind; circumstances made that inevitable. If, as was often the case, the Modernist was an official teacher of religion, he had an additional incentive to proclaim his convictions, be they never so destructive, since he was acutely conscious of the fact that many of the world's wisest and best were being alienated from Christianity by those elements in its orthodox presentation which cannot be accepted by men who are abreast with the results of modern enquiry.

I was not converted to Modernism by a study of Modernist literature; rather, I found in the works of the men of this school the matured results of a process similar (*magna componere parvis*) to that which was going on in my own mind, although I hardly realized the fact. I think I should have become a Modernist even had I not made acquaintance with the literature of Modernism; but my reading in this direction gave some form and order to

271

efforts which would otherwise have been but the blind groping of the amateur.

Acknowledging these obligations, as I gladly do, I must yet record my conviction that Modernism has been more successful in its efforts to destroy that which needed the ruthless hand of the iconoclast than in its endeavour to raise a new and better structure on the ruins of the old.

I think, too, that the Modernist hardly realizes how great and apparently impassable a gulf exists between orthodox Christianity and that which he holds to be true. He has attacked, with a large measure of success, the Catholic Creeds as generally understood; but that which he conceives to be the essential reality enshrined in (or, perhaps, obscured by) the symbol appears to the Traditionalist as but the shadow of a shade. The claim that any such vague idea adequately represents what is intended by the precise statement of an article of the Christian Creed seems to the Literalist simply disingenuous. I was in the happy, or unhappy, position of being able to see something in both sides of many such disputed questions. I held with the Modernist that much in the Traditionalist interpretation of the Christian religion is untenable in the light of present-day knowledge of Christian origins. I agreed with him also in his kindly contention that, though the mode in which the orthodox believer rationalizes his convictions and experiences is faulty, yet there is a core of absolute reality in the convictions and experiences themselves. But I was on the side of the Traditionalist when he asserted that his opponent's account of that reality was inadequate and unsatisfactory.

Thus, in that article of the Creed which affirms the resurrection of the body, I was one with the Modernist in his
rejection of the thought that on a certain future day the
scattered particles of disintegrated corpses will be miraculously reunited. But I sympathized with the aggrieved
Traditionalist when he was asked to surrender what was at
any rate a definite conception in favour of the vague thought
that it is just conceivable that there is a future life in which
our spirits may possibly be clothed in some sort of misty
wrapping, the nature of which is purely conjectural.

The necessarily destructive element in Modernism has
to make headway not only against the massive inertia of
custom, tradition and sentiment, but also to overcome the
desperate resistance which men must offer to any attempt
to tamper with conceptions which, quite erroneously, no
doubt, they yet conceive to be an essential part of the most
vital concerns and experiences of their lives. It is not easy
to disentangle the facts of spiritual experience from the
manner in which they are visualized. The majority of
people have neither the ability nor the desire to attempt the
task. Consequently, the complete revolution of thought
essential to the acceptance of the Modernist approach to the
problems presented by Christianity appeared to me at first
to be an impossibility for the greater part of mankind.

But later I thought that Biblical Criticism might prove
the solvent. So far, what is accepted to-day as axiomatic by
modern students of the New Testament is just a vague
rumour to the many. But, I argued, that which is only discussed amongst experts to-day will in time become common
knowledge. Already the progress made is astonishing. It

would, I felt sure, be true to say that but a few years ago the substantial historical accuracy of the Bible as a whole was accepted as unquestionable by every denomination of Christians. To-day we have the remarkable fact that the orthodox Christian conscience often remains singularly un-offended when the sacred writings are handled with the utmost freedom. I could not take my stand with those who are willing to accept the conclusions of a quite drastic Biblical Criticism whilst remaining entirely Traditionalist in theology and the forms and usages of public worship. It seemed, however, unlikely that men would go on using forms from which the meaning which gave them reality had largely evaporated. It was, perhaps, permissible to dream that some spiritual genius might one day arise who would invest those lovely and heart-moving symbols with a deeper significance than they have ever yet held, and one which need fear nothing from absolute intellectual in-tegrity. Meanwhile, the outstanding fact seemed to me to be that orthodox Christianity and the traditional conception of the historical character of the New Testament were in-dissolubly linked together. Protestant orthodoxy was con-fessedly founded upon an acceptance of the latter. Catholi-cism, whilst claiming the right to teach through its own inherent authority, yet as strongly asserts that all it teaches is supported by the Bible, and that this support is an essential part of its claim to be heard. But neither system could con-tinue indefinitely to rest on an insecure foundation. Thus, it seemed to me, that the position was that the Orthodox was delightfully housed in a noble mediæval cathedral rearing cloud-cleaving towers but built upon gradually subsiding foundations, whilst the Modernist wandered coldly over territory made clean and bare, vaguely hoping that ultimately it might prove the site of a building which had still to be erected.

As far as I myself was concerned, these reflections began to produce in my mind a paralysing uncertainty and a painful bewilderment. I passed through a veritable dark night of the soul.

At one time I conceived it to be better to believe anything rather than stultify myself by this vain quest for something that I could believe and yet retain my intellectual honesty. I saw that a creed strongly held, be it what it might, gave a man force of character, a purpose in life, and enabled him to achieve things.

My earnest young Ritualistic neighbour believed much which I now regarded as incredible, but his belief, honestly and strongly held, enabled him to fill his church, to be active in all good works, and to be a real blessing to his people.

My other neighbour, the Baptist minister, wore a cheerful face, though fortune buffeted him cruelly. His lively faith enabled him to hold Bible classes on a week-night in winter and to make them magnets of such supernal power as to attract the toil-worn labourer from his fire-side and compel him to trudge two miles through the mud and snow to hear his pastor expound Exodus. I have sat at his feet and marvelled as I listened to his accounts of the conversations between Moses and Almighty God which, under his treatment, often developed into an interchange of petulant recrimination.

18-2

Would it not be best to make up one's mind to believe something—anything—and so recover one's spiritual and intellectual vitality and effectiveness? But reflection revealed the futility of the thought. What gave those men their moral and spiritual force was conviction, however misplaced. Feigned or forced emotion could achieve nothing even if one were willing to sacrifice one's honesty in attempting to acquire it.

I walked in darkness and had no light. My former confidence in one after another of the constituents of the Faith I had once so heartily (but so unreflectingly) accepted was rudely shaken by the shrewd blows of a criticism whose fairness and honesty I could not deny, and whose convincing force it was impossible to resist.

My memory dwelt with wistful fondness upon that Christmastide at St Martin's when my faith in the event which the season commemorated was so complete and my realization of it so vivid. Then I turned to the story of the Virgin Birth as it appears when the New Testament narratives have been subjected to the intense scrutiny of modern scholarship. Two out of the four Gospels contain no reference to the event whatever, although both profess to tell the Good News about Jesus Christ. Of the two Evangelists who deal with the circumstances of the miraculous Birth, it seemed to me difficult to avoid the conclusion that the author of the Gospel according to Matthew, whose most cherished controversial weapon consists of proofs of the fulfilment of prophecy, and who elsewhere in his book undoubtedly forces his facts into conformity with his theory, may have done so in this instance also, anxious to show that

276

even in the circumstances of His birth his Master conformed to the marks of identification of the true Messiah.

The highly literary and imaginative element in St Luke's first two chapters is obvious unless we are to suppose that three persons concerned in his story each burst extemporaneously into lyric poetry, and that each time someone chanced to be at hand with writing tablets and obtained a verbatim record of what was spoken. Were those narratives propounded for our acceptance for the first time to-day, I thought, would anyone be persuaded to believe in a miracle so stupendous upon such evidence as is given?

I thought, too, of the time when to me the fact that the Mass was the parting bequest of the Saviour and that it was the centre of the Church's sacramental and devotional life demanded for it a place in my mind and heart which I joyfully yielded. But now I saw that whatever the Master meant when He uttered those mysterious words, it was a sheer impossibility for me to suppose that the Galilean rabbi, sharing a parting meal with his friends, was instituting a rite identical with that which is expounded in Catholic sacramental teaching. Indeed, I was faced with the fact that one only of the Gospels asserts that he desired the sacramental meal to be repeated, and that in a verse which even some conservative scholars regard as an interpolation.

Thus I pondered one after another of the cardinal doctrines of orthodox theology, amazed and bewildered to find that fabrics of thought so stupendous were based upon documentary evidence so slight and unconvincing.

Where was truth to be found? It seemed to me that so many professed Christians had no great concern for the quest for reality. "The more the Church asks me to believe, the better I like it", said a keen young Ritualistic layman of my acquaintance, apparently having no conception of belief as a vital conviction that certain things are facts, but rather regarding it as an attitude of mind to be assumed unquestioningly and unthinkingly at the word of command. To so many of those whose conduct I studied, eager for light, religion appeared to be a matter of sentiment, or personal taste, of fancy lightly entertained and readily abandoned. A priest whom I knew to have long been dallying with Rome, one morning said Mass for the last time (as he supposed) in the English Church. He prostrated himself before the Body and Blood of the Son of God, and then, in the same week, asked to be admitted to the Roman Communion, thereby acknowledging that he regarded himself as no priest at all, and that the idea he had held at the commencement of the week that the Body and Blood of Christ were really present on an Anglican altar, under the forms of bread and wine, was a delusion. His reception by his new co-religionists was not cordial, and he soon rejoined the English Church, thus again completely reversing his convictions upon a matter to him of fundamental importance. An extreme case this, of course, but not, it seemed to me, without affinity to a prevailing sense of unreality, almost of make-believe, in so much that passed for religion. The critical faculties being dormant or non-existent, people were content to accept statements touching life's most vital concerns upon evidence which they would regard with contempt in any other sphere but that of religion.

At this period, therefore, I was in the position in which,

278

could their secret history be written, it would probably become apparent that, at one time or another, many official exponents of orthodoxy have discovered themselves. I became aware that I could not believe or teach with a clear conscience much that the Church appeared to hold.

When matters come to such a pass, the lot of a minister in most religious communities is a hard one. I suppose that a Roman priest must abandon his office, or eat his heart out in secret disillusionment, or, if he makes bold to speak his belief, be crushed by the relentless hand of authority. The Dissenting minister has an equally autocratic censor in the tender and sensitive conscience of the theologically disposed deacon. A priest of the English Church is in more fortunate case, since, on the whole, no one can deny to that body the claim truly to represent the English mind which stresses practical considerations and is uninterested in mere speculation.

I have heard an Anglo-Catholic dignitary pronounce over the remains of an advanced Modernist clergyman the warmest eulogies. It is true that the one flatly denied a great part of what to the other was of the essence of the Faith, but he had been a faithful and beloved pastor of his flock and Anglican dignitaries are not wont to be censorious of such.

This policy has its penalties. The Church of England is accused of not knowing its own mind, and of having no clear idea of what it desires to teach. The proximity of two churches belonging to the same religious body, in each of which a large part of the teaching and practice of the other is vigorously disputed, is certainly disconcerting. But, to my mind, at a period in human history when so many venerable beliefs must necessarily be abandoned whilst those which will take their place are not yet apparent, there is something to be said for the policy which refuses to impose a rigid censorship on honest questioning, but gives wide freedom to thought and discussion providing that these are accompanied by a zeal for personal and social righteousness.

My position, therefore, in the English Church permitted me to face my difficulties without external aggravation of my trouble. In preaching I avoided the discussion of those matters wherein I was unable to voice conscientiously the official teaching of the Church. I was thrown back upon Christian ethics, and in speaking of the spirit of the Master's life and teaching I felt myself upon firm ground.

I read again and with fresh vision the Synoptic accounts of what Jesus said and did, and conceived thereby a conviction that here was essential and fundamental truth concerning man's relations with God and with his fellows. I could with my whole heart acknowledge as speaking with divine authority One who displayed so intimate an acquaintance with the vital facts of human existence. It seemed to me, too, that Jesus laid all the stress on the practical acceptance of His message, evidenced by conduct, and that the only discipleship He valued was that which was the inevitable result of becoming possessed by the spirit which inspired Himself.

From the contemplation of this, which seemed to me the very heart of the Christian gospel, I turned in thought to Christendom, a battlefield of contending sects. I conceived that Christ-likeness was nothing else but that attitude towards the totality of existence which corresponds to the divine ideal and thereby enables man to co-operate most effectively in the divine purpose. But this was the monopoly of no single sect and could not be dependent upon any one particular standard of theological belief or the practice of a particular cult.

I was led, in an odd fashion, to extend this conception beyond the bounds of Christendom. One dreary day in November I chanced to begin reading Rudyard Kipling's *Kim*. For one week in my life I lived in the bland sunlight of the East for all that my body remained where mists and sodden leaves proclaimed the dying year in our desolate English countryside. Absurd as it may sound to those un-acquainted with the limited outlook of one living in the orthodox Christian surroundings of a bygone day, it was the picture of the guileless sanctity of the old lama casting its spell over the impish worldliness of the disciple with whom he was so oddly assorted which first opened my eyes to the truth of that saying of Erasmus: "Fortasse largius funditur spiritus Christi quam nos interpretamur".

Along this curious bypath I was brought to a renewed and deeper contemplation of the thought that the vital fact of Christianity is that in the spirit of the life and teaching of Jesus Christ, and of that vast army of those His followers who have been possessed by it, has been made explicit that which is implicit in those vast processes by which man has been evolved. It followed that this spirit was identical with all upward-striving human effort wherever and whenever found. But was not that the conclusion reached well-nigh two thousand years ago by the seer who wrote "the Gospel

281

according to St John"?—"That was the true Light which lighteth every man that cometh into the world".

With this clue I re-read the book, no longer bewildered by attempts to square it with the Synoptic pictures of Jesus of Nazareth or to establish any sort of baldly literal historicity in that eagle sweep of mystic seeing. To me it seemed that here was the treasure-trove of one of the greatest of those adventurers who have striven to penetrate the external in search of the reality at the heart of things.

The results of the attempt of theologians to capture those rainbow gleams and build them, like bricks, into a neat edifice of literal fact and logical deduction appeared to me to have obliterated much of their significance for those who had been taught as I had.

Thus, at certain times, I fancied myself secure in an oddly assorted mystical-ethical faith, whilst, at others, I was overwhelmed by the rational and materialistic elements of my mind. Religion, I would say to myself, is the uncharted sea of the unknown, perhaps the unknowable. It is the sphere of vision, of fancy, of dreams. Men seek to soften the rigour of experience by feigning that this welter of mere happenings has a purpose, a direction.

An earthquake shatters a church in which the priest is holding up towards the God of love the Body and Blood of His Son, and overwhelms Host and priest and people in bloody ruin....

The shipwrecked sailor agonizes in prayer whilst the hungry surges of the good God weaken the grip of clutching fingers....

The sick man, writhing in the intolerable torture of a

282

malignant disease, babbles yet of the loving wisdom of his Creator....

What possible proof is there, I thought, when in this mood, that the Christian interpretation of existence is the true one? Is not one's point of view in these matters governed largely by emotion? Wordsworth, exhilarated by the beauty of a spring morning, imagines the vernal wood to exude morality. A man of scientific training beholds the same phenomena and perceives in them a ruthless and non-moral battle for existence, bird, beast, flower and tree seizing every opportunity for self-aggrandizement, even at the cost of the suffering and death of its rivals, in a deadly struggle for existence.

Under the influence of such broodings even the moral and spiritual teaching of Jesus became of questionable validity. If it be true indeed that not even a sparrow perishes apart from the knowledge of God, well then, that does but increase the difficulty as one studies, say, Hudson's pathetic account of the loss of bird-life in Cornwall during that fearful frost described in *The Land's End*. What proof of fatherly love is discernible in so wanton a profusion of creative effort accompanied by such reckless destruction? It is the conduct of a petulant child who models with infinite pains a miniature garden, and then, when the task is completed, obliterates its work with a sweep of the hand.

The Mind which planned the little songster whose artless warbling heard unawares cheats the fancy into a momentary dream that God is good, is the very same which conceived the superb efficiency of that swoop of hawk's

283

beak and claws which, in a flash, changes the scrap of pulsing life and liquid music into blood-bedraggled feathers and limp death.. . .

Happily for me, the urgent duties of my calling prevented my being reduced to utter impotence by speculation which seemed to lead no whither. Whatever might be the ultimate truth about this inscrutable existence of ours, it was obvious and insistent that the sheep entrusted to this bewildered shepherd should be tended as best could be in circumstances so untoward. It was a most gracious discipline which compelled me frequently to relinquish that alluring, baffling quest at the call of duty. The fact that old Master Rayner is in need of pastoral visitation brings me, enveloped by the sickly mists of doubt, into healthful contact with reality.

I set myself to school in the presence of old Master Rayner. We sit and look at each other silently; we are living in different worlds as to our minds, for all that our bodies inhabit the same remote East Anglian village.

Old Master Rayner, with kindly friendly eyes, his upper lip shorn, his chin and cheeks covered with a mat of grey whisker, stirs the fire with shaky hand splayed and knotted by more than seventy years of unremitting toil. Starting work when about nine years old, he has laboured all that while since, in summer's fiercest blaze, and, in winter, even when the snow, as he tells me, once obliterated the very hedges, and the countryside was one flat sheet of gleaming white. For Master Rayner was cowman and his work never ceased. His charges defied all Sabbatic distinctions and, in consequence, he who tended them had perforce to

284

do the same. Thus, not from choice, as he is eager to explain, he never was a church-goer.

Master Rayner's theology consists of chance-gleaned fragments. "I trust in His precious Blood", he says, "and I pray to Him as well as I can. I don't suppose He will be hard on me. He knows what I have had to put up with from her, poor dear." He indicates his wife, paralysed and tearful, nodding on the other side of the fireplace.

Old Mrs Rayner was always of erratic tendency. She would rise at midnight and wander miles over the country-side, causing much anxiety to her husband. A stroke confines her to her chair now, but she struggles to maintain her reputation for contrariness by falling out of it, in a most alarming fashion, on all possible occasions. "The Lord have been very good to me" is old Master Rayner's verdict on life as he knows it. "I have had fourteen children (least, I think so; I ain't quite sure of the exact number), but not one of them ever been in gaol or broke the leg."

Perhaps Master Rayner's genial view of Providence is due largely to the glorious health he has enjoyed. "I never had a headache in me life", he assures me; "I never been ill, and I never took no medicine. There! I'm telling you a story. Once I poisoned me thumb, and the doctor he say, Rayner, he say, I'll send you a bottle o' physic. Very good, sir, I say. Well, he send it, and it stood on the shelf for two year, and after that I dunno what become of it. But that's all the medicine I ever took in me life, and I didn't take that, if you rightly understand me."

One day, when he was eighty-four years old, and still engaged in his lifelong toil, Master Rayner suddenly measured his length on the ground. He was brought home and the doctor pronounced that the sturdy heart that had ticked away so cheerfully since the time when Queen Victoria was a slip of a girl was worn quite out. Its owner must sit through the rest of his days, uncomplaining, yet a little regretful, by his cottage fire, to dream of the past; that gallant past in which the background of toil and privation is relieved by sunny recollections of the copious flow of beer at the hospitable farmhouse. "The barrel stood in the hall, and anybody what liked could help himself."

I pray with old Master Rayner before I go. He repeats with me the Lord's Prayer and the Grace. We remain silent for a little while. I look at him. His eyes are closed, his horny old hands are clasped on his lap. His lips move; he is still praying. "For ever and ever. For ever and ever", he repeats, as would a Buddhist priest the sacred Mantra. "Oh, ain't that beautiful! I often think of that when I can't sleep at nights. For ever and ever."

The ritual concludes with my presentation of the customary offering of tobacco, which he acknowledges in terms which have now become a sort of liturgical formula. "Oh, thank you, thank you. I do like a piece of tobacco. That amuse me when I'm a sitting here. When I was a young man the doctor he used to say, 'I like to see you young men smoking. That keeps the diseases away!'"

I take my leave of Master Rayner, and enter the cottage of old Widow Spareman. I find her poring over a tattered paper. It is, she tells me, a letter she received from her brother when he was serving in the Crimean War. Old Widow Spareman gives the lie to that hoary imposition which teaches that cleanliness is allied to godliness. Who could maintain this foolish doctrine in the presence of one of the dirtiest and most godly of our village ancientry?

Old Widow Spareman's piety is, truly, of a somewhat lachrymose type. "I'm a getting old", she says, "and no one wants to be bothered with an old 'oman like me." I hasten reassuring disclaimers. "No, they don't," she persists, "and I wish the Lord would take me home. Sometimes as I sit here all by myself I think I can hear them blessed angels a-singing." Then, as her glance chances to light on the tea-cup of ale, duly sweetened, which is warming on the hob for her breakfast, she eyes it malevolently and says, without any pause between the two sentences, "This here beer we get now is wonnerful horrid old truck, ain't it? Why, in the old days a glass o' beer got more hold of you than six-penn'orth o' whisky do now".

But old Widow Spareman does not rashly charge God with the ills that flesh is heir to. By some subtle reasoning she can harmonize the omnipotence with the love of the Creator.

"If it hadn't been for Him", she says, "where would I have been? I know where to look for help."

I am thankful for that much of the grace of humility which has prevented my ever assuming the air of teacher in the presence of such folk. They are the teachers; I have been content to sit at their feet and try to realize what must be the amazing courage, and faith, and kindly humour which have preserved their confidence undimmed through all the changes and chances of their stern battle for mere existence. I seemed to catch glimpses of an essential goodness at the

287

heart of things as I reflected that it was part of the scheme that qualities so gracious should mature in such unpropitious surroundings. "God moves in a mysterious way His wonders to perform...."

At other times, the utterly unintelligible character of human existence hung upon me like a nightmare in which one is impressed with the inexorable necessity of solving a puzzle combined with a sense of paralysing inability to do so.

One day I was waiting for the arrival at church of a funeral party. The great tenor bell boomed sullenly every minute, the majestic beat of the drum of destiny. Two strokes were sounded each time, denoting to those acquainted with our local customs the funeral of a woman. Three strokes are given to a man, for even in death we are Hebraic in our conception of masculine supremacy.

The registers were lying before me. Ours begin in 1538, the very year in which Thomas Cromwell, that appropriate instrument of Henry's abominations, achieved his one title to grateful remembrance by ordering each parish to keep a record of Baptisms, Marriages, and Burials. I turned over those earliest parchment pages, from the red-letter heading, "Liber Registrarius de Barnelandes in Com. Suff.", and exquisitely written Latin entries, on towards the sprawling flourishes of my predecessor in the days of Charles the First. These were followed by the neat, clerk-like hand of the lay official who kept the registers during the Commonwealth, and thus the record continued through the eighteenth century, when various curates serving absentee rectors made hasty entries of ceremonies perfunctorily performed amid the more congenial labours of cultivating their glebe land.

There is nothing arresting in the baptismal registers of Barnlands ("Catalogus nominum eorum qui in parochia dicta de Barnelandes baptiz."), for as far back as record goes we have been an undistinguished community. Here and there a quaint name caught my eye. Roger Graygoose smacked of the yeomanry of ancient days. Had the father of Hamlet Plume, who was baptized in the reign of the first James, by any curious chance visited London and carried home memories of a play he had witnessed? "Persenel" and "Mirabel" suggested romantic affinities not to be expected in the parents of farm labourers. But, for the most part, the entries consist of a monotonous catalogue of Johns and Marys destined at birth to poverty and obscurity, to many sorrows and unending toil.

I had the curiosity to look back to the entry of the baptism of the woman the closing record of whose little span of life I was shortly to make. It was this: "Jane, the bastard daughter of Betsy Sparrow, domestic servant, baptized March the thirtieth 1879".

Further search gave significant hints of the career of Betsy Sparrow. She was baptized in infancy in the year 1864; her child was born in 1879; she died in 1890. The entries recalled village gossip which I had forgotten. She had "had a misfortune" at an age somewhat earlier than that at which our girls are wont to deviate from the path of virtue. She had lingered on eleven years afterward, a hopeless invalid. She left a sickly child who, growing to womanhood, and becoming united to a delicate husband, had, with the accustomed fertility of such, produced a numerous progeny.

I looked again at that last cruel entry. How hugely disproportionate to the act were its results! There, in that musty parchment, is coldly furnished forth to future ages the damning witness of a transient emotion, a momentary declension.

It must have occurred about the month of June, perhaps on the evening of a day when the world was all life and light. But now night had fallen and the little village girl is wending homeward beneath the stars, aglow with the pulsing vigour of youth and health when the blood flows a golden stream, and just awakening to consciousness of impulses not understood.

There is the meeting in the lane; the lad's arm stealing round her waist; the tightening clasp; the surging up of hot blood; the mist over the eyes; the wild throb of the heart; the half swoon; the dream that faded; the cold awakening. ...And here, on this wan winter's day, the last word of the insignificant little drama....I go out to meet the procession. Four labourers in their Sunday clothes bear the coffin. Behind it, two and two, the string of mourners, feeble old men, and aged women in rusty black.

I turn and head the procession on its way toward the church. Overhead the monotonous tolling, and my voice, strangely thin, repeating the opening sentences of the Office for the Burial of the Dead.

There is the slow tramp of feet up the church, the shuffling and scraping as the mourners take their places. They crouch forward uncomfortably, muffling their faces in black-bordered handkerchiefs, as I read the Psalm. "O spare me a little that I may recover my strength before I go hence and be no more seen." But that pathetic cry for respite, for just a little longer tarrying in the light of the sun and the friendly warmth of the homely familiar ways, has been disregarded, and the soul has voyaged out into the unknown.

There follows the appointed lection from St Paul's First Epistle to the Corinthians. I wonder what these rustics, with that patient, listless expression on their faces, stamped there through succeeding centuries of experience of the harsh buffeting of fate, can make of the bold imaginings of the Eastern mystic. What weird significance do they give to his record of "fighting with beasts at Ephesus"? What, to his reminder that "Evil communications corrupt good manners"? Do the words suggest to them memories of a copy-book aphorism laboriously penned during their brief youthful sojourn at the night school with which my predecessor's piety provided the village? Even as I, by some whimsical association of ideas, am invariably reminded by them of a bib with which I was adorned at meal-times in my early youth, whereon was depicted a clown feeding an elephant with buns, beneath which ran the legend: "May good digestion wait on appetite".

We duly thank God for removing this our sister out of the miseries of this sinful world, from which we ourselves are so unwilling to be separated; and then we go down the church again, past the font where Betsy Sparrow, pallid, gaunt, the ghost of a child herself, had once held the offspring of her shame.

Out into the churchyard where yawns the open grave. Beside it the pile of earth beneath which are hidden the skulls and bones which the sexton was obliged to disturb, for our churchyard has been completely buried over not once nor twice during the past six hundred years. "Wonnerful fine mouthful of teeth them old people fared to have", the sexton had said to me that morning, displaying with gloomy pleasure a brown jawbone.

The coffin is lowered into the mud and water which so soon collects at any depth in this sodden soil. "Earth to earth, ashes to ashes, dust to dust." The sexton punctuates the clauses with a threefold tribute of clay which rattles on the coffin lid. He wipes his hand on his trouser leg.

"In sure and certain hope of a glorious resurrection unto eternal life...."

We stand in silence for a few moments after the Grace, and then, according to the accustomed ceremonial, the undertaker leads forward in turn each couple of mourners, who solemnly peer down into the grave. The old men lean on their sticks and gaze with weak watery eyes; the faded bonnets of the old women shake with the emotion of their wearers. They make their way down the churchyard path, and the favoured few resort to the house of mourning for tea and the utterance of sentiments appropriate to the occasion.

Later on I pass the grave where the sexton is shovelling in the last spadefuls of earth, attended by a group of village children who delight in the agreeable sensation of beholding the re-interment of the late-disturbed bones.

I felt overwhelmed by an acutely painful sense of the

futility of human life. Was it for this, I thought, that man has been evolved through countless aeons? Was that amazing thing, the human body, painfully built up, through millions of years of preparation, from the formless amoeba to the glory of that cunningly compacted structure of nerve and muscle, of graceful limbs, the bloom of a maiden's cheek, the blown soft hair, the laughing loving eyes, in order, at length, a mass of fetid corruption, to rot in this oozy bed?

Is there indeed to be a glorious resurrection of this corruption? Paul, as I had just read, strenuously denies it, but speaks impossibly of the magical evolution of a living body out of dead matter. By what authority and with what proof? Can I reckon upon a miracle so unbelievable on the bare *ipse dixit* of an oriental visionary?

And what of the spirit, the living being with whom I had so recently been conversing? Where was it now? A pale wraith tossed to and fro on the eddying winds? A meagre ghost inhabiting an underworld of eternal night? An immortal soul, translated now to Heaven, chanting unceasingly before a throne?

I looked up at the grey and lowering sky; about me, where the rising wind stirred the skeleton arms of the gaunt elms; beneath me, where the uneven turf marked scores of nameless graves. Vanity of vanities! In the face of the silence unbroken since the dawn of human history what proof had I that man's spirit survives the dissolution of his body?

"Man's immortal soul!" "A mere secretion of his brain!" confidently asserted the scientific materialist. "Point but to one verifiable fact that indicates the contrary, and

293

I will believe you. But for your dreams and visions, the pathological fantasies embodied in your sacred writings, I have no use whatever."

Were they, indeed, I mused, subjective imaginings? No scheme of thought claiming to explain the meaning of human existence could be more convincing than that of orthodox Christianity, providing one granted its premises. But the critical study of the documentary evidence available had convinced me that, standing alone, the evidence did not provide the necessary foundation of ascertainable fact.

In matters so momentous could I base a firm conviction upon the sole witness of a collection of writings, the authenticity of which was, for the purpose of supplying objective fact, open to so many and such serious objections?

Thus, as evidence of survival of death, the Evangelists' accounts of the Resurrection of Christ appeared so confusing and so contradictory as to be appropriately denominated, according to many critics, "The Legend of the Empty Tomb". Paul vehemently repudiates the idea of a resuscitation of material particles where man is concerned; thus (unless Christ's resurrection is different in kind from that of all others, in which case it has no bearing on the problem of human survival) he would appear either to have rejected or been ignorant of the Easter narratives as they have come down to us.

Human ingenuity has exerted its utmost effort to explain this and a thousand other difficulties, but, however nearly to the discovery of the facts critical skill may have penetrated, precise knowledge of what actually occurred is, in

294

the nature of things, unobtainable by man's normal faculties after the lapse of nineteen hundred years.

The conclusion of the whole matter, so far as I was concerned at this time, was that I felt an ardent longing for a really satisfactory conception of God's plan and purpose for the world, and of man's part therein, based upon a foundation of observable fact. I was sufficiently acquainted with the difficulties of the problem not to desire the impossible, nor to look for proofs as compelling as a mathematical demonstration. I knew that the heart as well as the intellect must be thrown into the scale where a religious conviction is concerned.

But I did desire that my attitude towards life's most vital questions should be based upon a solid foundation of facts capable of demonstration and exercising a reasonably compulsive power upon a candid mind. Consistently with intellectual integrity, I could no longer accept the orthodox Catholic scheme of belief on the grounds upon which I conceived its acceptance proposed. It was in no spirit of contemptuous self-sufficiency that I found myself adopting this attitude of mind towards a system so august, and one with which most of my spirit's response to the highest concerns of life had been bound up.

I was profoundly convinced, strange as it may appear, that Christianity was "true", in the sense that it interlocked with the facts of human existence, so admirably was it adapted to man's universal needs. Yet, at the same time, I was totally unable to accept the Church's rationale of its beliefs and practices. The idea of a unique Revelation from God superimposed upon the normal order of existence, supernaturally attested, recorded with absolute inerrancy, mediated by an infallible authority, and, therefore, so compulsive of unquestioning belief that to offer less than that implied moral obliquity—this, to me, had become unthinkable.

Thus, the only source from which every impulse of my heart and mind had, for long years, been accustomed to look for light and leading on the pathway from birth to death seemed to have failed me.

Use and wont enabled me to continue my official duties. I clung desperately to any and every fragment of Christian belief which I could honestly accept, and made the most of these. I never obtruded my doubts and hesitations upon the simple folk committed to my charge, who would, of course, have failed utterly (happily for them) to understand any such conflict as that in which I was engaged. Their hold upon God and essential religious truth seemed to be intuitive, nourished by the tender ministries of the natural things amongst which they lived and moved, matured under the buffetings of trouble and sorrow most patiently borne, owing but little to mere intellectualism. To each of us his task. Mine, at that time, to suffer a bleak perplexity, to pass through a dark night of the soul; upon which, nevertheless, day, I hoped, would some time dawn.

XI

LIGHT ON THE PATH

AT length, light came, but from an entirely unexpected quarter.

There is a class of phenomena, instances of which have been reported from all parts of the world from the dawn of recorded human history.

These alleged occurrences are intermittent, unusual, and not readily accounted for by what is generally observed to be the normal sequence of cause and effect.

I had had no personal experience of any happening of this kind, but in the course of half a lifetime of fairly extensive, even if sometimes rather desultory, reading, I had come across reports of the occurrence of events alleged to be supernormal. Towards these I had unthinkingly adopted the attitude of mind prevalent amongst those by whom at the time I chanced to be chiefly influenced.

In my early childhood, being troubled by something I had read of ghosts, I consulted my mother. She comforted me by deriding the possibility of the existence of such objectionable beings, basing her conviction on a dictum of my grandmother's to the effect that when people die they go either to Heaven or Hell. If to the former, they are too well off to desire to return to earth again; and if to the latter, Satan sees to it that they do not get the opportunity. This appeared to me to provide for all contingencies and satisfactorily to dispose of the possibility of any unwelcome visit from the inhabitants of another sphere, and I was convinced and comforted.

My youth was passed under the influence of orthodox Protestantism, a system of thought which is rational rather than mystical. The theory of an infallible Bible has in the past compelled Protestantism to admit the possibility of happenings which it has designated supernatural. But that is the limit of its concession, and for allowing even this it recompenses itself by a vigorous repudiation of the possibility of any such occurrence ever taking place except as recorded in Holy Scripture.

Catholicism, which had the allegiance of my early manhood, accepts, of course, the Bible accounts of supernatural happenings, and, in addition, credits what are known as the ecclesiastical miracles, that is, such supernormal events in the lives of its saints and heroes as it considers to be duly authenticated. But, by a certain economy of belief, or influenced by its sensitiveness concerning its prerogatives, Catholicism is strenuously opposed to the acknowledgment of similar occurrences having taken place outside its own particular sphere of observation and interest. If, perchance, such events do occasionally happen, which the Church does not readily admit, then they are the work of demons, the same sort of demons, one supposes, as bewildered mankind by causing rites similar to Baptism and the Eucharist to be prevalent amongst certain pagan peoples.

As an Anglo-Catholic I adopted this point of view without reflection, and, on grounds so insufficient, presumed to warn people against any dabbling in the occult.

298

Last of all, when strongly influenced by Modernist methods of thought, I adopted (again without question) the attitude of the scientific materialist towards this matter, that being the standpoint to which the mentality of the Modernist inevitably and probably quite unconsciously inclines him. The Modernist is sometimes accused of being still obsessed by pseudo-scientific presuppositions which have long been out of date. There is, I think, some ground for this charge to be found in the refusal of most Modernists to give adequate consideration to the evidence alleged to have been obtained by Psychic Research.

Modernists, impressed by the victories achieved by the physical sciences in the effort to bring all phenomena within the sphere of observed cause and effect, are unwilling to acknowledge the existence of a class of alleged happenings which, if they really occurred, must be considered super-natural and destructive of that ordered scheme of thought which supports the validity of man's mental processes and has been the foundation upon which so imposing an edifice of knowledge has been reared.

In these later days orthodox Christian believers and sceptical materialists have found themselves occupying com-mon ground, for the Church has welcomed the assistance which science seemed to offer in its effort to dispose of a branch of enquiry which appeared to threaten some of its most cherished prerogatives. It is now no longer convenient to assert that all these strange occurrences are figments of the imagination, or else the work of demons. For, in the face of a storm of opposition and ridicule, a number of persons had strenuously asserted that these things did occur, for they themselves had witnessed them under circumstances precluding the possibility of deception or hallucination. Their pertinacity attracted the attention of a few thinkers of outstanding ability who possessed the true scientist's spirit of open-mindedness (perhaps, the rarest of human endowments), and who determined themselves to investigate and report upon whatever appeared to be credibly affirmed.

The difficulties were enormous, for the probability of fraud, credulity, misunderstanding, and imperfect observation disposed of a not inconsiderable proportion of what had been alleged to be observed fact.

But the net result of these enquiries, extending now over more than half a century, appeared to establish beyond question the claim that various phenomena of a supernormal kind do actually happen, and some of those occurrences seemed to throw light on the problem of man's survival of bodily death. This was unwelcome news to the orthodox, whether scientist or theologian; to the former because he generally regarded the idea of a life beyond the grave as a figment of the imagination—it was, at any rate, incapable of scientific demonstration; to the latter since that was a question about which he alone spoke with authority. But it could not be gainsaid by the thoughtful observer who patiently studied the evidence that a *prima facie* case had been made out. However, a possible escape from the difficulty presented itself. The phenomena were accepted but they were explained away by the simple method of pronouncing in an impressive fashion certain words originally coined by Psychic Research itself merely for purposes of classification. "The sub-conscious", "tele-pathy", "collective hallucination", and other fair-sounding vocables were employed in a manner suggesting that, in some strange fashion, they accounted for occurrences which (assuming the description to be correct) they merely de-signate by a convenient symbol.

> O wondrous power of words, by simple faith
> Licensed to take the meaning that we love.

This, and much more, I was, of course, to discover sub-sequently, for at that period of my life recorded in the last chapter I was (strange to say) but slightly acquainted with the history of the sustained and careful attempt to survey, examine, co-ordinate and give some rational account of the mass of evidence purporting to authenticate the existence of this class of phenomena.

I am unable to remember exactly what first attracted my attention to the subject, but, once aware of its existence, I followed it up with ardour, reading, in the course of several years, a good many of the best books published in England dealing with the problems involved in this infant science.

In my study of the nature of the evidence for, and the conclusions to be drawn from, psychic phenomena I was fortunate at the outset in reading the great classic of the subject, *Human Personality, and its Survival of Bodily Death*, by Frederic Myers. Thus equipped, I was no voyager in an uncharted sea, no wanderer in a fantastic realm of unwholesome prodigy. Myers taught me that in this sphere, strange and bizarre as some of its manifestations may appear, there is nothing supernatural, fantastic or un-accountable. All is strictly under rule and law; there is as orderly a sequence of cause and effect in matters psychic as in things material. Another class of phenomena has been brought within the sphere of scientific enquiry, thus actually increasing our conviction of the validity of our mental processes and making for the unification of all thought.

The chain of evidence which led to conclusions involving something like a revolution in my outlook on life may be summarized briefly as follows.

I became convinced, first of all, of the objective existence of certain phenomena. In itself, the movement of a material object by other than mechanical means may be as unim-portant as the upward propulsion of a kettle lid by escaping steam. Yet, just as the one suggested the undiscovered possibilities latent in the fact that water vaporizes at a certain temperature, so the other indicated that there was some power at work the importance of which was not to be gauged by the trivial means through which it was mani-fested. The point was that something actually occurred, even if it were but the movement across the room of a tambourine propelled by an unknown force. The happening was objective. It was not a trick of the imagination.

The evidence for the existence of the phenomena is overwhelming and it is no longer the custom to dismiss it in the contemptuous fashion with which it was received when first it came under public notice.

The cause, or causes, of these occurrences is the really debatable matter.

Every possible known cause must be considered before

one which is unknown can be advanced. The individual who supposes himself to have observed the tambourine moving across the room may be the victim of trickery, malobservation, or misunderstanding. If these, and every other explanation of a normal kind, should be ruled out by the facts, a supernormal cause is posited. Is the phenomenon due to some extension of, or addition to, normal human faculties? That there are such faculties is shown by the convincing proof which exists of the reality of the phenomena of clairvoyance, clairaudience, "psychometry" and so on.

Here is no case for hasty generalization. It is a matter of the accumulation of reliable and first-hand evidence, of its analysis and careful co-ordination, before the theory is tentatively suggested. Suppose, then, the possibility of an occurrence, duly attested, having its origin in some supernormal human power is ruled out by the evidence, then, and then only is some force outside man suggested.

I choose purposely to consider a crude and altogether elementary instance. Rappings, let us suppose, are heard in a room, which occur apart from the conscious volition of anyone present. Some force other than that which we ordinarily recognize as human may be suggested tentatively to account for them. What cause is at work? Is the phenomenon brought about unconsciously by anyone present? Is it a supernormal and quite unaccountable manifestation of the action of blind and unintelligent matter? These possibilities cannot be ruled out without consideration.

But suppose it occurs to someone present to test the probability that the rapping may be due to an unseen yet intelligent force: "If someone is there," he says, "will he please" (for courtesy is always becoming) "rap three times". Three distinct raps follow. Thus encouraged, a clumsy and rather tedious code is suggested, and, very slowly, an intelligible sentence is rapped out.

This is distinctly a step forward. It would appear that the force behind the phenomenon is intelligent.

Our friends, now interested, proceed to question it. It, or rather he, asserts that he is a man who used to live at a given address in a certain town a hundred miles off, and who died suddenly a few months ago. He gives particulars about himself, and is extremely anxious that a message should be delivered to his wife, for he is uneasy owing to a misunderstanding between them, the clearing up of which was prevented by his unexpected decease.

Somewhat impressed, but decidedly sceptical, they address a letter to the person alleged to be concerned, who replies that the facts are as stated, that they were known to no one but her husband and herself, and that the message sent is one of indescribable consolation.

There is the problem. What is its solution? I did not rashly attempt any answer to that question in the early stages of my enquiry. I would increase my stock of facts before seeking the hypothesis to account for them. But the one thought ever before my mind was the possibility that this study which I had undertaken might afford me that conclusive proof of man's survival of death for which I had first experienced the imperative need when Hallam died. My need of really definite and, indeed, of overwhelming evidence safeguarded me from rash assumptions and hasty conclusions. I had the will to believe in a life after death, but the urgency of my desire was the measure of my caution in accepting the conclusions to which the evidence pointed.

Thus, for over ten years I made the subject my especial study. I had no conscious psychic experience of any kind whatever during this period. That, of course, to one who is favoured with it, is the most conclusive of all evidences.

I can well believe that a person who has witnessed what seems to me the most impressive of psychic manifestations, that of the Direct Voice, would chafe at the cold formality of the statement that the "spirit hypothesis" is the only suggested solution that really covers a certain class of psychic phenomena. Probably, had I been privileged, as some now appear to have been, to converse audibly, time after time, with a departed friend, in all the intricate and unexpected twists and turns, and with all the casual allusiveness of intimate conversation, I might express myself less guardedly.

But, as it is, and knowing myself as I do, I am not without wonder that I was able to arrive at the conviction that the evidence gathered by Psychic Research which I myself had read and studied afforded an almost overwhelming probability that man's existence is not terminated by bodily death. In stating this conviction I am preserved from an uncomfortable sense of singularity by the fact that my belief is shared by a choice body of persons of wide experience and distinguished by the highest intellectual gifts, who, after devoting half a lifetime to the closest scrutiny of the alleged facts, have reached at first-hand the conclusion which I was nearing through their testimony.

A distinguished Anglican divine has said that he is compelled to accept the evidence for certain occurrences of a psychic nature, but that he does so with extreme reluctance. It is a feeling which I do not share, but one with which I can sympathize. The orthodox thinker, be he scientist or theologian, has fashioned his philosophy of existence and created a mental world in which he moves with the ease and freedom of long familiarity. Psychic Research presents him with phenomena, and with inferences derived therefrom, which he can in no wise fit into his scheme of things. To accept them would involve a drastic rearrangement of his mental furniture. His instinct compels him, therefore, to put up a desperate resistance against ideas so anarchical.

The theologian's is, perhaps, the harder lot, for this pseudo-science, he feels, intrudes upon holy ground, with its claim to speak with authority of the state of the departed.

It is a kindly human instinct which presents all our departed friends with a halo, and invests their present condition with an awful sanctity. That beings removed so far above us could resort to undignified rappings, the uncouth antics of some commonplace medium, or the gyrations of a lead pencil, in order to attract our attention and get into touch with us is to many unthinkable.

This aspect of the matter presented no difficulty to me, to whom it is no offence that Bach and Beethoven communicate their ideas through lengths of wire and catgut. And I possess just this much, at any rate, of the scientific spirit; I am prepared to consider any alleged facts, in however unaccustomed a guise they present themselves, providing that the evidence advanced for them possesses any kind of cogency. I have not yet completed my universe, and I certainly should not on *a priori* considerations shut out of it any fresh experience clamouring for admittance, seeing that my philosophy is compelled to accept the amazing and inexplicable oddity of so much in human life the existence of which is acknowledged by everyone.

The powers and possibilities affecting and affected by the Unseen World, conceivably latent in all men, the actual existence of which in some seemed to me to have been amply demonstrated, appeared to open vistas for the future of the race compared with which humanity's past achievements are, in certain respects, perhaps but the gleams that herald the dawn.

But mine is not the prophet's mantle. I am concerned now only with that which may be proved by processes similar to those by which all matters of scientific fact are established.

Whether man survives bodily death or does not, is the question which, of all questions, is surely the most immediately vital. Upon the answer given to it depends the validity of the greater part of our belief in a moral purpose governing the world. A conclusive reply in the negative (if such were possible) would shatter for ever the better part of humanity's hopes. An answer finally establishing the fact would set the seal to the glowing testimony of the prophet, to the rhapsodies of the poet, to the visions the artist saw but could not paint, to the musician's most ethereal intuitions.

For, repugnant as such an idea may be to minds scorning necessary human limitations, it is certain that even man's most exalted spiritual and mental strivings ultimately involve

307   20-2

him in sheer moonstruck fantasy unless they keep in contact with actual matter-of-fact. Man's mind, with eagle vision, scans the empyrean, but his feet must be firmly planted on the homely solid earth.

The facts which are capable of satisfying that side of our nature in which the senses, the evidence reaching us through the senses, and the inferences derived therefrom are rightfully supreme, do not encroach upon, far less supersede, those intuitions and moral certainties which in the past have led humanity to posit a life beyond the grave. But they do give them a rational confirmation without which they cannot, in these days of enquiry and unrest, assert a compulsion upon our nature in its entirety. The child's question, "But is it true?" falls, a cold chill, upon the unsupported rhapsody of the visionary.

The facts already accumulated are, to many of those acquainted with them, of the nature of overwhelming proof. But they possess no coercive power upon satisfied ignorance, nor, I think, should they be accepted merely on authority. The investigation of the evidence is open to all; first-hand experiment is profitable to those suitably equipped. The body of evidence receives additions almost daily, and it can be approached for verification at any time. For Psychic Science presents no static system to be swallowed at a gulp, at the word of command; it proposes for acceptance no closed record of long-past happenings, the evidential value of which it is impossible to verify save with approximate accuracy.

A tenth part of the evidence for the conclusions reached in this matter would, if it were available for the purpose, be regarded by most orthodox Christians as finally establishing the authenticity of almost all the Biblical and ecclesiastical miracles put together. But man's essentially conservative nature shrinks from the extension to the strange and unaccustomed of those principles which he applies unhesitatingly to the familiar and the known.

Thus, the Christian apologist fails to recognize the help that Psychic Research offers him. Christianity claims to be a historical religion and its records must, therefore, be tested at the bar of historical criticism. If its alleged facts are thought to be uncertain or incapable of tolerably conclusive demonstration, its claim on the allegiance of man is proportionately weakened. It is indisputably the fact that this is now actually occurring.

Biblical Criticism has dealt some staggering blows at what was once conceived of as an impregnable citadel.

Of the three Synoptic writers no single one was a first-hand witness of the events he describes. Both Matthew and Luke, it is demonstrably certain, freely adapted their material to the furtherance of certain preconceived ideas.

Thus, the narratives of Christ's resurrection are in many particulars irreconcilable with one another, and large numbers of thoughtful persons to-day find it difficult to accept upon the often contradictory evidence of untrained observers, recorded at second-hand, a fact which they conceive to be so improbable as a series of reappearances after death, alleged to have taken place in a remote province of the Roman Empire nearly two thousand years ago.

If, however, the New Testament narratives are corroborated even to the extent that the unusual occurrences they record are shown not to be *unique*, then, at least, there is a reasonable case for discussion. The narratives concerned may be examined again in the light of the new knowledge, and tested for the residuum of actual fact, on the lines customary to historical criticism, and the results thrown into the scale along with those moral and spiritual considerations which tend to establish the probability of the event upon which Christianity may be said to be based.

Thus, tentatively and provisionally, I reasoned. When I came to sum up what my knowledge of the new science had given me, I found that I had become acquainted with a body of phenomena which had been subject to the closest scrutiny, over a period of half a century, by trained scientific observers and other level-headed and trustworthy investigators, who, in reaching conclusions as to its meaning, had employed exactly those methods of observation and legitimate deduction which have achieved such prodigious results in the sphere of the physical sciences.

It is hardly necessary to say that this knowledge did not solve off-hand all my previous doubts and perplexities concerning life and its meaning, but it did send me back to the study of the riddle of existence, and of the phenomena of religion, with a sense of the strong probability, to say the least, that certain of the main presuppositions on which the Christian religion may be said to be founded are scientifically demonstrable. These are, that this world of visible phenomena is interpenetrated by another world, equally real though normally invisible, and that the spirit of man possesses supernormal powers and is able to exist and function independently of the body.

This indeed was light on the path.

XII

GATHERED THREADS

CAN it be I, that odd, and not very attractive little boy, who once wandered through the green lanes of pleasant Gloucestershire, dwelling all the while in another land in which anything might happen? On the stage of memory the child re-enacts his part, moving about a silent country of which he is now the only inhabitant. Across the gulf of nearly fifty years I observe him with a curious detachment. Is that strange being myself?

Am I that cockney clerk, a pale, shy dreamer, caught up into the roaring life of a great city; in it but not of it, an exile from home?

Can that be I, the young priest between whose fingers the beads of a rosary drop one by one, whilst, with closed eyes, and lips that murmur the oft-repeated prayer, his mind is far away in the Holy Land where, beneath the trellised vines, Elisabeth, awe-struck, beholds the approaching figure of the Mother of her Lord?

Can that indeed be I, the anxious seeker absorbed in the study of "the Word of God", at times convinced that for him the issues of Life and Death depended upon the validity of a particular interpretation of a disputed text?

And was I once the sceptic imprisoned in a meaningless world of blind material forces, and doomed to grope in a trackless wilderness, yet, by inexorable fate, pushed daily nearer to the edge of the precipice beyond which was annihilation?

A thrilling thought possesses me as I scan the events of my life—it is, that if I could but understand the true significance, the inner reality, of the experiences through which I have passed, I should hold in my hand the key to the riddle of existence. Illusion and all half-lights would be gone and I should see things as in themselves they are. "Flower in the crannied wall...."

As matters stand, however, a humbler task awaits me than to explicate all knowledge and all mysteries. I desire in the closing chapter of this book to glance back over the half-century of existence which I have been privileged to enjoy in this well-nigh unbelievable world, and to indicate the position to which I have been led.

I do not look upon my present standpoint as unalterable, for I hope never to make a trim little house for my soul by refusing entrance to whatever fails to fit in with some petty scheme. With all my heart I echo Goethe's cry: "Light! More light!"

I think myself fortunate, therefore, that I did not in my younger days attain to a closed system of religious convictions. Had I done so I should have missed invaluable experience and lacked the material necessary in the endeavour to look out upon life from a standpoint not altogether provincial.

It has been said that to have progressed is to have changed, and to have made great progress is to have changed often. I may be said to have changed my religious beliefs; I think it would be more true to say that I have developed them, as the necessary data became available. Having acquired a wider experience I adjusted my mental attitude to it.

I had been brought up as a youth under Nonconformist influences. Had that which my Independent teachers gave me proved a satisfactory explanation of the problems I encountered I should have been saved an infinity of trouble, but I should have remained in ignorance of much that has helped me to realize the glory of existence in so splendid a world as this.

But Fate (or was it, rather, some plan worked out for me from Beyond?) made me acquainted with wide fields of knowledge outside that which I possessed in my Dissenting youth and I did but adapt myself to the successive stages in which it reached me.

I am glad to have seen a sect of English Nonconformity from the inside. As a particular system of belief and practice that followed by Independency made little impression upon me, since I was not at the time interested in such matters. Its chief value to me is that through it I became acquainted with men and women who influenced me for good and whose memory I honour. Indeed, they were amongst the first who showed me what real goodness is. The memory of the gentle old ladies of Fairchild House has saved me from sectarian prejudice. And so with my other Dissenting teachers; but it was because of their innate goodness and not as exponents of a theological system that they helped me. Indeed, what little I understood of their purely denominational affinities rather repelled me, for did not my otherwise kindly Sunday School teacher once refer to a minister who had sought Holy Orders in the Church of England as

"a scoundrel who has gone over to the Establishment"?
And was not our humble-minded and affectionate Pastor
led to pour forth unseemly invective in his much admired
course of sermons "Protestant Truths and Romish Errors"?

My nearest approach to adopting as my own certain
features of a particular system of Dissenting theology was
made at the time when, in a condition of mental overstrain,
I came upon a volume of sermons by the Baptist preacher
Spurgeon, as I have previously related. My state of mind
just then was almost pathological, and, though I look back
upon the experience now with a kind of horror, I realize
that I was thereby enabled to attain to a measure of mystic
exaltation, alternating with darkness and despair, and to an
overwhelming sense of the paramount importance of religion, which gave me personal knowledge of a wide sphere
of spiritual experience of which I should otherwise have
been but a casual and uninterested spectator.

I was ordained to the ministry of the Church of England
when that experience had become but a memory, and it was
not until Hallam had fired me with some of his enthusiasm
for Catholicism, as it is understood and practised by a
great and growing party in the English Church, that I
became really a believer in a definite variety of organized
Christianity.

But I have endeavoured to make it plain that I did not
accept that system after any careful personal study and
enquiry. I was drawn into it through the emotions of the
heart rather than by a rational compulsion.

As long as Catholicism was represented to me by Hallam
it held me, and I became acquainted thereby with much of

314

what is best in that august system, for which I can never feel anything but a profound veneration when I recall the appeal it once made both to my emotions and (since I assumed its premises) to my reason, and when I remember the opportunities of service which it afforded me.

In Hallam's successor and his assistant I saw Catholicism in another light. They were earnest and devoted men, but the religion they taught and practised resembled a corpse from which freedom of movement, colour and heart-glow had fled. It appeared to me a mere resuscitation of the Pharisaism which had nailed Christ to the Cross.

But of Catholicism as interpreted by my friend I had, at first, no doubts. It was still the divine plan for the world's salvation. It was merely misinterpreted and misrepresented by Hildebrand and Forsse. I did not realize that for me it was, perhaps, as much Hallam and his like who made Catholicism as Catholicism which made them. As is true also of the greater part of the varieties of Christianity, the system works well enough when administered by the Christlike. It is the men who matter; the peculiar denominational form in which their ideas are moulded appears to be of secondary importance.

My study of Christian origins, it may be remembered, began not very long after Hallam's departure from St Martin's, and the result of a course of earnest enquiry conducted solely with the aim of ascertaining the facts was to demolish in my mind the foundations upon which a large part of the Catholic system appeared to rest. I was left with a strong sentimental regard for a religion which had meant so much to me, and out of the fragments of faith in it which

315

I retained I constructed a precariously balanced scheme of belief of a liberal, æsthetic, Utopian sort. This appeared to be a working faith, although the effect on my mind of Hallam's tragic death dealt it a staggering blow. But I recovered temporarily, and my imperfectly grounded belief served me until further reading and study enlightened me as to the Modernist standpoint. Modernism, of course, is not a carefully constructed scheme of belief; the word is used roughly to describe the outlook of a small body of able, candid and earnest seekers after truth, who, living in the twentieth century, desire, in their search for truth, to take into consideration all the relevant data which the twentieth century has made available.

I have acknowledged my indebtedness to these thinkers who so ably explicated the ideas which were also at that time agitating my own mind. But their work with me was mainly destructive. I felt, and still feel, that the circumstances make it at present inevitable that they should break down more effectively than they build.

I was left, it seemed, with little more than the ethical teaching of Jesus Christ. I reached the lowest depths of unsettlement and intellectual despair, when, from time to time, oppressed with the heavy and weary weight of all this unintelligible world, I doubted whether even Christ's doctrine of the Fatherhood of God and the Brotherhood of Mankind, and all that that involved, could be squared with the facts. Was it not purely fantastic to picture as a loving Father whoever or whatever was responsible for a world of apparently blind and pitiless material forces? Against the cold logic of the facts laid bare by scientific research faith had but a dim hope to offer; and I, sometimes, had not even faith. The universe seemed a soulless machine, and the apostles of materialistic philosophy assured me, with passionate conviction, that it really was what it seemed, and that no account of the world was in the least degree credible which did not assume its ultimate annihilation, involving, incidentally, the blotting out of mankind, with all its glorious hopes and high ideals and noble achievements, as though the human race had never existed.

It was at this period of masterful negation and collapse of almost all my religious convictions that I began to take an interest in Psychic Science. I have already narrated the stages by which I became convinced of the validity of the evidence available within this comparatively new sphere of enquiry. Persons but little acquainted with the subject are usually bewildered when such matters are referred to. They feel it to be a kind of departure from good taste. And experience has shown me that, unless a mind has something within itself congruous with any particular new idea to which it is introduced, that idea is unable to effect a lodgement. It was my good fortune to possess a mind not bolted and barred against the assault of good evidence, even if it witnessed to a range of facts startling in their novelty.

I am not engaged in propaganda and do not propose, therefore, to justify myself by setting out in detail the evidence by which I obtained conviction. Nor need I fortify my own insignificance by enumerating the names of those men of brilliant gifts and cautious scientific temper (whose witness on any other matter would command a hearing) who have testified that, approaching the subject with a strong bias against it, they have been compelled, after years of close and careful investigation, to agree that the facts are as alleged, and that the interpretation given them by earlier workers in the field is, on the whole, the only one which adequately covers the ground.

But I desire to bear witness to the fact that through the gateway of this infant science I have entered a new world, or perhaps I have rediscovered an old world in which dreams have come true.

To me, the fact that convincing proof is afforded that man outlives his body's death is alone of stupendous import to humanity. It sets at rest the age-long controversy between those who assert survival as axiomatic and those who regard it as a crazy speculation begotten of ignorance and an overweening vanity.

I regard this as a question of evidence, of simple matter-of-fact. Man's instinctive conviction that he was not born to die, and all the arguments which have been elaborated to support it, carry weight, but however impressive they may be they fall short of actual demonstration. I am so constituted that for me authentic instances of the survival of human beings outweigh all purely philosophic or theological considerations in power to produce conviction.

The orthodox Christian will assert that we have that evidence in the story of the Resurrection of Christ, and, in the light of the knowledge afforded by Psychic Science, I agree. But it is notorious that the unsupported testimony of the Resurrection narratives has failed to carry conviction to large numbers of educated and thoughtful minds, by whom it is relegated to the sphere of legend. To me it appears that it is mainly by contemporary evidence, capable of being examined and tested, and by experiments which can be made, to a certain extent, at will, that proof can be obtained as to the fact which is perhaps of all facts the one of most vital importance to man—that he really is a spirit who survives the death of his material body. And this is the achievement of Psychic Research.

I am, of course, aware that this would not at present be admitted by the majority of scientific men. The history of Psychic Research is following the normal course of all advances in human thought. It was first derided and its assertions rejected as beneath contempt. It continued to press its claims and constantly added to the amount of evidence by which they are supported. Here and there a scientist of the first rank, or persons distinguished in other walks of life but equally possessed of the scientific temper, thought the matter worthy of investigation, and, after ex-haustive enquiry, announced their conversion. And now it is attracting the attention of an increasing number of thoughtful people in all grades of life, who realize that, unless a considerable body of persons otherwise notable for their intellectual pre-eminence have taken leave of their senses, conclusions of an importance not easily measured have already been reached about man's nature, powers, and destiny. For, to my mind, the evidence is conclusive of much more than survival. It is, of course, obvious that reports on the nature of life beyond the grave cannot normally be tested in the same way as can the evidence for survival itself. But if it be granted that communication with the departed exists, and the truthfulness of messages thus

319

obtained is established in matters capable of verification, then it is, at least, not improbable that information gathered from the same sources, even if at present unverifiable, may yet be true. And when the information given at various times through half a century, and in all parts of the world, is in substantial agreement, and is, moreover, though often of a kind unexpected by a particular recipient, yet inherently probable and consistent with that given to others, then, as it seems to me, the cumulative effect is weighty.

At any rate, after long and careful examination, the evidence has produced that impression upon my own mind. I have been introduced thereby to a universe conditioned throughout by sequences of cause and effect as orderly as mind of scientist could desire; a sphere in the ordering of which there is nothing arbitrary or irrational. Yet it is a universe in which the mental and emotional faculties have free play, and all that the saint, the philosopher, the poet, the artist, the musician have accomplished here has its counterpart on the other side.

We pass at death, it seems, into that particular sphere for which the characters and dispositions we have formed on earth have fitted us, there, normally, to follow up, under more favourable circumstances and with far greater opportunities, the interests which have previously occupied the better part of our minds, and in the company of those of natures congenial with our own.

This is the Next State, the first stage of the journey, which lies just across the barrier. But the evidence points to this being but the ante-chamber to regions of adventure and discovery, of growth and opportunity and advancement, beyond our dreams.

A wild fantasy? Crazy speculation? So I should once have described it. But, to me, the evidence, solidly based on ascertained fact, has carried conviction and set my feet upon a rock. At last I have that without which any philosophy of life would be for me incomplete. Science and the scientific method have given the same response to my questioning as that which was offered by mystic intuition, religion, and the arts. The circle is complete.

This particular branch of enquiry is in its infancy; it is difficult to set a limit to its possibilities. I remind myself that the achievement of Madame Curie in isolating radium was described at the time as a nine days' wonder. Yet it not only led to discoveries concerning the value of radium which are probably merely the first-fruits of the harvest still to be, but it opened up a whole field of research, so that scientists, I understand, speak now of over sixty "octaves" between the gamma rays of radium at the one end of the scale and that of "wireless" at the other.

What vast potentialities are indicated as awaiting investigation! And when the sphere of enquiry of which I speak has attracted in sufficient numbers men endowed with the true scientist's enthusiasm for discovery tempered with his infinite patience and skill in achieving it, man will, I expect, be on the way to surpass all his previous triumphs.

If I ask myself in what ways this knowledge has affected my attitude towards the Christian religion, I find that it has given back to me much which I had lost, but in a form which is consistent with, and not opposed to, the world of facts to which modern scientific discovery has given us access. For, I suppose that all Christian teachers, and, indeed, the exponents of every religion of the civilized world, would assert that a great part of their purpose is to show mankind how best to take its share in forwarding the purposes which lie behind the scheme of creation, and thereby to fit itself for further achievement in the world which is conjectured to lie beyond the grave.

The records of the life of Jesus of Nazareth which we possess, scanty and imperfect though they may be, clearly indicate that His teaching was of this kind. He taught that the true service of God consisted in pure devotion to His will manifesting itself principally in the service of man. One's position in a future life depended upon that. A life inspired, as His was, by the spirit of concern for the will of God and the welfare of humanity developed the highest in us here and opened up the way to greater things hereafter. That teaching (as to which there is, at any rate, a theoretical agreement) is supported in the fullest possible manner by what the new knowledge reveals to us of the conditions of life in the Next World. But much of that which has divided good men here is gradually discovered to be of little importance there.

Thus, the light of the knowledge of actual fact begins to dispel the twilight throughout wide regions of thought in which men have often struggled hitherto, stumbling and guessing, mistaking friend for foe, and being afraid where no fear was.

As one who has experienced so much of the particular con

322

tributions to religion made by good men as widely separated as are Catholic and Protestant, I do not look forward to the establishment of a reduced Christianity, a mere system of ethics. I know that religion must be infinitely more than that. It must include not only the intellectual integrity of the best Protestantism, but also Catholicism's rich corporate life; all for which its sacramental system stands; the treasures of its vast experience; the dignity and beauty of its ordered worship. It must share the daring flights and intuitions of the mystic as well as assimilate the painfully acquired stores of the scientist. I believe that religion will inspire once more the poet and the musician, and cause the artist, the builder and the craftsman to achieve the yet unattempted. It is my faith that to this desirable consummation Psychic Science offers an indispensable contribution. The discovery of Copernicus and all that resulted from it demolished our little sky-topped world and opened up the entire material universe to man. Psychic Research will, if it fulfils its youthful promise, provide the material for bridging the gulf between science and religion, and make us free of the spiritual universe by putting us in ever more fruitful contact with the accumulated wisdom of those who have progressed beyond the sweep of earth-bound man's imagination. I do not anticipate that the religion resultant upon such a conjuncture will be of a lesser content than any we at present know.

We have not yet attained. The foot of man is at a lowly place on the pathway to the stars, but he is moving forward, and the possibilities are infinite.

To me, it imparts a miraculous element to my life's

experience that, being essentially a sceptic, I have been able to write with conviction what I have written.

Once more I have visited the seaport town in which the early years of my ministry were spent. I write these words amid the downs that lie inland and whither I came some twenty years ago upon the day in which I heard of Hallam's death. It is the same landscape upon which I look; the same, yet how different! For now it is transfigured because I look upon it with other eyes. I view it no longer as the background of a few fitful years of restless and frustrated endeavour soon to be swallowed up in utter annihilation. It is now the setting of but the opening scene of the drama of man's life.

And how lovely is that setting as I behold a fragment of it from the top of this steep green hill. The rounded chalk downs, clothed in warm fragrant turf, enclose a wide plain marked out into fields of every shape, each bounded by an ample hedge. The sheep in the distant meadows are a cluster of pearly dots, the bell-wether's movements recorded by the softly clear tinkle. Amid the clustering trees is the sturdy tower of a little thirteenth-century church, around which lie the bodies of those who since the Norman Conquest have tilled the fields upon which I am looking. But the sight does not oppress me, as once it did, with the thought of a succession of toiling generations doomed to death after a few years of labour and sorrow. I do not faintly hope, but I am sure that the scheme is nobly planned, for I know that man was not made to die, that experience is garnered, that a rich harvest awaits the ages of preparation.

324

The little plot of earth that lies encircled by these green downs and hanging beech woods was the sole scene of the joys and sorrows of most of that small community the bodies of whose dead have for seven centuries been laid to rest beneath the shadow of the cool grey shrine. But I lift my eyes. A single gull floats white in the still, sunny air, and vanishes through an opening between the hills. Following its flight, I look out upon the blue distance of the weald which stretches away to where land touches sky. I perceive that this little scene lies in a wide setting. It is good and gracious in itself (its beauty brings the tears to my eyes), but its significance is chiefly manifested and its value infinitely enhanced by what lies about it and beyond.

It is a parable of my quest for reality, and whither it has led me hitherto. I have not learned merely to pronounce a fresh formula of belief; I have been admitted into a wider world. My position is secure in a boundless universe and I know whither my steps are tending. Doubtless life holds for me still my share of trial and suffering, but I think it will be endurable in the light of what lies beyond it all. Doubtless, too, I shall experience many perplexities still to be solved, for I am seised of no stock of facile answers to life's problems. Yet, in possession of certainty in regard to what are to me the more immediately vital issues, I can approach the lesser difficulties without haste or anxiety.

Thus, I now at length enjoy periods of leisure of heart and mind, seasons of calm weather in which I can look around me, and take deep draughts of delight in the glory of this amazing world to which within a few years I must bid farewell.

Once, at a time when I was absorbed in the duties of a busy life, I received from a person possessing psychic gifts, who knew nothing of me or of my circumstances, a message from "an old spirit who has passed over, who says he is sorry you have ceased to study Nature". The message was at least *ben trovato*, but there is good evidence that actual contact is sometimes established between two minds having a connecting bond of sympathy, even though one no longer inhabits this earth.

I should like to think that the poet to whom I am linked by so vast a debt of gratitude had indeed spared a thought for his poor disciple. He would be pleased perhaps to know that here on this autumn day, amid these hills, looking back over all the years of my life since first I became acquainted with his poetry, out of a full heart I record my gratitude to the master who opened my eyes to so much of the beauty and significance of this fair world.

I rejoice to know that my sense of wonder and delight in Nature is not dimmed by the passing of the years; rather it grows deeper as all I see is linked to growing knowledge and wider experience. This scene, this halcyon day, are richer through their association with other scenes and by-gone days, and, above all, by the consecration of a certain visionary splendour seen in those moments of insight that come even to me, unworthy, when heart and mind are stilled in quiet contemplation.

CAMBRIDGE: PRINTED BY
W. LEWIS, M.A.
AT THE UNIVERSITY PRESS

For EU product safety concerns, contact us at Calle de José Abascal, 56–1°, 28003 Madrid, Spain or eugpsr@cambridge.org.

www.ingramcontent.com/pod-product-compliance
Ingram Content Group UK Ltd.
Pitfield, Milton Keynes, MK11 3LW, UK
UKHW012329130625
459647UK00009B/164